Shades of Thorne Creek

Copyright © 2023, Alan Havorka
Front and rear covers copyright © 2023 by Alan Havorka

ISBN-13: 978-0-9794849-4-0
ISBN-10: 0-9794849-4-4

All rights reserved. No part of this publication may be reproduced, stored in a retrieval system, or transmitted in any form or by any means, electronic, mechanical, recording or otherwise, without the prior written permission of the author.

Printed in the United States of America.

The characters and events in this book are fictitious. Any similarity to real persons, living or dead, is coincidental and not intended by the author.

Shades of Thorne Creek

Introduction iii
The Plan of the "El" v
Emery, Circa 1974 vii
    Chapter 1: Ghosts 1
    Chapter 2: The Emery "El" 9
    Chapter 3: Andrew 23
    Chapter 4: Annie, Deferred 37
    Chapter 5: Annie and Bob 45
    Chapter 6: Lewee 55
    Chapter 7: Sunday Morning 63
    Chapter 8: Sunday Night 71
    Chapter 9: Andy Junior 79
    Chapter 10: The Lewee-Bird 87
    Chapter 11: First Meetings 97
    Chapter 12: Final Touches 111
    Chapter 13: Thursday's Prayers 125
    Chapter 14: Catastrophe 137
    Chapter 15: Business Deals 145
    Chapter 16: Sunday 153
    Chapter 17: Pretenders 167
    Chapter 18: Final Arrangements 181
    Chapter 19: August 8th, 1974 195
    Chapter 20: Unplanned Events 207
    Chapter 21: Aftermath 215
    Chapter 22: Judgments 229
    Chapter 23: Secrets 239
    Chapter 24: On Death, and Life 249
    Chapter 25: Longings 259
    Chapter 26: Redeeming Love Convalescent 267
    Chapter 27: Thorne Creek 279
Appendix: The Sixth Air Vent 287
Within a Sheltering Darkness 289
Excerpt from the pending *Shadows, Forward* 293
About the Author 299

Shades of Thorne Creek

Introduction

The Deadly Pentangle

Facilities that process and store grains face an acute danger; the operations they perform bring together five factors that pose a grievous danger of explosion. Those factors are a fuel, oxygen, confinement, dispersion, and heat (typically in the form of a spark).

The fuel, curiously enough, is simple grain dust. The loading, unloading, and moving about of common grains such as dried corn or wheat, generates a very fine, and seemingly harmless, dust. Air scrubbing schemas will remove much of this dust, but like all systems, such scrubbers can degrade or even fail outright.

Oxygen is, of course, ever present. The workers do have to breathe.

Confinement is almost essential when dealing with perishable consumables like grain; there must be confinement to keep out moisture and impurities.

Dispersion, however, can be combated. Grain dust settles over time. As long as it remains settled, as a film or even a thick layer, it poses no danger. But before it is settled, or when it is dispersed after settling, it mixes with the air and can reach critical concentrations. Air scrubbers, working to remove as much grain dust as possible, can be effective in keeping the concentration of the airborne dust below this critical threshold.

The wildcard in this scenario, as in so many others, is an ignition source. Sparks, electrical arcing, a cigarette, any number of things can provide the final facet of the Deadly Pentangle.

If these five elements come together at one time, grain dust is highly dangerous. Ounce for ounce, or worse, pound for pound, grain dust has five times the explosive power of gunpowder.

Introduction

A Note About Tumblers

A standard key-operated lock has a series of pins, called tumblers, of varying lengths. A key's teeth push the tumblers of the lock aside as the key enters. If the length of each tooth correctly matches the length of each corresponding pin, the ends of the pins align and the lock can be turned. If one tumbler is out of place—because one of the key's teeth is not right, or the tumbler sticks, or any other reason—the lock cannot turn. All the tumblers must be aligned correctly.

The circumstances of life resemble the tumblers of elaborate locks. If enough circumstances come together in the right way, in the right order, the lock that safeguards against disaster is opened.

In the physical world, all things make noise when they move, and the tumblers of a lock are no exception. But the unseen tumblers of life are not subject to normal physical laws. When they fall into place, it is true that they often do so noisily, almost with fanfare. But they sometimes move without any noise whatsoever. Sometimes they fall into place in total, unrecognizable silence.

Shades of Thorne Creek

The Plan of the "El"

This diagram is not essential to the novel. However, as various aspects of the "El" 's operations are referred to, some readers may elect to refer to this diagram for clarity.

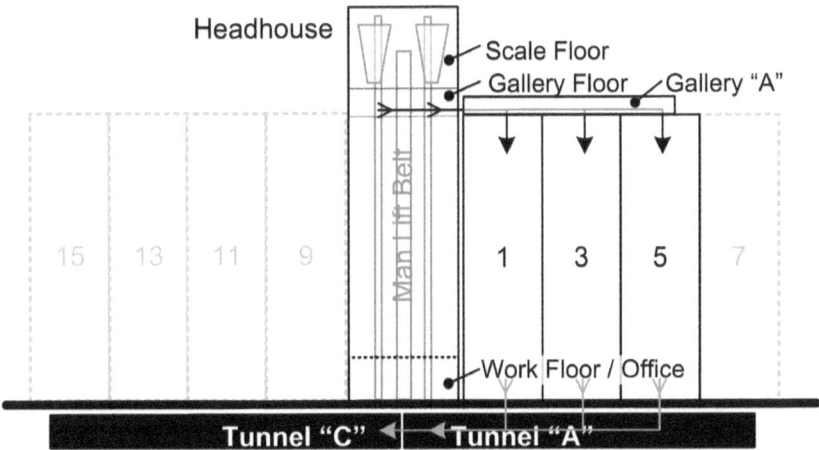

Shades of Thorne Creek

Emery, Circa 1974

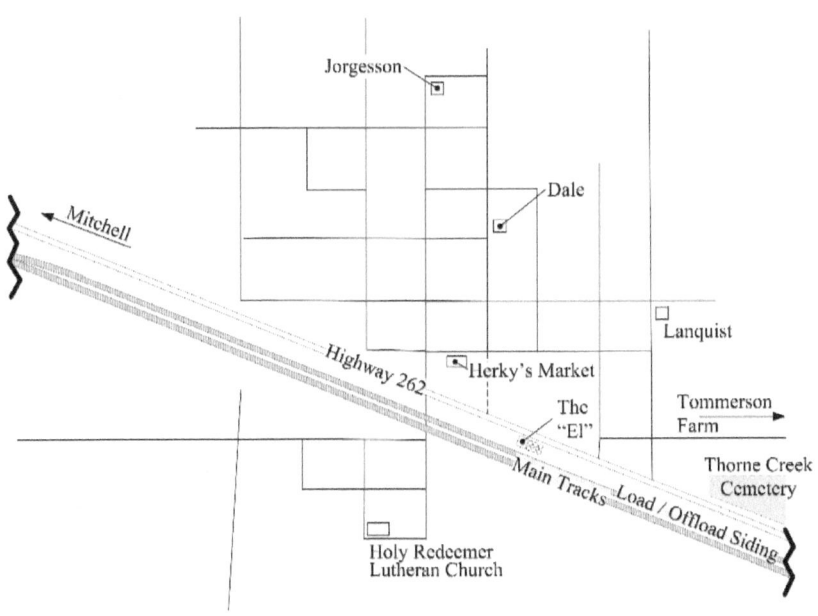

Shades of Thorne Creek

Chapter 1: Ghosts

Some ghosts just want to be forgotten. They are ashamed. Ashamed of who they were, of what they did. Or ashamed, perhaps, of what they did not do, even though they had the chance. But some ghosts, I am sure, do not want to be forgotten. They want to be known."

I began learning this lesson one chilled September day, in a small cemetery not far from Mitchell, South Dakota. Mitchell, home of the Corn Palace—a landmark second only to Mt. Rushmore in bringing tourism fame to the Dakotas. Thorne Creek Cemetery. Just a small town graveyard. The insignificant, drowning in the shadows of the unimportant.

All things, I have come to learn, come together in stages. Multiple series of small events working together. My decision to bicycle from Mitchell, South Dakota, to St. Paul, Minnesota—that was the first of it. Then choosing to go down Highway 262 to connect with Highway 42—that was the second. An endless chain of decisions brought me there, to those tombstones, in time for a mid-afternoon stretch—so that I might see a subtle thing, a silent thing, and be dropped to my knees by the horror of it. All of these had conspired to bring me to this story.

The plains of South Dakota and Minnesota are, for some bikers, a nightmare of flat, uninterrupted terrain. For me, they were a joy of flat, uninterrupted terrain. They were an endless canvas upon which my mind could play while my muscles stroked, and pumped throughout my body the naturally generated endorphins that yielded, for long stretches, the "bikers' high".

My route had been planned with care. Towns were frequent enough that I could find a restaurant when needed, and I carried survival rations to see me through if the diners failed to appear. Always

One: Ghosts

within striking distance there was either a motel with ample vacancies, or a campground where I could pitch the tiny tent compressed in my pack. The weather, monitored each night by radio, was holding steady.

So, unencumbered by the worries of survival that plagued the rest of mankind, my mind roamed at will as my body sailed along its preset path.

Mid-afternoon. Time to treat my body to a rest, even though it did not yet demand it. A town had been manifesting itself in the distance—a water tower first, then the tallest of its buildings. In time, I passed its welcome sign; an inglorious state-produced affair in plain green with off-white lettering: Emery. There were a few gravel driveways leading to recessed farmhouses, marked by mail boxes bearing names that, at the time, meant nothing to me. Then there were some suburban residences, then minor cross-streets, and eventually the town proper. I sailed through, slowing only as needed for traffic control pleasantries. I always scoped out the whole of a town's main drag, then looped back to handle whatever business was pressing upon me. The town's far side was a fair mirror of my approach, and as the cross streets and houses dwindled, I spotted a cemetery on the left. Lunch had been handled hours before, and supper was hours ahead. All that I needed from Emery was a rest stop, a chance to walk, to sit, to lie in the grass. A cemetery would be perfect, and I cruised into it.

Thorne Creek Cemetery, as its signpost declared it, seemed unusually large for the size of the town it adjoined. It even had a groundskeeper's house. It occurred to me that it might not serve merely the town of Emery, but perhaps the towns surrounding it as well—maybe even all of Hanson County.

For a time, I cruised Thorne Creek's meandering paths, noting how the markers ranged from the most basic flat plaque to a few ornate edifices with angels.

I stopped and dismounted, and hung my helmet on my handlebars. I briefly strutted, fearing I must look like an emu as I eased my legs down from their engrained routine. I flexed my back and my neck. I began a tour of the stones. Most were unremarkable, but a few

Shades of Thorne Creek

suggested their own little tales which I, with my writer's blood, could not help but flesh out.

A husband and wife, side-by-side. He had died in 1942, at twenty years of age; she had lived on until 1943. I saw him as a soldier, dying overseas. She, grief-stricken, had tried for a time to go on but had given up in the end. Her suicide might have been obvious (for women, pills were the most common avenue) or it might have been more ambiguous. Perhaps a single-car crash, driving into a tree. Accidental death, her doctor would have graciously declared on the certificate. Who knows? His pronouncement might even, by chance, have been the truth.

To the left, another stone, flat, in-ground. Born 1880, died 1948. Sixty-eight years; not an unreasonable span, even though shy of the three score and ten which many felt their due. But what struck me on this one was the aloneness of it. By now, any wife or siblings would have passed as well. If he had been connected to anyone in life, they had been buried elsewhere. But his was a cheap stone, to which no survivors seemed to have contributed. The absence of the same surname anywhere nearby suggested survivors did not exist at all, and that was the scenario I spun; a man who lived, and died, alone.

On the neighboring stone: Born 1920, died 1983. Twenty-one years of age when the Pearl Harbor attack brought us into World War II. If he were anything like his era's brethren, he had served. Most likely enlisted, rather than drafted. But unlike so many, he had survived. What horrors had he seen in those years? How had they affected him?

A traditional rectangular stone, with rounded top; a slightly pinkish stone. Born 1949, died 1974. Too young, I thought. Perhaps a car accident.

Beside it, the same type and color of stone, though with a different surname. Born 1955, died 1974. I looked to the previous stone; died August 8, 1974. Then back to this stone; August 8, 1974. I mulled that. A car accident, I surmised again. One accident, taking both lives. Buried at the same time, perhaps as part of the same funeral services. The stones had been purchased together. A twenty-five year old and a teenager in the same car? Perhaps. Or maybe separate cars, the inexperienced teen crashing into his elder.

One: Ghosts

The next stone was different, larger, plain in shape but with more elaborate carving. Beloved husband, father, etc., Born 1946. Baby boomer, I thought. Died 1974. My face tightened at that, and my eyes found the month and day. August 8. Something unspoken welled inside me. The next two stones were short, plain, pinkish. Rectangular; rounded tops. I felt dread creeping up on me. I read the date of death of both of them. August 8. 1974. I looked to the sky, to the September clouds crawling slowly by. What was this place where I now stood?

I became conscious of my breathing, and forced it to become regular and steady.

"OK," I said aloud, thinking I could shrug it off: "Something happened. Something bad." Then, thinking, *Something worse than you want to imagine. Just keep moving on till you get to the end of them. Get past these, make up a few more stories for the rest, and get back on your bike.*

Paying no attention to names, quotations, or dates of birth, I moved on so I could find the end of this… thing. This subtly embedded memorial. This cemetery within the cemetery. This terrible tribute to that one date.

The date of death kept repeating. I passed them, conscious of my effort to not count them, just wanting to find the end. But count them I did, on some level. I realize that now. Because when I reached a dozen, I stopped. I had just passed four in a row of the plain pink stones. Looking ahead, I saw there were at least a dozen more of the same type. Obviously, having the same style of stone did not prove they all had the same date. But they did have the same date. They had it. I knew that. I knew it.

The dread I felt earlier now lay across me like some choking dust; it grew heavier, and I even imagined my feet settling deeper into the grass under its weight. August 8, 1974. What had happened on that day? A kind of existential horror weighed down on me, as my mind raced to imagine what could claim so many lives. All in one day. A terrible imagining swept me. Even as I had imagined my feet had settled deeper into the grass, it suddenly occurred to me I might keep settling down, sinking down, and that these cemetery grounds might receive me, might swallow me whole. A new grave marker would appear. *My* name. *My* date of birth. *Died: August 8th, 1974.* But as my feet pressed down on the grass, they moved down no farther. Reality, it seemed, was still pretty much as I had always understood it.

I heard someone approaching from behind. He stopped near me. He waited.

"I see you found 'em," he said gently, in a deep voice.

I started to turn, but stopped myself, unable to move my eyes from the date in the stone.

"Yeah," he said. "They do kinda reach out and grab ya, don't they? Gets me too, sometimes. And I see 'em every day."

I turned to him. He was middle-aged, in a guard's uniform. His ancestry was mixed and hard to read. Very light-skinned African, perhaps. Maybe with some Hispanic. He stood about five foot eight, and held about a hundred pounds more than his doctor probably wanted to see on him, but he carried it well, as if he had carried it a long, long time.

"It's the ghosts, talkin' to you," he observed. "Some ghosts just want to be forgotten. Least ways, that's what I think. They're ashamed. 'Shamed of who they were, of what they did. Maybe 'shamed of what they didn't do, even though they could'a. But then there's others. Like these," he said, pointing to the row of headstones before us. "I think these don't want to be forgotten. I think they want to be known." He shrugged against the chilled September air. He stood for a moment, looking at me. More than that, though. Looking *into* me. Divining what sort of man I was, I later realized. "I don't know. Least ways, that's what I think. That's why I'll tell you. If you're of a mind to hear it. Hear it all, that is."

I looked to the sky. Mid-afternoon had flashed into early evening. Where had the time gone? It seemed it had been just minutes ago that I had stopped.

"No way I can bike to the next town," I said. "Looks like I'm here for the night. So, yeah. I'd like to hear it. Hear it all. If you can take the time."

One: Ghosts

"Time," the old man said with a smile. "I've got plenty of time. Just let me make my rounds. I'll be back to the house…" shrugging toward the guardhouse, "…in just a bit. Door's open. Make yourself to home."

I watched his tired frame trudge away, and looked back to the stones. I needed to know their story, or at least the groundskeeper's version of their story, before I could bear to know how many had died that day. And how they died. And why.

* * *

"Emery in the seventies," he told me in the tiny fiefdom of his guardhouse, after his rounds, "was pretty much like Emery today." The guardhouse had been marginally decorated; threadbare curtains with sun-fading stripes, framed flea-market prints of nature scenes, and the table where we sat—a little wobbly, with a walnut finish of separating laminate.

He poured coffee for us both, in large mugs. "Oh, you go inside homes now, you'll find cable TV, and computers, and all such stuff. But on the outside, things don't look much different. Same looks to things. Same businesses, in most cases. Styles of cars have changed. That's about it though."

He drew deeply from his mug. *Ducks Unlimited*, it had once read.

"'Cept for one thing, mainly. The El. The Barris Grain Elevator."

"Grain elevator," I echoed, and drew tentatively from my own cup. "That must be something from back then, not now. I didn't see any grain elevator. Saw a *water* tower…."

"You won't *never* see no grain elevator in Emery, South Dakota," he said firmly. "Not ever again. You can't even see the ruins of the foundation. It was dug out, and plowed under."

"Some kind of contamination?"

He shook his head. "Contamination. Nah." He drew more coffee from his mug, then looked up to me. I knew the look. He was a man making a decision. He was sizing me up, a final time.

Shades of Thorne Creek

"Digging up a foundation?" I asked. "Plowing it under? Sounds pretty radical. The sort of thing a person doesn't just do... not without a reason."

"A reason," he said with another draw.

I wanted to encourage him, lead out of him whatever it was he wanted to say. But I sensed that now was the time to wait. Again, his eye met mine.

"A reason." He sighed. "Yeah, they had a reason."

Over the rest of the evening, and the next several days (I eventually phoned my son and arranged for him to pick me up) the story of the Barris Grain Elevator—the El, as it was known—was assembled for me. Most of it I gathered from Ray Tucker, the groundskeeper at Thorne Creek—the graveskeeper, I came to think of him as. Other parts I got later from survivors. Some pieces I gleaned over the following months from the investigators' reports. And, of course, some parts I fabricated from whole cloth, to fill in gaps. But on the whole, I think that what I have committed to paper is a fair representation of what happened in the summer of 1974. I think it does justice to Thorne Creek's heroes, who were few, and its villains, who were fewer still. Most important, I think it gives voice to those who would want to be heard.

Shades of Thorne Creek

Chapter 2: The Emery "El"

The "El" had been a mainstay of Emery commerce for years. Becoming operational in 1963, officially named Emery Elevator Operations, it was instantly profitable and remained so for three years, functioning as a storage place for grain—primarily corn, secondarily wheat.

Changing economies and technologies altered its fortunes, however, and in 1967 and 1968 the "El" (as it was known by everyone, including its owner, Ed Gulleif) operated at or just below the break-even point. 1969 marked its first year significantly in the red, a condition from which it would never emerge during Ed Gulleif's tenure.

With no change in conditions brewing on the horizon, her owner began casting about for options in 1971, and in the fall of 1972 he connected with Barris, Inc., a company with many holdings in grain-related industries.

A brief meeting was held at the El, in the Work Floor office of her Head House, between Ed Gulleif and a foreman from a Barris Elevator in southern Minnesota. After the meeting, the Barris foreman was given a personal tour by Gulleif of all operations at the El. Later, a somewhat longer meeting was held, again in the Head House office, with extensive discussions regarding operations and history. Gulleif gave the foreman specifications for the elevator complex, copies of purchase orders for additional equipment, quotes for equipment being considered, as well as balance sheets and profit & loss statements that were obviously beyond the foreman's ken, but which he had been instructed to retrieve. Certain that that would be the end of the matter, Ed Gulleif returned to the day-to-day grinding down of his soul as he watched the "El" inexorably creep ever so slowly further into the red.

Two: The Emery "El"

In November of 1972, Barris contacted the El to arrange another meeting. Perplexed, but willing to grasp at irrational hope, Ed Gulleif arranged the meeting, again at the El.

"They're here, Ed," Annie said softly. Her simple, pleasing features were framed in medium length straight gold hair. Her eyes were a soft Scandinavian blue, and downplayed by a reserved, minimal makeup. Ed Gulleif did not respond to her announcement.

"Ed," she repeated, with no change in volume or tone. At times like these, she spoke softly—as though her words, if spoken too sharply, might crack some imperceptible shell holding him together.

Gulleif looked out his office window, across the snow-dusted prairie. His office was on the south, facing the tracks, away from the town. The placement of his office had been a conscious decision, so he could watch the trains load and unload. But it had also worked out well later, so that he was not burdened with a view looking across Emery's streets. He needed no reminder of how many families depended on the El– of how many families depended on him.

Ed's office was small, and unadorned with art. Papers were tacked up everywhere—charts, progress reports, even the original blueprints for the El. Near those blueprints, becoming surrounded and even covered over by other, more pressing data, were the sketches he had once drawn up himself, for expansion. The six original silos might have one day become sixteen, if only things had gone differently. Old ideas, he knew. Old, old ideas.

"How many men?" Ed asked.

"Four of them."

"Four?" He turned to her.

"Business types. Lawyer types, maybe. That's good, isn't it Ed?" She was imploring him with those clear, blue eyes. She knew it was good; she was asking the question so as to point it out to him, but still let him realize it for himself.

As he walked past her, he paused without turning to her, and touched her shoulder.

Shades of Thorne Creek

"Keep the good thought, Annie. Let's go."

In the main office of the Head House they passed the new intern—the Jorgesson girl, Lewee—as she sorted through the stacks of mail on one of the long folding tables. She didn't look up at them, instead keeping her focus on the piles she was creating.

"Knock 'em dead, Mr. G." she offered absently.

Ed Gulleif swallowed hard, and opened the conference room door.

"Thanks, Lewee," Annie said with a smile. She followed Ed in, and gently closed the door behind them. The conference room boasted the closest thing to fancy furniture the El possessed: a broad conference table which had been reasonably impressive, until the passing years had brought scratches and dings and a peeling of laminate on one corner. The chairs had not fared quite as well.

Introductions were quick and businesslike. Two men, Stonebridge and Brandt, were from the Barris Board of Directors. Stangdahl was a foreman from another Barris elevator, this one in Iowa. Petroci was a lawyer—an announcement that spiked Gulleif's pulse even more than the board members. Gulleif introduced Annie Dale as his Chief Financial Officer, an on-the-spot promotion that made her nervous; she barely felt capable of handling the El's accounting.

The preliminary small talk was even more concise than the introductions.

"Mr. Gulleif, we have reviewed all aspects of Emery Elevator Operations, and are prepared to offer to buy you out," Stonebridge said, as he slid a paper deliberately across the conference table. Gulleif scanned it without picking it up, leaving it turned so that Annie could read it as well.

Gulleif did a masterful job of masking his emotions, his shock. The numbers... the numbers. This would not only cover the outstanding loans that had built the El; it would cover all the debt that the bad years had amassed, as well. And it left... a balance. He might be able to retire. Not extravagantly. But comfortably. Gulleif came from strong Swedish stock, and he was not inclined to excessive optimism. But the numbers... the numbers were there.

Two: The Emery "El"

Gulleif had spent his adult life farming. Most of the years were good. With the money he had saved, and the good will he had built with the financial institutions in the area, he had swung the loans necessary to build the modest grain towers of the El. He was no mogul. But the markets were good, his financial plan was sound, and he convinced a number of his neighbors—his friends—to invest. He would only need to run the El for a few years, build it up to make Emery a focal point for the economy of this corner of Hanson County. Then he could sell it off, and retire. But the El would go on—his gift to Emery, to the people who had helped him over the years.

It had started well. The El provided employment for those in Emery who were not so fully enchanted with farming. And when Emery could not supply enough men, the El drew in new people, people who added to Emery's ranks. After the first two years, he had paid off all the friends and neighbors who had invested; they had invested as a favor, not out of hopes of getting rich, and he was not inclined to let their investment "ride" like money on a roulette table. Despite the steep payoff rate Ed Gulleif insisted on for them, he managed to keep up on the payments to the banks.

Emery's economy had grown, with the El representing an ever increasing share of the action. And then, almost as soon as his neighbors had been paid back, things began to sour. The crops were still good. The economy was good. Too good, it seemed. Other elevators were springing up to store grain, and storage rates were falling. The El had always been a modest endeavor, run to make a profit but not a windfall. As the prices for storage dipped, the El's profit spiraled down, and then turned red. Ed Gulleif watched his investment erode. Soon he watched the money he already had set aside for retirement erode as well until it, too, was gone. His Swedish heritage also gave him a stubbornness, which had served him well during the occasional lean year of farming. Now, it was his downfall. The impact on the Gulleif household, and on Emery as a whole, would have been serious had he elected to fold earlier. But now he was well past that point.

Businesses had grown up, supporting the El, and supported by the El. People, and then families, had relocated to Emery because of the growing commerce that all revolved around the El. But despite all that had grown around it, the El remained the lynchpin. None of it could be self-sustaining. All of it would collapse, without the El.

Ruin was all that awaited him, and all that awaited the citizens of Emery he had wanted to help. Ruin, unless something dramatic happened.

He looked again at the paper. He looked over to Annie. She did not look up to him, but kept her eyes on the table. Across the top of her notepad, a roll of paper had been formed by all of the pages that had been flipped over. At the top of her current page, concealed by the roll from the Barris men across the table, she wrote in small letters: "go go go".

Taking his own pen, he wrote a check mark over the first, and the second, and then paused over the third. He looked to Annie. Then he closed his eyes, turned to the Barris team, and opened his eyes again. He swallowed. All his nightmares could be swept away with his signature on some papers.

Annie knew it, even though Ed had done his best to hide his personal finances. She ran the El's books, and knew from where the money had been coming. Annie knew nothing of Ed's personal finances, but she knew that the infusions of cash from him to the El were growing smaller— ever closer in amount to match each looming bill, ever closer in time to meet those bills' due dates. Annie knew how much he must have needed this, and how unlikely it was that a similar offer would come from any other quarter. What was he doing, she wondered, hesitating now?

Annie became aware of the sound of each of a half-dozen different machines running overhead in the Head House, their noises intruding into the conference room. They were not enough to fill the current silence. What was Ed doing?

"Gentlemen. Your offer is… entirely sufficient. I am most interested in proceeding. There is… one question."

The Barris team waited quietly, patiently, curiously. They had done their homework. They knew the Emery Elevator Operations' status, and prospects. More than that, they knew Ed Gulleif's personal

Two: The Emery "El"

circumstances, in more detail than propriety permitted. They also felt that they knew the man—that he would not be driven by greed. So they knew: This negotiation pause had to be about more than cash.

"Whatever your intentions regarding the future of the El," Ed forged on, dreading that he might sour the deal, "there are a lot of people employed here."

The lawyer Petroci nodded inwardly, but kept his reaction hidden. As Gulleif continued to speak, Petroci opened his briefcase, and casually navigated the pockets.

"I'd like to think," Ed said, "that my employees would have time to adapt. If you could agree to keep them on in their current positions. Just for a time. Six months, perhaps a year."

Brandt smiled, and he received a single sheet of paper from Petroci. Scanning the document, he said:

"Emery Elevator Operations will do us no good without staff familiar with it, ready to continue after we take over."

He filled in some blanks, initialing the document in each location.

"We can amend the main agreement to include this." He slid the paper to Gulleif. "It's standard boilerplate for our retention of all employees, current as of this date, for a period of 12 months. Excepting cases of extreme malfeasance or nonfeasance, of course, but I doubt that will be an issue. And as an unofficial aside, Mr. Gulleif, I would say that beyond that period, we have no intention of making any sweeping changes."

Annie struggled to ensure her mouth remained closed. The possible permutations of events she had deemed plausible for the next 60 days had all ended with the El in financial collapse. Even in her wilder fantasies, where Ed and his wife emerged without going into bankruptcy, Annie and all the El's employees were nonetheless still set adrift. Now, with a few scribbles on a sheet of paper sliding back and forth, all of that seemed to be changing. Her own, unique situation had moved from devastating to status quo. There was hope for her, and for her brother. *Too good*, she thought. *Too, too good....*

Shades of Thorne Creek

"And besides," said Brandt, snapping Annie back to attention, "we'll need time to explore this computer system your CFO has been developing."

Annie managed a smile, despite the chill that swept her.

Oh no, Ed, she thought. *What have you been telling them?* But she shook the thought off.

As Ed reached his pen across to Annie's pad and checked the third "go", Annie added more words to the hidden header.

"What's their plan???" she wrote. "Bad move".

Ed knew she was right. Barris had to be making a mistake. Ed Gulleif did not now write, but rather spoke to her:

"K & C". There was no need for hidden notes; this was private idiom, just between them. He used the phrase occasionally, but had never before used it for anything connected with El operations, or for anything serious; the phrase was too blithe for that. "K and C"; short for "IDK and IDC"; itself short for "I Don't Know and I Don't Care".

Committing to keeping all the employees meant committing to running the El as a grain elevator. And to Ed, that could only mean financial ruin. Not ruin for Barris as a whole; they were big enough to weather this kind of blunder. But the El, viewed just by itself, was a financial disaster.

Well, Ed thought, *if the Barris people were better businessmen than he was (most likely true) maybe it might mean breaking even. But no more than that.*

His better nature wanted to ask just what their plans were, how they planned to make a profit. But he had risked enough. He had risked souring them, to get an additional concession for his people. He felt he owed Emery that. But he didn't owe these people across the table. All things being equal, he would have helped them out. Would have asked the questions that could have saved them from a bad financial move. But this was his future on the line. More than that, it was Emery's future. Could he risk what he had just secured for them, all to play the Good Samaritan? He regretted that thought, with its implications in

Two: The Emery "El"

moral teaching. Barris was making a mistake and Ed Gulleif knew it. But there was too much at stake. Too many futures.

In that moment, before he said "Gentlemen, how do we conclude this deal?" in the silence when he could have asked "Just what is your plan?" but did not, there was an additional silence, a different type of silence, layered on top of the rest. It was a silence upon which no Head House machinery could hope to intrude. It was a silence Ed Gulleif would not recognize until hours later, when he thought back over the events in the conference room. It was a silence whose true and devastating meaning he would not understand for years. But it was a silence that would come to haunt him, haunt him like rows of stones that would one day be placed in Thorne Creek Cemetery.

* * *

When the men left, Annie insisted on seeing them beyond the Head House door, out to their car. Huddling within her cloth coat, she gathered her courage.

"Gentlemen, I appreciate your coming here, your making this deal happen."

"Our pleasure, Miss Dale. It's a win-win."

It was jargon she hadn't heard before, but she understood, correctly, that it meant this was a good deal for both parties, Barris and Ed Gulleif. She was as doubtful of that as Ed, but she let it go.

"I'm looking forward to doing all that I can for Barris. To giving you my best."

"I'm sure you are," said Stonebridge. He paused. "But there's something else on your mind."

She did not meet their eyes.

"Ed's really enthusiastic about what I've been able to do," she said. 'Full disclosure' was a phrase that flashed through her mind. Full disclosure would have required that she explain that she had never had any formal training in accounting. She had picked it up on her own, enough to fill in temporarily when Ed's bookkeeper had left. And she

Shades of Thorne Creek

picked up enough on the job that Ed felt less and less pressed to hire someone permanent. In time, he had settled into the notion that Annie would *be* the permanent. She kept reminding Ed that she was purely self-taught, and he kept reminding her she was smart, and had a natural aptitude, and that she needed to believe in herself. And in time she did.

She had always wanted to take some kind of classes, correspondence courses, maybe, but it seemed there was never time. She was always too busy doing her job. The balance sheets and the P & Ls were always plenty good enough for Ed. And then came the day that Ed asked for the Balance Sheet, and the P & L, so he could pass them on to Barris—and she was hit with dread. Surely the Barris accountants would know, once they saw what she had prepared. They would notice things she had done wrong. The little "accountant facade" she had built up would fall.

But no one had said a word. "Chief Financial Officer" Ed had called her, and still no one had said a word. "…keeping on all employees… for a period of 12 months," the amendment had said. And no exceptions had been declared. Nothing like "Except, of course, we'll have to hire a *real* accountant."

Perhaps it was the fact that she had thus far navigated these waters that caused her to leave that fear behind. But another fear pressed on her now, and she said the words:

"It's about this computer program I've been working on."

"Yes," said Stonebridge. "We're most interested in looking at it."

"If you're concerned," said Petroci, "about the work you've put in on it, I'm sure we can come to some understanding."

"Sir?"

"I imagine you've spent a lot of your own personal time working on it. If we feel our other facilities could make use of it, there would be some measure of additional compensation."

Annie's stomach knotted. Would vomiting in front of them be considered bad form, sending perhaps the wrong message? Sending just the *right* message, in fact.

Two: The Emery "El"

"Gentlemen," she forced herself to say. "It's not that, at all. It's just that... I am not a computer programmer. I don't really know what I'm doing. I've just been playing with it, getting it to do some things. I'm not even using a real computer. Not like big businesses use, not like banks use."

"Not a 'mainframe'?" offered Brandt.

Annie wasn't sure of the terminology, but she knew that that was probably right.

"You're probably using something like a Tandy, or an Altair," suggested Stangdahl.

"Altair, yes. That's what I'm using." At last, someone understood. She was just a pretender, not the real thing. She felt the burden lifting. "So you see, it's not like it's some big, major thing."

"Relax, Annie," said Stonebridge. "Is it OK if I call you Annie? The last thing we want is to invest in some kind of mainframe for each elevator we own. Something that runs on an Altair would be perfect."

"What are you programming it in?" asked Stangdahl. "VisiCalc? I've been trying to use VisiCalc." He was referring here to the first generation version of spreadsheet programs.

"My Altair didn't come with VisiCalc," she said. "It just came with Basic. That's what I've been using."

Stangdahl stared at her. Was she making fun of him? It didn't seem in her nature. But could she be serious? He had struggled for months to come up with something useful, and had gotten nowhere.

"Basic? But Basic is a programming language, not a program. Are you saying you've built a whole program, an actual *program*, from scratch?"

"I guess so. Like I say, the computer didn't come with anything else. I got it second-hand," she added, guessing that this *VisiCalc* thing was supposed to come with it.

"And you're not a programmer," said Brandt. "Never took any classes, anything like that?"

"Well," said Annie, trying to explain away her lack of training, "the whole computer thing... it always seemed like kind of a lark."

Shades of Thorne Creek

"Gentlemen," announced Stonebridge as he opened his car door. "We've made a terrible mistake today. We agreed to keep Annie on for twelve months. But we failed to get a commitment from her that *she* would stay with *us*. Let's hit the road."

Once they were all settled in, he rolled down his window, and said to her: "Miss Dale, we'll be in touch very soon. We'll have some of our computer people call you. Would it be better for them to come here, or for you to come to them?"

Reacting rather than thinking, she said: "Here. Here would be best, if that works for you, Mr. Stonebridge."

As they cleared town heading northwest, Petroci, from behind the wheel, said: "You sure that was smart?"

"Hmm," intoned Stonebridge, not taking his eyes from the road.

"Telling her that. That she could be looking elsewhere?"

Stonebridge looked over to him, with a smile.

"You ever think," Stonebridge asked, without a hint of the sardonic in his tone, "of going into trial law, instead of corporate?"

Petroci thought about it, and decided to answer in the way least likely to open himself up to ridicule. "No," he said.

"Smart move." Stonebridge returned his gaze to the road ahead. "You need to be able to read people better. I read her eyes. She wasn't going anywhere. Something's holding her here. She was afraid, really afraid, that we'd let Gulleif collapse. She can't move on. We don't need to keep her here; we just need to keep her happy. I made her feel good about herself. I made her happy."

Petroci nodded, approvingly. "And so, Amazing Kreskin?" he asked. "What is holding her?"

Stonebridge shrugged. "Family is my guess, something strong. Doesn't really matter. As long as it holds her."

Petroci gave an imperceptible shake of the head: "So we forge ahead, not even knowing what it is."

Two: The Emery "El"

Stonebridge smiled, a smile of some fair inward satisfaction, and replied playfully: "K and C."

Annie watched their car till it disappeared up Highway 262, west and north. She pulled her coat tighter around herself, uselessly. Her mind flashed to Stonebridge's words about their terrible mistake, how they should have made her commit to working for them, and of how her life had just miraculously stabilized. She thought of her brother Bob, and all the terrible tumult that had been looming over him these last few years without his even knowing it, and how now he might never need to know about it.

In the gravel of the El's parking lot, a small stone caught her eye. Stooping, she picked it up, and straightening, she held it up before her, turning it, examining it. She smiled, and slipped it into her pocket.

She turned back to the El, spinning like a leaf borne on the wind.

Her mind flashed to Stonebridge's later words: "We'll have some of our computer people call you." The wind died, and the leaf settled to earth. Heavily.

Head down, she moved back into the Head House. Over the next half hour, she made three trips to the bathroom, and finally managed to vomit out her anxiety. Oblivious to what was going on with her, Ed Gulleif gladly OK'd her request to leave early. He was leaving early, himself. Tonight was a night to celebrate.

In that meeting in the Head House conference room, Ed Gulleif could have asked, but did not, what Barris' intentions were—what plan they thought would magically change the financial reports they had been given.

Had Gulleif asked, Barris might have told him their plan, or they might not. Had they elected to tell him, Ed Gulleif might have recognized the significance of it, and the danger—or he might not. But all of those points were moot. He did not ask.

And in that silence, where he might have asked, but did not, and where all the further discussion might have unfolded, but did not, there settled that secondary silence—the silence of a tumbler, falling into place.

Shades of Thorne Creek

Chapter 3: Andrew

Under Barris, little changed in terms of organization. Ed Gulleif was gone, immediately and by his own choice. He and his wife retired to a trailer park in Flagstaff, Arizona. From there they remained studiously in touch with all the El's employees, though strictly by way of holiday greeting cards (Christmas, New Year's, Easter) directed through the El.

Andrew Lanquist, formerly the Plant Foreman, became the El's Manager (Head of Operations, officially; a title which simultaneously embarrassed and pleased him. Manager or Foreman was what he went by, on a day-to-day basis.)

When he had taken over Ed's office, Andrew had cleared the walls to restore order. He had kept the original El plans hanging where Ed had them, along with Ed's sketches for the expansion. Andrew had added some high school football team photos and a handful of mementos. But beyond that, things began stark and clean.

In time, postings began to encroach. In the end, the office looked much like it had in Ed's day.

Andrew's blue-and-gold high school banner was mostly covered now, but the team photo managed to hold its own. Andrew had been a good player—never a star, but a good player. There had never been even fleeting thought of professional play, nor serious thought of college ball. Andrew did not have the academics for a college career, nor the superior heart and talent for a sports scholarship. He had known, from his sophomore year on, that high school would be the end of his playing days. But they were good times, and good memories, and the photo held its place against the tides of management concerns that washed papers across the walls.

Three: Andrew

The family farm had been Andrew's obvious, and only, choice. He had been faithful to that course, in as much as life had allowed him. There was a brief detour through the military during the Korean War. He had never seen combat, nor even been shipped overseas; he served at several stateside bases till the war ended during his stint. After that it was back to the farm, which he eventually inherited when his father retired from the life. But a back injury from Andrew's fall from a silo had ended that. Prospects of moderate middle-America prosperity slowly dissolved into eking by, by renting out their acreage to nearby farmers.

It was Ed Gulleif's dream of the El that had rescued Andrew from his slow financial death spiral, landing him a position as foreman.

There seemed to be a pattern in Andrew's life, a pattern of which he was becoming vaguely aware—a pattern of new promises that always seemed to founder. Sometimes it was his own shortcomings that caused it; sometimes it was circumstances beyond his control. But it always seemed to happen. Football, the military, farming. For reasons within or without, things just never clicked. But there was no reason now to think the pattern would continue. It had taken a long time for him to hit his stride, but this seemed to be it. He was a success. A modest *success*.

The job suited Andrew well, revealing management strengths that his days on the football team and in the military had, by chance or momentum, left untapped. When Ed bowed out in the wake of the Barris deal, there was no serious doubt that he would name Andrew to succeed him.

Apart from some requisite shuffling of responsibilities, the organization held steady. Officially, there was no Plant Foreman. One employee essentially slid into the role, but Andrew bided his time in making it official.

The tasks that had consumed most of Ed's time during the final dark years, drumming up new business and trying to find buyers for grain that was already stored, were handled invisibly by the remote powers at Barris. And in that, the change was dramatic.

Shades of Thorne Creek

Emery Elevator Operations had been a grain storage facility, whose income was derived from the rental paid by farmers for the storage space in the silos, from harvest time until a profitable buyer could be found. Once the grain was loaded, it stayed, sometimes for months. Idle money, locked away.

The Barris plan was different. The El was merely part of a chain of elevators across the Midwest. Barris made their money not so much in the storing of grain, as in the moving of grain.

Formerly, charges for loading and unloading were minimal; storage was where Ed Gulleif had tried to derive income. Barris boosted storage rates to where no one wanted to keep their grain there. What the customers wanted was a place to put their grain for a day, perhaps a week, until a buyer with a good price, or a silo with a better storage price (and there were always silos trying to beat out other silos on storage prices) could be found.

And with Barris' extensive contacts in the markets, there were plenty of customers to be found. By the politically tumultuous summer of 1974, Barris had transformed the El's fortunes.

The El's success was just a footnote to the sea change in the grain industry in the seventies. Mobility was key. The markets were changing, and the silos were changing, too. Elevators were being designed with the market changes in mind. They were being designed to move grain faster, and more frequently. Shifting more grain meant generating more grain dust, and the newer elevators were laid out in ways that allowed more handling with minimal increase in dust.

The older surviving elevators, of course, had been designed according to the older concepts. They had been designed for longer term storage, and were susceptible to excessive dust when impacted by frequent moves. They did not lend themselves well to the developing technologies for controlling dust.

The Emery El, of course, was among these earlier designs.

Andrew Lanquist was familiar, through reading if not through experience, with the problems posed by these differences.

"Lousy two-bit chiselers" Andrew muttered as he banged his fist on his desk.

Three: Andrew

Lewee Jorgesson jumped, reflexively.

Looking up in surprise, Andrew's faced softened for a moment, but only a moment, as he addressed her: "Sorry, Lewee. Not your fault." Then, snatching up the letter, which she had just delivered to him, from the spot on his desk where he had just tried to nail it, his face screwed up again. "It's these lousy Harkin people."

"What'd they do?" asked Lewee, honestly wanting to know, always eager to grasp more aspects of the operation. Lewee understood a lot of the goings-on around the El. But she wasn't as smart as she wished she was. She wasn't as smart as Annie, which is what she really wanted to be.

Andrew shook his head.

"Ah, that scrubber they sold us last year. And installed, at a tidy little fee, thank you very much. It had a bunch of dandy little features. Problem is, turns out they don't all work. Like that ever-lovin' external bin gauge that Hector was so hopped up about"

"Well, can't we make them fix it?"

"Oh, they'll fix it all right," Andrew said sarcastically, dangling the Harkin letter. "For a price."

"Mmmm," Lewee nodded. She knew Andrew wasn't angry at her. But it sounded like he was, and angry voices always knotted her up inside. It mattered to her, what people thought of her, and what Andrew thought mattered to her more than most. More, even, than Annie. Certainly, Lewee thought, more than what her mother thought of her. Mother was about all Lewee had these days, and Mother wasn't much. Father had been out of the picture for a long, long time. Which, although Lewee reflexively resisted admitting it to herself, was a large part of why Andrew's approval mattered so much.

Andrew looked up from the letter, and saw that Lewee's mind was someplace else.

"Don't worry about it, kiddo," he told her. "We'll straighten it out." Lewee left, and continued delivering mail.

Shades of Thorne Creek

Good kid, thought Andrew. *She's no Annie, but she's no dummy, either.* Letter in hand, he stood. Time to visit Hector, and review scrubber procedures. In person.

"Andrew?" Annie's voice came from out in the main office.

"Yeah." He slipped on his floor jacket.

"*Mrs*. Lanquist, on two."

His shoulders slumped. Midday calls were never good. Could be Andy. Or the car. Or the washer again. Or Andy. He picked up the phone.

"Joanie, I've got a lot on. Can it wait till tonight?"

"Oh." She sighed. "I… I guess so. Can you come home early?"

"Yeah, probably." The high school had called, he just knew it. Andy. This was not intuition; just experience. "I'll see what I can do. OK?"

Sitting at the kitchen counter, Joanie said "OK," and hung up without taking her eyes off of Andy. Her son rolled his eyes.

"Aw, come on, Joanie," he told his mother. "He'll think it's funny."

Joanie Lanquist felt the unease in her stomach, imagining Andrew's reaction to their son's new 'look', and calculating how many days, how many weeks, they would live with the reminder of this day.

Joan was Irish by descent, and in appearance; her hair was tinged red—though not the fiery red of her forebears. Hers was softened somewhat. Her demeanor was tempered even more, carrying none of the tempestuousness some would expect of her heritage. She was a calm and quiet woman, and when she spoke, she spoke softly. But despite this aura of reticence, or perhaps because of it, she had learned to speak her mind with conviction, even if her tone suggested timidity.

And so as she moved off through the house, silent as some disembodied spirit, young Andy began to sense that others might not treat his lark as lightly as he had intended.

Three: Andrew

Ignoring the lunch hour, Andrew headed down to the tunnels to track down Hector, and Annie took her usual lunch place at one of the long tables in the main office.

Uncharacteristically, Lewee joined her. Together they opened the brown paper bags they had prepared for themselves. Annie waited patiently for whatever it was Lewee wanted to discuss.

"Andrew was upset today," Lewee said as she arranged her sandwich and orange and crackers. Annie nodded, knowingly. Lewee continued: "Something about the air scrubber we bought from Harkin. Something about a gauge."

"The scrubber's just a big vacuum cleaner, Lewee, cleaning the dust out of the air. And the bin is like the bag."

"You've gotta keep it empty," Lewee observed, "or the vacuum clogs up. The gauge he was talking about, it measures how full the scrubber bin is?"

"On the nose, Lewee my dear. Previous models, you had to stop the system and lift the lid every once in a while, to check it."

"And that's what Hector liked about this new one," Lewee speculated. "The thing Andrew said he was so hopped-up about, why we went ahead and bought it. It has a gauge, so you can see without shutting it down, without opening the lid."

"That was the idea," Annie said. "I didn't read the letter, but it sounds to me like the gauge doesn't work. At least not always. Not enough so you can count on it."

"But they can fix it," Lewee announced.

"Oh?" Annie said, lowering her chicken salad sandwich.

Lewee smiled, rubbing her thumb and forefinger together: "For a price."

"Oh boy," said Annie. "That explains Andrew's mood."

Lewee smiled more broadly now. It felt good whenever she enlightened Annie on something.

Shades of Thorne Creek

Annie saw the flash in Lewee's eyes, and it made Annie smile. They were large, dark hazel eyes, by far Lewee's best feature, the sort of eyes a girl could drive boys mad with, if she were of a mind to.

Lewee's hair ran that middling ground between blond and brown, less attractive than either, but she had been blessed with a natural waviness that compensated. She wore her hair just short enough to lose most of that advantage, though. Annie wondered if the hair length was Lewee's choice, or her mother's. Lewee was old enough to live on her own, but she was still with her mother. Annie sensed it might be a somewhat stifling relationship, affecting Lewee's style. And her clothes.

As they ate, Lewee saw that Annie was watching her, watching her wrists, her tightly buttoned sleeves.

"I'm sorry," Lewee said.

Annie stopped eating, surprised. "Sorry? Sorry for what, Lewee?"

"About the blouse you bought me. I like it. I really do. It's just that...."

Annie had not realized till just then that she had been staring again at Lewee's shirt. Annie had tried to get her to loosen up, wear things a little more feminine, had even made her a present of a half-sleeve peasant blouse. Lewee had never worn it.

"No, Lewee. It's OK. It's just not your style. That's OK. You wear what you want to wear."

Lewee nodded. Quietly, subtly, during the rest of lunch, she rechecked the buttons on both her wrists, and the one tight up on her collar. Then, confident she was secure, she inhaled deeply and puffed herself up—a glorious bird safe within her protective cloak. *What would Annie think*, Lewee wondered, *if she really knew me? If she knew what this blouse concealed?* She straightened herself as if she were a preening peacock, smiling as her skin stretched and shifted over her muscles and bones.

* * *

Three: Andrew

The El received its grain at the top of its silos, and disgorged it from the silos' bottoms into a pair of underground tunnels running the length of the complex. The tunnels had long, continuous belts to carry the grain back to the Head House. There the grain could be raised as high as needed, and disbursed to waiting railroad cars or to trucks.

In the process of disgorging grain from the silos, and moving that grain along the belts, a great deal of dust was generated. And owing to the enclosed nature of the tunnels, this was one of the prime areas of focus for explosion control.

In a specially constructed room off one of the tunnels, the room housing the Harkin air scrubber, Andrew explained the new problem to Hector.

"I understand what you're saying," Hector shouted over the roar, "but the gauge is working."

"But this," said Andrew, holding up the Harkin letter "says we can't trust it."

Hector nodded with exaggerated range, as if the gesture might otherwise somehow be masked by the noise.

"I understand. I got a copy too, in the mail today. I'll check the bin. Every couple of days. Take it off line, open the bin."

"*Every* day, Hector."

"She builds up real slow, Andrew."

"*Every* day, Hector." Exactly the same inflection.

More nodding. "Every day. I got it."

Andrew looked at Hector levelly. 'I got it', as in 'I understand'. Not necessarily as in 'I'll do it'. Andrew knew Hector wasn't being evasive, exactly. He just wouldn't casually commit to things; he had to fully mean them. And actually, that peculiar sort of honesty formed a great deal of trust between the two.

It was over a year ago now that a party attended by many of the El's personnel ran late, and more than a little too wild. Four men had come in to work drunk the next morning, Hector among them. Andrew brought them all in to his office, one by one, to fire them.

Shades of Thorne Creek

One protested he wasn't drunk. He was the easiest of all; 90 seconds and out the door. Two had made elaborate and earnest pleas for their jobs, with expansive promises: Always to be on time for their shifts. No absenteeism. No more drinking, ever. They had gotten about ten minutes each, as a courtesy, and then out the door; Andrew had no use for employees who would lie to him, and he did not believe for a moment that the two would never drink again. Hector (who had actually been the first of the four to appear before the High El Court) had been different. Every bit as apologetic as the two resolute reformers, but without any false promises. He had said he wanted to cut back on his drinking, and that he was trying to. And that he would try never to be drunk on a workday morning. But if he ever was, he had vowed he would call in sick rather than show up and try to pass for sober.

Andrew hadn't been sure Hector would be good to his word, but he at least deemed it possible. And so Andrew had spared the axe. And he had gotten a valuable, and grateful, employee in the bargain, for the expense of just two sobriety-sick days in the time since.

With this history, Andrew knew that an 'I got it' was not a firm commitment to comply; it was an acknowledgement that Hector understood the depth of Andrew's concern. And that was better than just an unkept promise. Andrew would need to follow up, but at least he *knew* he would need to follow up.

So two unspoken, even unconscious decisions were made as the two men parted:

Hector, knowing from the letter that a bin gauge retrofit would become available for sale from Harkin in a few days, made no specific mental note to be sure his crew all knew about the daily check. It was Hector's job anyway. It didn't make sense to confuse things with a new official procedure that was going to go away anyway. But he would do the daily check, as best as his overburdened schedule allowed.

Andrew, while knowing he had not the slightest intention of paying more money to Harkin for them to fix something that had been delivered and installed non-functional, knew that safety required that the new daily check be codified in the El's operations handbook. If it was in the book, it would get done. While he would normally return to

Three: Andrew

the Head House to make a note to himself, or to mention it to Annie, he had other rounds to make around the facility, and Joanie waiting for him at home with some kind of news that he just couldn't *wait* to hear, thank-you-so-very-much, so he decided to save the making of the note for tomorrow.

And the engines of the Harkin scrubber listened patiently to both silent decisions being made, and rumbled on, slowly filling the bin.

* * *

At 6:05 PM, Andrew Lanquist rolled into the unattached garage, and made his way to the kitchen of his home, his castle, his sanctuary.

Joanie stood over a bowl, whipping something with a whisk, as though she had been mindlessly whipping it for days.

"OK, Sweet Stuff," Andrew said, with just a touch of resignation in his voice. "What is it? What's the news?"

She kept whipping, almost as though she hadn't heard. Then the whisk slowed slightly, and she half looked up to him.

"Andy..." she began to say, and then stopped herself. The whisk sped up. "Andy's in the living room."

Andrew pondered that. This was going to be bad. Maybe Andy had been in a fight? Got all bloodied? That would upset her like this. But then Andy wouldn't be in the living room; she wouldn't have him messing up the furniture, and the new carpet.

The new carpet. That's why he was in the living room. She had told Andy to wait there, so he could show his father what he had done to their brand new carpet. Did Andy know how much it had cost? Why, the installation alone....

Andrew shook off the thought. This was nuts. Time to find out. Go see what the fruit of your loins has done, Andrew.

Crossing the house, he heard the TV was on in the living room. That science fiction *Star Trek* crap Andrew hated.

Shades of Thorne Creek

"Oh, Andy," he muttered in anticipation, "you sure know how to set a stage." And then Andrew was at the living room. The two younger children, Julie and Eric, were nowhere in sight. Upstairs, doing homework. Or hiding.

No one was in the living room except Andrew Lanquist's first-born son. Andrew Lanquist Junior. Dressed in his very finest school clothes, immaculately pressed, clean. Sitting there before the TV, as it displayed a starship captain with his pointy-eared side kick. Andy, looking up from Andrew's favorite chair, saying nothing, smiling at him. Everything perfectly normal. Except that his son had not one hair on his entire melon-shaped head.

Andrew stood silent and still, like a god looking down from heaven upon his corrupt creation.

Still, Andy said nothing. Rather, he simultaneously arched both eyebrows—or what would have been his eyebrows, had they not been completely shaved off as well. The words were clear, in their silence: *Cool, huh Pop?*

Andrew said nothing. Turning toward the TV and beginning to walk all in one motion, he pushed the "Off" knob. Without pause he turned around and returned to the kitchen. Joanie sat at the table, the bowl of dark glop in front of her. She looked up at him balefully.

Images and ideas were beginning to move through Andrew's mind: Andy's clothes.

"Andy's clothes," he said. "This was picture day. At school. The makeup day for the school pictures, that he missed before."

She nodded.

"Did they take them?"

She nodded again. "The photographer was only at the school today. He had to take them."

"Did he say anything. Did he say why."

It took Joanie a moment, in her current state, to shift gears between talking about the photographer and talking about their son.

"Andy said," she began cautiously, "that he and his friends had been having trouble. In school. With Mr. Koch."

Three: Andrew

"Koch?" Andrew echoed. "Koch." Recognition dawned. "Koch—the gym teacher...." And it hit him. Koch was bald.

"The boys thought it would be funny," Joanie said, as if it all made perfect sense, "to have their pictures taken, you know... to make fun of him."

Andrew nodded, and nodded, and nodded.

"How many?"

"How many pictures?" Joanie asked, confused.

"How many boys shaved their freakin' heads?" Andrew clarified.

"The other boys chickened out. Only Andy."

"Is supper ready?"

"What?"

"I said 'Is supper ready'?"

She looked out to the dining room, then around the kitchen, then let her head bobble a moment or two, and finally said: "Yes. I guess so...."

He turned and went to the center of the kitchen. Finding a hanging fry pan he took it, along with a large metal spoon, and went to the stairs that led to the second story. There he clanged the pan like a dinner bell. In moments, two pair of puzzled eyes peered fearfully over the upstairs railing.

There had never been anything like a dinner bell in the Lanquist home, but all recognized this clanging pan for what it was: The first unspoken pronouncement in a night of wordlessness. They descended the stairs, and all gathered to their established places around the table, last of all Andy.

They ate well that evening—ate of anything within reach, or that could be covertly signaled for. But anything that had to be asked for, or that required some overt signal, was understood to be taboo.

In the brief wordlessness at the El that afternoon, proper procedural recordkeeping had been skipped. In the oh-so-long wordless stress of the Lanquist evening, the thought of a task to be done was lost.

Shades of Thorne Creek

And under the covering rumble of the faraway Harkin scrubber, as a bin slowly grew fuller and a gauge neared its ill-defined limit, no human ear could hope to detect the soft click of one more tumbler dropping into place.

Chapter 4: Annie, Deferred

A large portion of Andrew's next morning was spent on the phone. This would not have been his first choice; there was much to do in preparation for his coming vacation. The official plan was for it to be a Friday-evening-start weekend trip, but he harbored the idea, as yet not shared with Annie, to take Friday off. Doing that would require some extra time to be spent preparing things. He would have preferred to have spent his time on that, rather than on covering old ground with Stonebridge at Barris.

Andrew kept his door closed. Partly, this was to filter out the noise from the office, which itself filtered out noise from the Head House work floor of which it was a part. But mostly, the shut door was for Annie's sake. She didn't need the stress of knowing this call was happening, of knowing what was being said. Andrew himself would be the filter running in the other direction—letting Annie, again, know the basics of what Stonebridge was asking, but without the hype and the flourish and the pressure. Annie didn't need that. She didn't deserve that. She had given Stonebridge what she had promised him, what he had contracted for. That she drew the line there, and did not elect to give him everything he wanted, was a choice that was hers to make. Andrew might disagree with it, but he understood it at least in part. More importantly, he respected it.

"No, sir, I'll be sure and let her know. Today, sir. Yep. I'll do lunch with her, lay everything out."

As he listened over the next few minutes, Andrew's face took on subtle changes, changes that he was careful not to reflect in his tone.

"No sir, I really would prefer not to go that route. I am her boss. I am the Head of Operations at this facility." Invoking his official title was something Andrew did so seldom that no one in the office had any

Four: Annie, Deferred

definite recollection of it being done. "I believe it is proper for a proposal of this nature to follow the chain of command." Andrew knew Stonebridge had served in wartime, as he had. A different war in a different theater of operations, but a common understanding of, and respect for the value of, military procedure and courtesy. Even so, Andrew was reluctant to use the "chain of command" line again. If he relied on it too often, it would lose its power.

"Yes, sir, I can promise you that. Most definitely. I see the problems myself. I know the shortcomings. More to the point, Mr. Stonebridge, you need to understand: Annie Dale sees those problems too. Every day. She built this system. She knows what it can do, what it should be able to do." Now the tricky part—holding his tongue, so as not to insult the investment that Stonebridge had thus far been wasting: "I'm sure she wants to help turn things around, make them better. I know she wants that. But there are some complex issues on her end."

Andrew let his head rest in his hand, and massaged his forehead.

"No sir. I don't think so. In fact, I'm sure it won't. Money isn't the issue. Yes. Yes. I understand. Oh. I see. Very well, I'll be sure and let her know."

Andrew leaned his head back, and with eyes closed, he let the fluorescent light stream through his eyelids, like sunlight. He leaned back in his chair, as if it were a chaise lounge. The undifferentiated roar of the workings of the El became distant outboard motors plying the waters—some lake, some river, anywhere.

"Well, sir, what time will you be back from that? I see. I see. Well, I'll call you this afternoon. Either from here or from home. Yes sir. Very well. Thank you."

He returned the receiver to its cradle far more gently than his will directed.

Head of Operations. The title echoed in his mind. *Manager* of Operations. Subtle difference. Just a word here or there. The role of Manager fit him, but it didn't fit him well. He would rather run the operation than run the people. When he did have to manage his people, he would rather do it like this. Protector, defender. White knight.

Shades of Thorne Creek

But the rest of it? Dealing with employee absences? Correcting attitudes? Figuring who deserves a raise, and who does not? Who gets fired, and who stays? All of that was like an emotional meat grinder. In ninety-five percent of what Andrew did, day in, day out, there was nothing... heroic. Not at work, certainly not at home. It wasn't a matter of appreciation. Joanie and the kids appreciated him. And Barris ran his paychecks—what more appreciation could one expect at work? No, the problem was that he never did anything... never had the opportunity to do anything... that was truly *big*.

His eyes moved across the wall's photos and pennants.

Pathetic loser, he thought. *Longing for the glory days of high school football.* But he could not chide himself out of it; he did long for those days. Those days were filled with the prospect of heroism. Oh, there weren't many really big plays. Not many times when he made a difference—though there were some. But what made it special was the promise. Each play had the promise of greatness. Each time he crouched on the line of scrimmage, he knew: Maybe this time, I'll be a hero. And sometimes... not often, but often enough... he was.

He was being heroic now, stopping Stonebridge from pressuring Annie. But it was a low-grade heroism. And the chances even for this bargain-basement valor came too seldom.

With a sigh, he arose and moved to the door. As he did, as he passed his photos and pennants and framed clippings, he reached out to the wall; with his fist he gave a soft tap to one of the pennants. It was gesture he himself didn't fully understand. Part affection, part anger.

Outside his office, the general office chatter and the general work floor drone were louder. Annie sat at her desk, glaring at her computer screen, frustrated by the same sorts of problems that plagued Stonebridge.

Andrew was about to bark out her name, but checked himself. *Stonebridge* could start off *that* way, he thought. Time to add some value to the discussion. *White knight time.*

"Annie?" he called, loud enough to be heard over the din, but pleasantly enough not to make anyone jump.

She turned to him, dropping the frustrated look from her face.

Four: Annie, Deferred

"How 'bout a late lunch today?" he offered. She thought of the sandwich and apple and carton of milk she had brought in, stored away in the office fridge that morning.

"Sure," she said. "One o'clock?" Inwardly, she sighed. Andrew didn't take her to lunch on a regular basis, and when the offer came after a twenty-seven minute phone call, and he wanted to eat late so there would be no crowd even though there was seldom much of a crowd at a dive like the Dew-Drop Inn, it only meant one thing. Time to face the music again.

* * *

"Mushroom and Swiss burger," Andrew said, without consulting the menu.

Annie folded hers: "Chef's salad. Italian dressing, on the side."

The waitress didn't write anything. Separate or together, Annie and Andrew always ordered the same things. She took their menus and she was gone.

"So how bad was it?" Annie asked.

"Why, Annie. Whatever do you mean?" Andrew asked with a smile.

"Oh, Andrew. I'm sorry to put you through all of this."

"Annie. You aren't putting me through anything. This is all Stonebridge's doing."

"But I have the power to stop it. If I'd just go along."

"All right then. Let's go through the paces, just to keep old Stoney happy. Anything changed on your end?"

Annie shifted her water glass.

"OK then," Andrew said. "See how easy?"

"Oh, it can't be that easy. Not quite."

Andrew shrugged. "Okay, not quite. Two things. First, I need to run through the situation. Just in case you've developed a sudden amnesia. Or in case you think the program is running smoothly, like if you're in a coma or something."

She partly smiled, partly winced. She felt to blame for the problems, no matter what Andrew said.

"The Barris programmers have made another round of changes to Ella," he said, referring to the program that Barris now called "Elevator Operations Master Program". It had started as the program Annie had written, but, with every improvement the programmers tried to implement, it was becoming an increasingly problematic mishmash of computer code.

"I know," she said. "I got the latest diskette this morning, and installed it."

"How bad? Is it worse than Stoney is saying?"

"That depends. How many users does he say have jumped off bridges so far?"

Andrew cursed, but quietly enough that the specifics were shared with no one.

"That explains a lot," Andrew said. "Stonebridge's offer is this. He's willing to scrap everything that they've done to tweak the thing. Set it back to square one, the way it was the day you handed it over to them. He'll let you take it over. The Barris people will give you input, make suggestions, tell you what they want. But they won't touch the code. You'll have complete control."

"I wonder how many man-hours of programming they're talking about throwing away."

"Don't wonder about it. *Stoney's* not thinking about it. He's just thinking about the fact that nobody's using it. And the few that are, are getting their numbers so screwed up that they're going to drop it soon. If nobody's using the thing, then the programming money is shot anyway. So he figures, why not just admit it?"

"But the deal's the same, isn't it Andrew?"

He sighed. Seeing that the waitress was assembling their order, he waited till they had been served and she had moved off.

Four: Annie, Deferred

"You'd have to relocate to Kansas City. That's the only way they can see this working, as far as your interacting with the staff."

Annie smiled as she poked around at her salad.

"I told him, Annie. I told him, your moving from the area is a non-starter. I didn't tell him why. But I can. It might make him back off."

Annie shook her head, stabbed some lettuce, but kept the fork hovering in the bowl.

"I understand, Annie. It's none of his business. I'm just saying, if you do change your mind about telling him. You can tell him yourself, or you can give me the word, and I'll explain it to him. However you want to play it."

She looked up at Andrew, as he dug into his burger. She smiled at how football sometimes intruded on his speaking; it was like he was discussing the next play on the field.

Then her thoughts turned more serious. His face, his hands, the balding on his head, all showed him old enough to be her father. That was a good thing. She needed a father about now. And a mother. Her throat constricted; wrong time for such thoughts.

"There's more," he said, swallowing. "Don't know if it makes any difference, but here it is. They're upping their offer." His tone lowered. "Another five thousand. And the guarantee? It's *three* years."

She abandoned the fork to the bowl.

It was more than she would ever make at the El. More than she was likely to make anywhere. It might even be enough. If she got a really tiny place. Not a home; maybe a studio apartment. With the money Barris was offering, maybe she could afford the cost. She closed her eyes. Money would solve only half the problem.

Pushing away from the table, she sat staring at the salad.

Andrew set down his burger.

"Annie, this is the place where I have to pick which kind of a jackass I want to be."

She smiled, without looking up.

Shades of Thorne Creek

"I have to decide," Andrew explained. "Am I gonna be the kind of jackass who doesn't tell you how much I want you stay? Who doesn't tell you how much your being here means to the El, and to me? Or. Am I going to be the kind of jackass who *does* say all of that, and by saying it, just adds one more thing into the mix. Makes it that much tougher for you to decide what you're going to do?"

He picked up the burger, and took another bite. Speaking through the food, he added: "I dunno. Haven't decided which way to play it yet."

She looked up, but he couldn't meet her gaze. He focused on his plate as he chewed.

"You'll let me know," she said, "when you decide how to play it?"

He nodded. "Sure."

"I'm sorry, Andrew. I can't eat. I should get back to work."

"Annie. Stonebridge... he's never going to understand. You could explain it all to him, and he still wouldn't get it. He'd just throw more money at you, figure that would solve everything. No. Scratch that. If you told him what was really holding you, he'd just tell you to move to Kansas City. You. Just you. He'd tell you to leave Bob here."

It was the first time Bob's name had been mentioned, in all the discussions on the topic that had gone before.

"But that's just not going to happen," Andrew said. "And old Stoney's never going to get that. And don't even think about explaining it to him. Just let me run interference for you. And you do what you have to do."

She nodded, and was gone. Andrew waited a few moments, and then went at his burger again, silently cursing Stonebridge for adding another layer of stress into Annie's life. Andrew had met Annie's brother Bob a few times. Bob Dale was entirely a creature of habit, of routine. The slightest disruptions could turn his disposition. And whatever Bob felt, he acted on. That was part of his nature. Annie could have been so much, Andrew knew, without the responsibilities that she elected to carry for her brother.

Four: Annie, Deferred

Stonebridge would consider it all a waste. Andrew cursed him again—out loud this time, and catching the waitress' ear—and then he finished his meal.

Shades of Thorne Creek

Chapter 5: Annie and Bob

On that Friday, as on all Fridays, Annie Dale left work early at 3 pm, driving up Highway 262 toward Mitchell rather than straight home.

Outside of Mitchell, she came to Redeeming Love Convalescent, a Catholic-run facility serving some private but mostly county and state funded residents—the permanently infirm, the temporarily disabled. Mostly, the very, very old.

Cruising past the front entrance, she waved to the tall gaunt figure that waited, patiently as a puppy, for her Friday arrival. Wearing an incongruously warm jacket for the late summer evening, she knew he was not uncomfortable. He never was. Friday, 3:30. Annie was here, and all was right with the world.

"Howdy, Bob," she called cheerfully as she exited her car.

"Annie-Annie," he called out concussively. "Friday afternoon, what time. Time. T-t-t-time?"

She approached as he waited for her at the end of the sidewalk, where the concrete turned to grass, and his world ended. Beyond was Annie's world. As she neared him she crouched, with her arms extended.

"Time is..." she said, pausing her words but not her advance, "...three thirty!" Her hands went up, as did his, and she was at his side. Together they returned to the front door.

"Three-thirty it is," he said, shaking his head as if disbelieving his good fortune. "Three-thirty, three-thirty. Time to go."

"Time to go, Bob ole boy," she said. She noticed his close-cropped hair was clean, just washed this afternoon. The staff tried to get him all cleaned up on Fridays, if time and circumstance allowed. His dark hair

Five: Annie and Bob

was flecked with grey, and she sighed. *You've only got three years on me, Bobby. You can't be turning grey already.*

"Afternoon to you, Miss Dale," said the receptionist, traces of her Irish lilt still enduring after a lifetime in the Midwest. "Someone's been waiting for you!"

"Going to Annie's for the weekend, I am," Bob told Annabel, as though it would be some great revelation to her. "All weekend going to be gone!"

"Ah Robert. We'll do our best to hold down the fort without ye." Turning her attention to Annie, Annabel pulled out a small plastic bin of medications. "Sam's on rounds, so he left things with me. Friday and Saturday night?" she asked, pulling out two small envelopes and leaving a third.

"That's the plan," Annie confirmed. "And early enough on Sunday so we shouldn't need to worry about it." Annie only took the third packet on the rare occasions when they planned to be late on Sunday. But they avoided that if at all possible. Bob liked The Carol Burnett Show, and he liked The Carol Burnett Show *here*. As eager as he was to go with her, he would be eager to come back. Because that was the routine, and the routine was everything.

Annie completed the sign-out sheet and they were off. Weekend with Annie. Scary movies, and drinking coffee.

"Goin' to McDonald's we are! McDonald's. Having supper!"

And McDonald's, thought Annie, with a smile that was about as insincere as she ever got. They drove toward Mitchell proper to hit the McDonald's, and then back to Emery, back to home.

They always ate at home—never at the McDonald's, never in the car. Usually on the drive home she played the radio, so he could hear some top forty hits. Top forty wasn't all that popular in Redeeming Love Convalescent; the median age at RLC was a little too high for that. But this Friday she kept the radio off. She wanted the time, and the quiet (if Bob would oblige, which was doubtful) to think. To ponder her good fortune.

Shades of Thorne Creek

The Barris El was doing well, better even than in the early years. The El might not be flush with cash, but it was definitely, solidly in the black.

Her accounting, it had turned out, was entirely up to current standards, except in the most trivial of matters—which she had long ago rectified. She was even teaching Lewee some of it, and the kid was picking it up; it was doubtful Lewee would ever be able to take over, but she could probably handle most of the day-to-day entries.

And the program debacle had not been Annie's fault. Her programming, while crude and awkward in design, had proved quite competent in execution. The programmers that Barris had brought in had helped her clean up and lean-up her design; she, in turn, had taught them quite a few things about how the grain industry really worked, and had given them some off-kilter but oddly effective insights into how Basic could be used to handle it.

Stonebridge had phoned her from time to time, though he never again came out to the El. Without harping upon it, he had let her know that if she ever wanted to relocate to the Barris home office, there was a place for her there.

When it became clear that she would not take the programmer position in Kansas City, Stonebridge had made the fated decision to hand her creation over, fully, to his in-house programming people. That was when things turned for 'Ella', as they dubbed it. They had changed a lot in the program. Never with malicious intent, despite what the results always seemed to suggest. Now there was no way to fix it, short of resetting everything.

Annie looked to Bob, his head dipping almost imperceptibly in time with the gentle rhythm of the road's asphalt ridges. She knew she wouldn't be relocating.

Making Robert Dale a ward of the county had been a good move, the only move, back when it was clear that he was too much for their parents to handle full time. His mental retardation, though a heartbreak, was in practical terms only a nuisance when he was still a child. During his teens it was a trial, but Annie was there to help out. But once he reached adulthood things had changed, in ways that were not good. He

Five: *Annie and Bob*

was never violent, not exactly, not with people—but his anger could be close to it. Things got broken. Rarely, holes got punched in walls. The doctors experimented with medications, but Bob always seemed either too angry or too doped up.

By turning him over to the county, the Dales were still able to see him whenever they wanted, could take him home every weekend and every holiday, could even take him on vacations. The county agreed to place him in RLC, so he was just minutes away.

With Bob's move to RLC, Annie had something like a normal life for the weekdays for the rest of her teen years, and a huge load was lifted off her parents. In time, the doctors found the right medications to make Bob mostly normal, in terms of his mood.

Life was good, as good as it gets for a family with a retarded son, until Annie and Bob's parents died.

Bob didn't understand much about the dangers of automobiles and ice, and even less about the permanence of death. But he quickly learned what it was like to be at RLC always. As soon as Annie got past the funeral, and the financial arrangements, and got her own head settled with the new circumstances, she began taking Bob home with her, to what was once their parents' house and what was now her house, every other weekend. It went well, and she settled into making it every weekend. Sometimes for holidays. Never for vacations, though. She loved Bob, but she needed to breathe, too. She turned onto Highway 262, for the final leg to home.

"Turn like this, it was, where they died," Bob said to himself.

Annie's eyes widened. He couldn't know. It wasn't a turn *like* this where they died. Through the tears, she looked in the rear view, back to the intersection.

"Shouldn't drive in wintertime. Dangerous." Bob was looking ahead. He turned to her. "You don't drive in wintertime, Annie, do you."

"Gotta drive in wintertime, Bob. Gotta get to work."

Then, mostly to himself: "Quit workin'. Quit. Quit." He turned to her again. "Why don't you quit your job, Annie. Quit working."

Shades of Thorne Creek

"I've got to have a job, Bob. Got to pay the taxes. Got to pay the bills."

"I don't have a job. Nobody's got a job at 'Deemin' Love. You could come live with me. Quit. Quit workin'."

She shook her head, more to herself than to him. "Just doesn't work that way, Bob ole boy."

Nothing else was said till they rolled into the driveway. And then, for Bob, the universe changed.

"Coffee, Annie? C-Coffee? Coffee?" he said, clutching the McDonald's bag as they got out. "Make us some coffee for when we're done with McDonald's?"

"Coffee it is, Bob," she said, following him to the door. She tested him: "How much coffee you going to have?"

"One cup," he announced with conviction. "One cup. Just one cup. Till later. Till it's movie time." He held the screen door open, and she pushed the unlocked door open.

"Sounds like we've got a plan."

"Movie plan. Scary movie. Drink lots of coffee to stay awake."

* * *

Dinner was disturbing, but no more disturbing than usual. Bob had the intellect of a five year old, and the social skills of a twelve year old. That made him quite affable and very friendly in crowds, and with new people. But etiquette, apparently, fell more into the realm of intellect than that of social skill; Annie found watching her brother eat to be a very effective appetite suppressant. At times, it was almost an ipecac. By meal's end it often seemed there was as much food on his hands and face as had made it to his stomach. And the condition of his hands deterred him not in the least from eagerly grabbing things, so it was always a race to get him wiped down and then washed off as soon as the meal was done. His Friday night medications were taken at this time, so as not to collide with the midnight coffee that awaited them.

Five: Annie and Bob

As always, Annie set him to listening to the radio while she went upstairs to take a long hot bath. Showers were for mornings, but the long hot bath, that was a Friday night staple. And, while leaving Bob unattended for an hour was technically inadvisable, whatever mischief he got into was generally correctable. And for Bob, the freedom of an unattended hour was sort of a vacation in itself, after the structured, supervised week at RLC.

Later, they would sit on the porch, and talk about Bob's week. He loved to talk about it, and she loved to try to imagine RLC's side of things—for he usually had some complaint about unfair rules. It was, for her, sort of like a detective's puzzle. An idle amusement. Sometimes, like this night, they would doze, off and on, sitting idly on the porch.

As it grew dark they would clean up the table from supper—together, after a fashion—and then take a slow drive around town. Their equivalent of Sixties cruising.

By ten o'clock they would be home, so Annie could watch the news. Bob survived this half hour ordeal by Annie's expedient of breaking the program up for him into news, weather and sports; shorter chunks of time that did not, quite, pass the extreme limits of his patience and attention. She treated each segment like a new program. It was silly, and inelegant, but it worked.

At 10:30 it was The Tonight Show. Bob understood nothing of Johnny Carson's monologue, and little of the interviews, but he always understood laughter, and joined with it without either equivocation or the need for comprehension. He really liked funny people. And music, when it was performed on stage, was even better than on the radio.

During the penultimate commercial break, Annie began the big pot brewing, the movie coffee. She cut it with a 50% mix of Sanka, though she didn't tell Bob this. He needed some caffeine, she knew, to stay awake through Monster Theatre.

At midnight, with Johnny and Ed and Doc signed off, a local station ran their production of Monster Theatre: Some local personality sitting in a quasi-spooky set, instructing all twenty-three viewers about some arcane trivia of the horror film about to roll, and then the movie

Shades of Thorne Creek

ran. Limited commercial interruption (before, after, and two breaks in between). It was a black and white resurrection of the glory days at Universal, and on rare occasions a Hammer Films color gore-fest to shake things up.

Tonight was *Creature from the Black Lagoon*. Somewhere around the gill-man's being drugged and captured by the expedition's scientists, Bob dropped off to sleep. Annie watched on as the Creature, transfixed by Julie Adams, spirited her away to his lair. Richard Carlson, risking all, rescued her as always.

As the credits were closing, she pushed the "off" switch. She covered Bob with a blanket on the couch where he had first slumped and then later sprawled. Turning off all but a few faint lights, so Bob could see should he stir, she stood a moment at the bottom of the stairs.

In the dim hallway that paralleled the stairs, her eyes found the worn end table that had once stood guard beside a couch, then served as a keys-and-mail repository in the hall, and had somehow, without conscious plan or even thought, evolved into an odd sort of display stand. All that the table held now was a crudely woven basket, and the treasure of stones she had collected over the years. She suspected she had woven the basket herself, at some time in the misty past, but she could not recall that. What she could recall was bringing it in to her Sunday school class, to be part of a project. A stone-gathering project, based on David and Goliath. She had gathered five stones—no more, no less. That was what the project called for; five smooth stones. Annie remembered some debate with the Sunday School teacher about that, but five smooth stones it had been. Initially. So many, many more had been gathered over the years. None of them smooth like the initial five, but all of them interesting—in color, or texture, or shape. The years went by, and the number of stones grew. Milestones, of a sort. They were like markers of the passing time: Her work at the El, the program she had written, her caring for Bob.

She surveyed the living room. A perfect evening, really. There had been many perfect evenings, and near-perfect ones, and there would be many more. Life was good. Life was *stable*.

Five: Annie and Bob

Watching Bob sleep on the couch, she thought back. Years ago she had had someone over. Richard... Richard *Twelling*. She smiled and shook her head. She hadn't thought of him in years. They had sat on that couch, in the near dark, and kissed. Had begun, she imagined, to make out—though she wasn't altogether clear on what that phrase would entail, nor that she was ready to learn. Something happened, some interruption. Had it been Bob? Her mother, her father? No matter, really. Not much had happened, or would have.

But she wondered, what would it be like to have Richard Twelling in her life? Or *some* Richard Twelling.

She thought of Bob's grey-flecked hair, of growing old.

Maybe this life, she mused, was better than that other one would have been. But even if this were better, where would it lead? Bob would get old and gray. Someday they would both be in Redeeming Love. One of them would die first. She would leave him, alone for each and every day of sameness. Or he would leave her, leave her wondering if being an old woman living alone in RLC had really been worth it. She turned to face the carpeted stairs, but she did not move. She was too young to feel trapped. Too young to feel her life was all decided, and determined, and that there were no ways out.

She felt an unease in her stomach. She took one step up, and stopped. She remembered how she had felt on a recent early-winter afternoon at the El, also when life was good, but also when circumstances seemed beyond her control.

She took another step, and waited. Tears welled in her eyes, and her stomach shifted again. Her mind returned to the basket of stones; it only reminded her of her childhood, of the time that had passed since then, and the crush of responsibilities that adulthood had brought onto that young, young girl who had fixed the cloth liner in place, who had selected with youthful care those first five stones. She tried to push the basket from her mind. But it would not go.

Methodically she climbed the stairs, much as she had methodically trudged back into the El on that cold day.

And she spent the early morning hours of Saturday much as she had spent that winter's afternoon at the El.

Shades of Thorne Creek

Saturday dawned early—brighter than any Saturday, even the best of Saturdays, had any hope of being. It was a glorious day, a day of familiar adventures for her and Bob, and a day worth enduring the night before.

But the night before was not forgotten, and would not be forgotten. She resolved to pursue the questions that had clung to her that night. Patiently. Calmly. Most of all, in their time. But not on a Saturday. And least of all, on *this* Saturday.

Chapter 6: Lewee

"Child, you can't sleep the day away," Mother Jorgesson called up. Lewee twisted deeper into the tangle of sheet and blanket and comforter. In a normal volume of voice that she knew would be muffled in the point blank bundle pressing her face, she answered:

"I'm nineteen and a half years *old* Mother. I can *so* sleep the day away, if I choose."

"I got pancakes about to hit the griddle!" Mother called up.

Lewee's eyes opened, even as every other muscle froze. She pulled the bundle away from her face.

"You got buttermilk?"

"While it lasts, I do!" and Mother Jorgesson retreated into her kitchen, her lair, knowing her task had been accomplished.

Lewee flung off the covers, resisting with all her will the urge to yell some insipidly childish exclamation of joy. She fairly leapt from the bed. Grabbing her robe from behind the door, she bolted for the bathroom. She leaned into the tub. Hot faucet. Cold faucet. Adjust. Test. Readjust…. Perfect. She flipped the lever up, and the water streamed from the showerhead, grazing the curtain.

She turned, and saw herself in the mirror. The pajamas, with the buttons she had awkwardly added, still secured her wrists, her ankles, her neck. She smiled at the thought of shower time.

Pushing the bathroom door fully closed, she listened for it to click, then pulled back to confirm it was secure. She pushed in the center lock button, and when it clicked, she turned the knob to ensure it resisted her. Near the door's top, she slid the bolt, and dropped its handle down into place, then slid her fingers across its length, smiling.

Six: Lewee

She flew at the buttons, and shed the pajama top and bottoms onto the floor. There, before the mirror, she stood, and turned, and arched and stretched, mostly faced away from the mirror, looking over her shoulders. She felt glorious. She *was* glorious. And every week she was more and more glorious. More and more the Lewee she wanted to be, and less and less the Lewee her mother understood, or thought she understood. Less and less the Lewee of her mother's dreams; more and more the Lewee of Lewee's dreams.

Her eyes moved again to the door, to the latch, securely in place. Taking her robe from where she had carelessly cast it, she hung it right by the front edge of the shower, right where she could grab it and clothe herself with it, if Mother got it into her head to suddenly, somehow, enter.

Stepping in, she dipped her face into the shower stream, swallowing, spitting, swallowing, spitting. Then she let the water run over her, as she moved her soapy hands over herself, just the way she wanted Billy's hands to move over her. Just the way Billy's hands would, someday. Somehow. When he came back.

She was nineteen and a half. But she felt like a woman. She felt wanted.

Buttermilk pancakes, she thought. She hurried through her shower. Then she quickly, but carefully, and thoroughly, dressed.

Bounding down the stairs, she smelled the cakes. She smelled melted butter. And syrup… Mother had heated syrup on the stove.

Sailing into the kitchen, she slid noiselessly into her chair, in front of a plate with two six-inch pancakes. Her mother had eaten; her soiled plate had its steel flatware laid across it.

Lewee dug out a big hunk of butter with her knife, and began working it across the two.

"Keep 'em comin' Ma."

"Oh, Lewee. You've got yours," her mother said, frying up more pancakes for leftovers.

Shades of Thorne Creek

Lewee spoke as if she didn't know where the conversation was headed: "Gotta have more than two 'cakes, Ma. Lots to do today. Gotta stoke up."

Mother Jorgesson moved to the table, stood in front of the place setting where she had eaten.

"*Bulk* up is more like it. More than two cakes and you'll start to balloon out. You know that."

"Mother, I am *not* fat."

"Not *too* fat. Just." She returned to the stove and flipped the cakes. "You've got to watch that kind of thing, Lewee girl. Got to watch that figure, keep it trim. Got to catch the eye of a good man, and marry well. These days some women can make a go of it on their own. The really smart ones. You're smart, Lewee, but not that smart. Not smart enough to make it alone. Not smart enough to do better than being a go-fer girl at the Emery El."

Mother was too busy attending her pancakes to notice that Lewee had emptied the cup of heated syrup onto her two pancakes, and more syrup from the bottle until the pancakes fairly swam. She was eating with a spoon, slowly, so as to be sure she did not finish before her mother saw.

"Men want a trim body. Not much a woman can do about her face, but she can sure do things to.... Lewee Jorgesson! Goddammit, girl, what do you think you're *doing* with all that syrup! You clear out of here right now!"

She shooed Lewee away, but not before Lewee grabbed the quarter-carton of juice from the refrigerator. She guzzled it as she piled out the back door.

"You think it's funny now!" Mother Jorgesson yelled out, not caring if the neighbors heard. "You see how funny it is when you're sitting around on your fat butt! With *no prospects*!"

Mother let the screen door slam behind her as she moved back into the kitchen. Taking the pile of pancakes she had prepared, she dumped them into the trash. She snatched the half empty bottle of syrup and threw it there as well.

Six: Lewee

The phone rang and she jumped. Then, setting herself like a tigress, she swept into the living room to get that phone.

Lewee finished what she wanted of the juice, then tossed the near-empty carton in the general direction of the neighbors' open trash can.

Lifting her bike off the grass, she pedaled away. She would have preferred to drive, but she'd left her keys in the house, and she wasn't going back in there, not just now. Her bike was a three speed, but only one speed worked. It was a speed that suited her, though.

Taking beauty advice from a frumpy old crow, thought Lewee. *Advice on how to land a man, from a woman who...* she let the thought go. She didn't want to think about her father's leaving. Father didn't leave her. Father left *Mother*. There was nothing wrong with Lewee, Lewee knew. She knew that. She knew it. Her memories of her father were mere fragments—but what memories survived were positive, and warm, and good. She nurtured them; they were all she had left of Father.

She pedaled toward the store, and she passed Annie Dale's house, and she watched Annie and her brother playing Frisbee in their back yard.

It must be nice, Lewee thought, being perfect just the way you are. And having a perfect life.

At Herky's Market Lewee bought an icy Coke from Rachel Saunders, the reliable fixture behind the counter. It was a transaction without conversation. She liked Rachel, but Lewee wasn't in a mood to chat. Before stepping out, Lewee made a quick scan of the comics rack. She hadn't bought a comic book in almost three years, but scanning the covers, even just reading the titles, set her in the mindset she wanted. Carefree youth; the joy of a secret place. She slid the Coke can into the hand-crafted wire basket she kept affixed to her handlebars, and she was off.

She followed a meandering route through the shaded streets of Emery, working her way to where the streets faded into crumbling asphalt, and the grass—first lawn grass, and then wild grass—reclaimed its dominance. A trail, too narrow to have been formed by foot traffic, but the product rather of bicycle tires, had been worn all the way up to a vague parting of brush. Following the path, she emerged from the de facto hedge onto the perimeter of a corn field—what had once been part of the Tommerson farm.

Her well-worn path led up the long, slight ridge in the farmland, then turned and followed the property line. Eventually it led to a grove of trees. Lewee always thought these were the last remaining trees after countless acres had been cleared to make way for farmland. In reality, the land had, for countless generations before the farmers came, been a vast treeless prairie. The trees had been planted by the farmers in strategic places to serve as windbreaks, as snow drift stoppages. Now, even as they served the farmers as a kind of shelter in winter, they served that same purpose for Lewee in summer. Coasting to a stop within the tiny strip of forest, she took her Coke and laid the bike on the ground at the foot of a slight rise.

She moved between the oaks that stood on the rise. On the far side, as the ground sloped back down, was a treeless patch perhaps twenty feet across. Within that area a collection of boards had been laid, covering the man made hole that was the cave, the shelter, the pit, or whatever its current occupant chose to call it.

The hole had existed long before Billy had found it. There was no telling how many "owners" had claimed it, and perhaps even unknowingly concurrently shared it, as their domain. During Billy's reign, it had been his alone—until Lewee had caught his eye, and he brought her to it.

One end had no covering boards, and had a sloping edge of dirt that one could navigate down easily. Stopping halfway down, Lewee reached over and banged on a covering board. She was always concerned about the errant badger, or woodchuck, or who-knows-what, which might have taken up residency. But nothing ever had.

Hearing no response to her warning, she descended into the dark. In minutes her eyes adjusted to what light came in through the entry, and between the loose fitting boards. There was almost enough room to stand upright. But this was not a place to stand. This was a place to sit.

Six: Lewee

She nestled into a spot along one wall, and leaned back. The cool damp soil welcomed her as she settled back against it. She gently twisted the Coke can into a standing spot. She closed her eyes.

This was a powerful place in her memory. It was the first place she had kissed Billy. Not the first place he had kissed her, because he had rashly snuck kisses twice before then. But this was the first place she had returned the act, and where they had explored just what a kiss could be, beyond a stolen peck.

Billy had wanted to explore a good deal more in the dark seclusion, but Lewee had managed to control him, and herself, so that things never got too far beyond what she was comfortable with. For his part he had remained gentlemanly, within the limits his hormones would allow.

The place had thus remained a place bordering on the forbidden, yet a place of fond memories, rather than of shaming ones.

When Billy had disappeared, she had continued to come here. At first, she hoped he would rendezvous with her, explain his absence, and lay out his plans for their flight and their future life together.

Later she came here in order to relive the memories of being close to him, of the heat of their breath mixed with the cool of the earth, to wonder if she should have stopped those advances she had stopped, and how things might have been different, might have somehow ended better, if she had not.

Finally, she had reached the point where she came here simply because it was a place she liked to be, in the here and the now. A quiet, cool, alone place, with no pressures, and no demands. A *Fortress of Solitude*, as Billy had called it, in a term she believed he had gotten from a comic book.

That morning, in her own good, sweet time, she shifted the square of plywood that concealed the hiding place beside her—the hiding place that had once concealed a bottle of whiskey that Billy had nursed for three weeks, and still had not come close to finishing—and she drew from within that space the double-padlocked box in which she kept her inmost self. In it were her short stories (*her* short stories, her private ones, not the ones she had written for class in her school days) and the letters she had written to Billy in the days when she still hoped he would return to read them, and, of course, her drawings. All the evolving drawings of her glory, from the earliest sketches to the final plans she was now executing.

Taking the box over to the light streaming down through the entrance, she flipped through the three-ring binder of her writings and the drawings, and reveled in the wonder, the marvel, that was her.

A short way away—yet endlessly distant from the sunshine where brothers and sisters played Frisbee, and young girls hid in earthen forts—in the tunnels beneath the El, Hector went about his weekend maintenance routine.

Over his workbench, behind the battered metal door that guarded a workman's treasures, Hector slid aside a large and oil-stained box, which bore a gaping tear.

The box housed a one-way air vent, a vent that should have been installed along with the other five of its kind that *were* installed with the air scrubber. But there was a loophole, an accounting oversight, in how Harkin tracked what parts had been installed and what parts had been deemed damaged beyond repair and then destroyed. It was a loophole large enough for an unwitting El employee to carry a supposedly extraneous air vent through[1].

That El employee had seen pointless waste occurring, and had secured for his company a near-perfect free spare vent assembly for use some time down the line, and all had seemed right with the world.

And in the tunnels of the El, five ducts were secured against the unexpected, and one was not. And the scrubber chugged away, drawing air out of the tunnels and into the scrubber room. There was no interruption of the system, no blockage that would have made the presence or absence of a one-way vent an issue, and thus the air flowed exactly in the direction it was meant to, and all seemed right with the world.

---

[1] The details of this oversight appear in the Appendix.

Six: Lewee

And there was no sound of a tumbler falling into place, and neither was there a silence to mark a tumbler's fall. Because this tumbler, signified by a spare assembly that was not a spare assembly, had fallen into place long ago. This tumbler had fallen into place before the purchase by Barris of the El, with a spare-tracking policy that assumed a seemingly sound, but, flawed, equation: Items Shipped minus Items Returned equaled Items Installed.

Shades of Thorne Creek

Chapter 7: Sunday Morning

What might well have been the most anemic rendition ever of *A Mighty Fortress Is Our God* doddered its way down the center aisle of Holy Redeemer Lutheran, past rows of unpadded wooden pews, and out through the large oak doors at the rear.

Bob Dale didn't mind; he charged on with singing it, getting all of the notes and most of the words right.

Annie didn't mind, either. What the presentation lacked in dramatic power it made up for in familiarity, in predictability, in the sameness of one organist playing the same tunes on the same instrument for as long as Annie remembered. Like endless reruns of *Davey and Goliath* stop-motion animations, or flannel graph cutouts of indistinguishable disciples, the melody carried a promise, perhaps imperfectly expressed, of something important, beyond the here and the now.

"Did we in our own strength confide / Our striving would be losing," she intoned with those around them. The Appletons. Rick Snell and his wife. Andrew and his clan—uncharacteristically near the back, this Sunday. And Andy Junior wearing a hat through the whole service. She could ask Andrew about it tomorrow, but thought better of it.

"...from age to age the same / And He must win the battle..." Her eyes rested, as they often did at such moments, upon the small but fantastically brilliant stained glass windows that Holy Redeemer boasted. Of all the colors of all the bits, there was one piece of blue, in the halo about the dove of the Holy Spirit. On this late summer morning, struck dead-on by the sun without, it fairly glowed. It sang, in its own right. Everything in these glassy depictions was glorious, and

63

Seven: Sunday Morning

important. They were a reality heightened; depictions of scenes of inexpressible import, of events that had happened long ago.

But when they happened, were they then so surreal? Did the colors sing at that time? Or did they seem, to those who watched, or even to those who participated, to be just so much more daily life? Did those events, in their time, feel like the events of Annie's own life now?

"The body they may kill / God's truth abideth still / His kingdom is forever."

And on that happy note the hymn ended, as did Annie's reverie. She maintained a mask of dutiful attention for the balance of the service, but all the while worked over and over in her mind what she would say to Reverend Ackermann. Before she left, she would ask him for a chance to talk. A time to consult. She had refused to dismiss the thoughts that had haunted the early, early Saturday hours—for they were the sorts of thoughts that were certain to return at some point, and she was not about to stand helpless before them again.

The service staggered forward, reaching its predetermined end. Annie and Bob lingered as the others filed out, till they could be the last to depart, the last to greet the pastor as they left. The transaction of the request, when it played out, was awkward. Annie was uncomfortable with asking for spiritual help; Reverend Ackermann was unaccustomed to congregants seeking it.

But her mission was accomplished, and the Reverend asked her to return that evening, at seven, which worked well for her because by then she would have just returned Bob to RLC. So her mind was free from burden for now, and she and Bob returned home to change, so they could wander about the fields, and along the tracks between Holy Redeemer and the El, and could look for adventure and for treasure. And, if time and circumstance were with them, perhaps they could make some treasure of their own.

* * *

Shades of Thorne Creek

Lewee lounged at home, uncertain what to do with the morning. She needed to leave by five p.m., but what to do till then? She had her keys in her pocket this time; that was the main thing.

The phone rang. Lewee's eyes locked on it, then flashed across the room. No sign or sound of Mother. Before it could ring twice, she made her move for it. Her hand was extended, just inches from the handset, when her mother's voice came:

"What the *hell* to do think you're *doing*?" Mother was just outside the rear screen door, a pile of laundry in a basket under her arm.

Lewee stopped and straightened, and prepared for the assault. The phone rang again. Mother set down the basket—dropped it, nearly—and flung aside the screen to bluster in.

"You heard me, child. What are you *doing*? You know better than that. You know the rules. *I* answer the phone."

Ring.

"Ma, for God's sake, I live here too."

Ring.

Mother's eyes went wide, and wild: "You pay the taxes? You pay the phone bills? *I* pay, Lewee, and I make the rules." Ring. "*I* answer the phone."

"So answer it!"

Mother's expression grew less angry and more uncomfortable. The rationality of the suggestion was hard to avoid.

Ring.

She snatched it up: "Hello." It was a flat, affectless greeting.

Lewee folded her arms.

"Wendy, I'll have to call you back." She set down the handset without waiting for a response.

"God forbid," Lewee muttered, "I should wind up talking to Wendy."

"When it rings you don't know who it is," Mother said, without looking up from the phone. "You don't know that it's Wendy. Or that

Seven: Sunday Morning

it's your boss. Or who it is." She looked up, and held Lewee's eye: "It could be anybody. It could be somebody wants to do you harm."

"Jeez Louise, Ma."

"Might be somebody, wants to *do you harm*."

Without unfolding her arms, Lewee cocked her head, trying with some fair success to look like a dog that had just heard some incomprehensible noise.

"Someone who wants to *do* something to you," Mother said. Then, almost as an afterthought: "Like that Billy."

"Ma, Billy never *did* anything to me."

Mother's eyes widened. "Not hardly, he didn't. He *scarred* you."

"It wasn't a scar, Mother. It was a butterfly. A butterfly tattoo. And it was pretty. And besides, Billy didn't make me get it. I *wanted* it."

"You never wanted to pollute your body before, disfigure it, like some darky savage from Africa," Mother scolded. "Not before you got mixed up with him."

Body art, Lewee wanted to scream at her. *Mutilation,* her mother would shout back. All of this, ground that they had covered before. Lewee just stood and fumed. And then, like some evil spirit bent on tormenting them, the phone rang once again. Mother stood burning her glare into Lewee, as if not hearing it.

Again it rang.

"Well, Ma? *I* can't answer it."

Ring.

"Nobody needs to answer it, child. Let it be."

"What are you afraid of, Ma? Billy coming back, to take me away?"

"Ha!" she grunted, and then spoke right over the ringing: "That one's gone for good. Won't be seeing the likes of him 'round here."

This was Mother's not-so subtle reference to the infamous court order. She had found a sympathetic judge in Mitchell who would let her lie to him about Lewee's age. And so she got her paper; a restraining order for Billy to stay away from her "minor" child, and that had done

Shades of Thorne Creek

her dirty work for her. Billy was gone, disappeared into the streets of Mitchell. Or maybe Sioux Falls, or even Fargo. Lewee had no way of knowing. And Billy had made no effort to contact her. Victory for Mother.

Ring.

"God damn it, Ma," she said as she stormed out the front. Then, yelling back through the slamming screen: "Answer the flippin' phone, will ya?" and she piled into her battered VW Bug.

Without taking her eyes off Lewee, Mother waited for the Bug to begin to move, and then she snatched up the phone—by now somewhere between rings ten and fifteen.

"Hello!" This time, the word was not without affect. She listened, and her expression changed. The hard anger fell away. But in its place came not peace, or joy, but rather a kind of sickened revulsion.

"Why are you doing this? What did I tell you?" The anger was beginning to return. "You stay away from here, away from Emery. And you stop calling." She listened. "I'm her mother, that's what gives me the right. She's my daughter. You stay the hell away from my daughter."

* * *

"Makin' money. Like crooks!"

"Not exactly like crooks!" Annie yelled to be heard over the roar of the train. She kept a firm hand on Bob's shoulder, in case his enthusiasm started him moving toward the tracks too soon.

The wind from the passing cars blew her hair wildly. Bob's crew cut seemed to take no notice. The train was moving fast—faster than she remembered. With a slight change of pressure, she eased Bob back a step. Then two. Box cars, hopper cars (perhaps with grain, but if so, not destined for the El), tanker cars, all hurtled by. The rails undulated beneath their weight, straining at the spikes that held them to the creosote-soaked ties.

Seven: Sunday Morning

For a moment it flashed through her mind how helpless they would be if something went wrong—if a spike failed, and a rail shifted, and a car derailed. But she did not ease Bob back yet another step. It was a foolish musing, and enough of Bob's life was being ruled by fears of death. She looked to him, saw his face leaning forward into the blast of wind from the rocketing cars. As it should be, she thought.

When at last the train had passed, she gave him a gentle pat; he rushed to the tracks to search for their freshly minted currency. The former nickel had fallen off the rail, but he found it soon enough, holding it overhead like a prize.

"For my collection!" He ran up and showed it to her. She thought of the battered cigar box he kept at home, filled with such flattened relics. What did that make him? A philatelist? A numismatist?

Bob ran ahead along the tracks, scanning for more glorious debris.

Fred Sanford, Annie thought with a smile, and followed him. As she did, she scanned the ground—scanned the stones that formed the rail bed. The stones were all the same, either from the same quarry, or from near-identical quarries. But here and there a different stone could be seen; some may have been brought in when the tracks were laid, or kicked up from the nearby native soil. But most of these irregulars, she figured, had gotten lodged in a rail car somehow at some distant location, and had simply chosen this place to fall out. Strangers, in a strange land. One stone, in particular, caught her eye. It was reddish brown, and had the look of frozen foam. Volcanic, perhaps. Crouching, she picked it up.

Annie heard Bob's voice, now some fair distance ahead of her. Mystery rock in hand, she stood.

"Fire!" Bob announced. "Burned it all up. All burned. Burned."

Annie came up beside him, and they surveyed the patch of blackened earth, two yards wide and running five yards along the far side of the tracks. Jet black.

"Burned. Burned right up. Annie? A-A-Annie-Annie? What for did it burn up? Why."

Shades of Thorne Creek

Annie smiled and walked on. She wondered how many times over the years she had explained it to him. The concepts were just a little too complex for him to retain. But he liked hearing things explained, anyway.

"Train wheels," said Annie, enjoying the smell of the burned grass. It was the smell of burning leaves, of autumn, intruding just before its proper time. "A bearing must have worn out. Got too hot, and melted. Little bits of molten metal, spewing out along the tracks. Caught the grass on fire."

"And burned it up. Burned it all up. Burned it *fast*."

Annie smiled again.

"Not this train, Bob. Some train yesterday, or Friday. It always burns slowly, when it happens."

"Moten... moten... moten metal," he muttered, working over her earlier words, as best he could, committing them to memory.

"You might be able to find a piece, if you're lucky."

"Moten! Add some moten to my collection!" He moved on ahead of her now, scanning the ground.

"If you see anything glowing," she warned, "don't you dare touch it!" The bits of metal had to be long cooled by now, and probably indistinguishable from the rocks along the tracks. Best to be safe, though. Always best to be safe. Her own reddish treasure she slipped into her purse. If it had once been molten, that was centuries ago, maybe even millennia. But just as Bob had a place for his manufactured treasures, Annie had a place for her natural ones.

Less than a hundred yards away, in Tunnel B of the El, a worker stooped down and, with a leather glove, carefully scooped up a glowing metal bearing. The metal scorched the leather of his glove, yielding an odor unlike burning leaves, and unlike autumn.

Shaking his head he moved back and forth along the conveyor, looking for the roller that he knew must be moving erratically. He found it easily—the roller that had spit out the bearing. With the bearing missing, the roller moved unevenly, and that caused the grain

Seven: Sunday Morning

to bounce ever so slightly upon the belt at that point. With a hunk of chalk he marked the wall nearby with the date, so he would know on Monday where to find the roller again, so it could be replaced.

But his task was not yet done. Dutifully he made the long walk to Hector's shop, and set the now cooled glob of former-bearing metal on Hector's desk. He was about to leave, but then decided to take that sort of extra step that Hector, and Andrew, and the never seen memo-writers at Barris, were always asking for. Scanning the wall, he found the battered Floor Handbook—a collection of three-hole-punched papers, with bolts run through the holes in an impromptu binding. He flipped through it to the page, pressed it open there, and laid it out on Hector's desk. He even set the bearing, now far too cooled to threaten to ignite the paper, smack in the middle.

Best to be safe, he remembered their oft-quoted adage. Always best to be safe.

That page of the manual was, itself, a kind of a tumbler. To an outsider it looked like a fine example of proper caution being taken:

"Report any damaged, and especially displaced, bearings. Rollers that are short of bearings are likely to throw more bearings, and thrown bearings can be a source of ignition. Report all roller problems so that recurring problems can be noted, tracked, and resolved."

To the investigators' eyes, the passage would tell a different story: The story of a problem—poorly maintained and inadequately lubricated rollers—that was addressed with reactive, rather than preventive, maintenance.

The passage clarified that someone knew that this problem was a source of heat, a source of ignition. A source of one of the legs of The Deadly Pentangle.

Chapter 8: Sunday Night

"I'm not sure what I'm looking for," Lewee told the librarian, casting an occasional glance at the clock. Plenty of time before closing, but not before her appointment. *Move it along*, she thought. "Fiction, I guess. But something... I don't know... important."

"A classic," suggested the librarian, pulling out some sheets from behind the counter. "If that's what you mean, we have classics of American Literature, or of Western Civilization...."

The American Lit sheet had some things she had already read. *To Kill a Mockingbird*. *Tom Sawyer*, and *Huckleberry Finn*. *The Great Gatsby*. There were collections of short stories by Hemmingway, and by Poe.

The Western Civ list held more appeal—fewer things she had read, and more that had a sense of greatness beyond the here and now. Homer. Shakespeare. Chaucer. Milton.

She had read one of Shakespeare's plays in high school. It was a tough go, but she had followed it. Scanning, she came upon another author she had experienced before. Dante.

"This one," she said. "*The Inferno*. I think I tried it once before. It's about Hell, right?"

"That's right. How did you like it?"

"I didn't," she said with a smile and a slight shake of the head. She had struggled with the book during the summer before her last year of high school. "It was too much."

"Too intense, too vivid," the librarian acknowledged. "A lot of people find it disturbing."

"No, it wasn't that. I didn't get far enough for that. I just couldn't understand it."

Eight: Sunday Night

"Were you reading an annotated version?" the librarian asked.

Lewee looked at her, puzzled.

"Were there footnotes in the version you had?"

"Yeah, I think so. I didn't read them, though." As she thought, the experience came back to her more clearly. "I mean, there were footnotes for everything. I couldn't get into the flow of the thing if I read them all."

"You know," the librarian leaned on the counter, full of thought. "We have a very good version, the translation by Longfellow. And it has excellent annotations. What you ought to try is reading a Canto, that's a chapter, with all the footnotes. Read every bit of them. Then as soon as you're done, go back and read that Canto right away again, without the footnotes."

"So I'd be reading it twice?"

"Sort of. But I think you'll find, it's like reading it the first time, both times through. One time to learn the background, and one time to enjoy."

Lewee remembered that summer telling Mother that she was trying to read *Inferno*, telling her how hard it was.

"Putting on airs," Mother had told her. "Trying to read above your level. Don't be trying to run a diesel engine on gasoline, child."

Lewee shrugged, and asked the librarian: "What else would you recommend?" But her eyes lingered on the line on the sheet: *The Inferno, by Dante Alighieri. A poet's journey through Hell.*

* * *

"I've been thinking about things," Annie explained. "About my life. Life in general, I guess. I know things are good, that I have everything I could ask for..." she wandered on.

Already Reverend Hunt Ackermann was breathing easier. No medical crisis. No confession of some uncomfortable sin. Annie was looking for an attitude adjustment. He patiently waited for her to work through the thumbnail sketch of her life and her fears, and he steepled his fingers as he studied her.

When it was his turn, he spoke in reassuring tones: How this sort of thing, these sorts of questions and feelings, happen to us all, and how they are normal. He even took a chance with her, and suggested an exercise he would not try with most:

If she could be... anywhere she wanted to be. Doing for a living... anything she wanted. And forget training and forget money and forget current responsibilities. If she were simply having a dream right now and she could dream right now that life was any way she wanted it to be... what would she be dreaming?

For most of his congregation, he would not suggest such a question; it would lead them to consider things that, for them, were better left unconsidered. But Reverend Ackermann thought he knew Annie Dale pretty well.

She thought about his question for a time, and then she smiled.

"I guess you're right," she told him. "This must all sound pretty silly, now. But you're right. There isn't any place I'd rather be."

Click your heels, Dorothy, he thought as his steepled fingers collapsed into an interlacing grasp. *Three times. Click. Click. Click. There's no place like home... there's no place like....*

"It just seems like... there should be something more."

The Reverend's gears ground for a moment. Then he adapted.

"Tell me what you're thinking," he suggested amorphously. "What you're feeling. What kind of a 'more'?"

"Something... eternal," Annie suggested.

He nodded, knowingly. He had been down this track with others. He released the interlacing grasp of his hands; this particular chess game was over. Since Annie wasn't likely to be headed for a seminary, the course was simple:

"The Bible tells us that we're all created with part of the eternal within us. It's in our nature. It's normal for us to long for it."

Eight: Sunday Night

She listened without reaction as he spoke into her soul. The eternal. Longing for the eternal. He understood her, she knew.

"The Bible also tells us that the eternal is where we are headed, where we are destined. That this yearning which we all feel—it will one day be fulfilled."

She knew he really wasn't saying anything different from what he often said from the pulpit. But it *was* different somehow, having it spoken just to her. Directly *to her*. Like the voice of God coming in a revelation.

"The Bible also tells us that we are *here* for a time, in an imperfect world, a world that only hints of the sublime eternal to come."

The sublime eternal to come, she thought. What a beautiful phrase. It reminded her of that one piece of blue in the stained glass window.

The sublime eternal to come, Reverend Ackermann thought. That was one of his favorites. He had come up with it himself, in seminary.

"And for this time, here on Earth, we are given much work to be done. Not just our daily work on the job...."

It was Annie's turn now to feel a grinding of gears. But she stayed with him:

"...but also the job of becoming who God wants us to be. The lessons of life, that prepare us for the eternity to come." The Reverend paused. "That's what I suspect you need, Annie. The focus that will help you through. During this time, while we wait for the joy that is to come, try to focus on how every experience of life can help prepare you, help make you more the kind of person that can enjoy more fully the joy of heaven yet to come."

Annie nodded, digesting. *Noble endeavor*, she thought. *Becoming what God wants me to be*. She tried working the thought around. But the whole proposition seemed like one more task, one more duty to be performed, to be fulfilled. One more responsibility. The thought would not digest, and she felt her stomach knotting again.

"I see," she said, hoping to stall while the conversation resumed its earlier tack.

Shades of Thorne Creek

"It's a glorious opportunity here, this life we are given, Annie." He laid his hand upon hers. "Revel in it. Glory in it. And all the while, use every moment to become the woman God wants you to be." She was single, which could be good or bad for this next bit, but he decided to toss one out along the biblical lines, since she seemed to like that: "Every day, becoming more the perfect bride. Awaiting her bridegroom, the glorious Christ who will return for her. For us, his Church." *Hallelujah, Amen* he wished for a chorus to respond; a musical exclamation point.

Somewhere between the additional chore of prepping herself for heaven, and being summarily drafted into the wedding party, something inside Annie withdrew. She smiled at the Reverend Ackermann. It was a wholly and uncharacteristically insincere smile; it fell across that bridal dress she had just imagined, like a splash of mud. All the darker, because the smile was convincing. She had to leave. She extended her hand, and someone with a voice very much like hers said:

"Thank you, Reverend."

"Any time, Annie. This is what I'm here for."

She drove across the tracks, to Highway 262. But she did not cross 262, did not head for home. Instead she turned south, and drove into the night. She drove past Thorne Creek Cemetery without even noticing it.

Five miles of sameness in the roadway calmed her, and she pulled over. She emerged, stood beside her car, and thought. Sliding onto the hood, she looked up to the sky.

"Why five stones?" The question seemed as clear as the day she had asked it. She remembered it, with a suddenness that seemed inexplicably reasonable. And she remembered the substitute Sunday School teacher, who had towered over her, but had not frightened her:

"Five stones is what David gathered up."

"But why five?" young Annie had persisted, concealing well her exasperation at not being understood. "Why did he gather up five? He only used one."

Eight: Sunday Night

"Well, I suppose he didn't know he would only need one."

Feeling the engine's warmth radiating up through the hood, Annie relived the long-past exchange:

"But he trusted God," young Annie had insisted. "David trusted God to help him beat the giant. So why did he think he would need five stones?"

Her inquiry had been met with silence.

"I mean, God knew David would do it with one shot. Why didn't David trust God enough to just pick up one stone? Why did he take five?"

If there had been an answer, or further discussion along that line, the memory of it remained veiled. The rest of her memories were more vague; she and her classmates on their outing to the dry riverbed of what had once been known as Thorne Creek. Each of them gathering up, as had the young David, five smooth stones. Annie had lined her homemade basket with the disused cloth, which she had trimmed to size and shape, and arranged the small stones within it. The stones had always seemed small, almost lost in the basket, and so she had added to them over the years. But, by happenstance or by unrecognized compulsion, none of the stones she added were smooth. They were rough, or jagged, or in some way—any way—irregular. Only those first five had been smooth. Only those first five had been worn down by years and years of flowing water.

Annie thought of the basket in the hall, and felt an urge to dig through those later stones, and to seek out the original five. She had no idea why. She wondered, then, why Thorne Creek had run dry. It had happened when she was very young, and the water never returned. If she had asked, she might have been told. But if she had been told, it was another memory lost long ago.

There still was no water in Thorne Creek, even to this very day. But there was water along the highway. The ditches had collected enough water to make home for some frogs, and they sang into the night along with the crickets. Rarely, a nighthawk called as it circled some distant target. There were no sounds that were human, no words of rational discourse. Just the sound of creatures, singing that night much as they had when God had created them long ago. And over them were the stars, singing in their own way.

And in that night, and in that dark, something not understood by Annie stirred, more forcefully than it had over the last few days, stirred as it had when she was a child. Something that would not be reasoned away—or be spoken out of existence by hollow words, or even, for a time, be comprehended—found for itself a welcome place inside her.

* * *

Lewee impatiently walked a sidewalk in Mitchell, watching, waiting. She was due for her appointment. She made a long circuit of this seedy stretch, not wanting any casual observer to notice what storefront was the focus of her prowls. She had discreetly parked two blocks away; even if she somehow managed to land a parking ticket, the connection to this place would be nil. As she passed the store front again, her eyes fell with annoyance on the posted closing time, and then to her watch.

Five minutes over. Let's go, let's go, she silently chided whatever lingering patron was holding things up. *He's paid by the job, not by the hour, so don't stand around and chitchat.*

She forced herself to walk two full blocks beyond, without looking back. When she turned, she could see that the shop lights were still on—their illumination leaking out around the drawn main shade. She paced out her return. She wore a light windbreaker, needless on the summer's evening. She carried no purse, having left it in her car. The cash she would need was stuffed in her jeans pocket.

Should have brought the book with me, she thought. Dante Alighieri's *Inferno* had been left on the front seat of her Bug.

When she was one block away, the door opened and the customer left. She waited for the man to enter his car and drive off. She resumed her approach. From across the street, she studied the place. Lights off. CLOSED sign posted. A quick flash of her eyes up and down the street, and she crossed. Without hesitation she opened the door, entered, and

Eight: Sunday Night

locked it behind her. Stale cigarettes, stale beer, and chemicals all mixed in their familiar way in her nostrils.

In the dim light filtering out from the backroom, she saw there was a small table beside the door, a table she did not recall from earlier visits. She flipped on the light. On the table was a crude wooden bowl, with one business card.

A. A. Anderson, Tattoo Removal, Minneapolis, Minnesota.

She crumpled it, and flicked off the light. Then she thought better of it, unfolded the card, and slipped it into her pocket.

She thought of calling out some comment, but elected not to. She slipped off her windbreaker, leaving it on a waiting room seat, and made her way to the back, unbuttoning her sleeves.

She took out the business card, smoothing it face down on the workbench beside the timeworn tools.

"Go ahead and write down the number of that preacher man," she said, unfastening the rest of the buttons.

Shades of Thorne Creek

Chapter 9: Andy Junior

Andrew Lanquist Junior daydreamed through shop class. This was not normal for him—not in shop class, anyway—because he was good with his hands. He liked making things, and breaking things, and fixing things. He actually liked shop class more than most other classes. Except for three things.

First, this was summer school. Summer school shop class, for God's sake. Whoever heard of such a thing? Andy's grades weren't bad enough to warrant serving time in summer school. He suspected it was more to keep him busy than to pull his grades up. Cs, with an occasional D, were enough to get him where he was going in life. Wherever that was.

Second, Mr. Koch, the gym teacher, handled shop class. Mr. Koch had always had it in for him, and his failure to appreciate the humor of Andy's head-shaving stunt had done little to improve relations. Mr. Koch tolerated Andy, and most days Andy tolerated ole Koch. But theirs was not a model for teacher-student relations.

Third, they were covering soldering, and soldering was for babies and city kids. When shop class, as the last class of the day, finally let out, Andy burst forth from school to do the real thing. Welding. Farm welding.

Without stopping at home to drop off books (he could set them someplace safe) or to change clothes (he knew how to be careful) he biked to the debris of the old Tommerson farmstead. Tommerson had died five years back, his only heirs being Sioux Falls city folk, and some nephew in St. Paul, none of whom wanted anything to do with a farm. Except the money, of course. Everything had been auctioned off, everything that ran or might be made to run. The land had been sold to various farmers around Emery, mostly neighbors who could just keep

Nine: Andy Junior

right on plowing and planting and harvesting, but now across the old property lines and onto their newly acquired land.

The house and the pole shed still stood, because nobody wanted to go to the trouble of tearing them down and clearing the trees just to squeeze out one more acre or two of land. Everything inside the two buildings had been stripped out, of course; everything of value. Or at least, everything anybody thought had value.

Andy dropped his bike at the power pole; he checked the old dirt roads that crisscrossed between properties to be sure no one was driving in the vicinity. And then he climbed. First he climbed the four small gaffs he had improvised and mounted himself, short enough and painted so as not to be noticed unless someone really tried to look for them. And who would bother looking, out at some old deserted farm? Using them, he reached the L-shaped metal rungs the power company had pounded in, and then climbed those to the top. Step by step, he made sure his school clothes didn't get stained by the pole's creosote.

At the top he used the few simple tools he always left there to reconnect the power, and then down he went.

Leaving his bike and his schoolbooks in a heap in the weeds, he raced to the pole shed. There, behind the bent sheets of corrugated steel, behind the disused timbers that weren't worth salvage, he found his prize: the submerged arc welder.

It had gone unsold in the auction for two reasons:

First, there were no welding rods left for it, and no local stores carried them. This posed little difficulty for Andy, as he knew right where he had hidden the rods before the auction inspections had begun.

Second, it didn't work. This also posed little difficulty for Andy, since with his electrical wiring skills it was relatively simple for him to reconnect those internal wires he had disconnected—again, before the auction inspections.

So here it sat, unused, unwanted, but now completely functional—and powered up, as long as the brittle lines between the power pole and the shed held. And if they gave out, well, there would be places a resourceful young boy could get more wire.

Shades of Thorne Creek

He scrounged through the shed for metal scraps, searching out what might make an interesting project. He found a few pieces, and spent time scraping off the rust—you have to have good clean surfaces to work with. He had figured that one out all on his own, even before ole Koch started the solder unit.

The rust came off easily, but both of the pieces also had some greasy goo that he was only able to shift around, not remove. No problem. In the back corner of the shed was a trap door—whose existence had somehow gone unnoticed during the auction inspections (perhaps due to *someone* doing some strategic last minute shifting of heavy debris). The door led down to a kind of a storm cellar. It was dank and musty and unpleasant smelling, except for the perfume of the magic goop-be-gone. Switching on the bare bulb, Andy brought his metal over to the large tank, with the faded sticker of Mr. Mercury on the side.

The contents of the catch-bowl beneath the spigot had all evaporated, so he would have to pour out some more. He used it sparingly, because once the tank was empty he had no idea where to get more. Then he'd be down to scrubbing with gasoline, which he'd most likely have to pay for somewhere, and then transport here.

But for now, Mr. Mercury's tank of Benzole still sounded almost a third full, and Andy knew how to be sparing.

"I will give you MORE MILES PER GALLON" Mr. Mercury was quoted as saying on the peeling sticker. But Andy knew what old man Tommerson must have known before he died. The National Benzole Company's gasoline additive, Benzole, was an excellent degreaser.

Opening the spigot, Andy rinsed the metal, scrubbing it with his hands, while the extra was collected in the bowl beneath. And like magic, the metal was clean. And his hands were clean. And the stale stink of the cellar was sweet again. Sometimes, even when he didn't need any, he would drip a few drops just to enjoy the smell.

Returning to the surface, Andy experimented, and he learned. And every day his welding skills improved. He had everything he needed. A goodly supply of welding rods. Trustworthy, steady power, care of the county electrical co-op. A farmyard full of scrap metal to work with.

Nine: Andy Junior

And a way to make it all clean and bright and ready to go. National Benzole had hit the target with their Benzole product. Gasoline additive. Cleanser. Andy wondered what else it could do.

It could do other things, of course, and it was doing other things, every time he opened the spigot, and breathed it in, and washed it over his hands. But what it was doing, Andy could not have guessed, even if chemistry class had been this year instead of next. Not unless he had recognized the similarity in the spelling, and not unless he had guessed that Mr. Mercury's Benzole had only one ingredient: the highly toxic, deceptively simple chemical compound known as benzene.

* * *

"I guess the main thing is," the young man said to Andrew, "I want what I'm doing to mean something. To last."

Andrew leaned back in his chair, studying the eager young man. The kid's crew cut suggested conservatism, of which Andrew approved, though in fact it was a hair style of necessity owing to the young man's profession.

"Not the sort of pitch I get from most contractors," said Andrew, with a smile. "So you don't get that kind of satisfaction, that kind of meaning, with what you're doing now?"

"My boss has an ongoing contract with Willabee Refining, in Minnesota. He's just one of a bunch of companies, working different parts of the same job."

Paul hadn't answered his question yet, and so Andrew waited.

"Willabee shuts down part of the plant, and we go in. We strip down all the paint, whatever's left from the last time it was done, and we put on the new paint. Then Willabee shuts down another part, and we go to work on that. Pretty soon the work we did, back behind us, is dry enough. So they open 'er back up again, behind us. Meanwhile we keep moving through the plant. Stripping, repainting, moving on."

"Sounds like honest work," said Andrew, not sure where Paul was going with this. Paul shifted his compact frame.

"It is. It's honest work, and it's hard work. And it's endless work. By the time we've finished the segment of the plant we're under contract for, a year has gone by. And it's time to go back and start stripping and repainting the place where we started. And it just goes on and on like that. Forever."

"That's nuts," Andrew said, shaking his head.

"I know. It's steady work. But after a while, it drives you kind of crazy."

"The paint job only lasts for a year?"

"We're talking about places that are constantly exposed to things. Yeah, it eats it away."

"Doesn't sound too pleasant."

"Well, that's the second part. They ventilate it pretty well, and we wear masks. But yeah. After a while, you start to feel like it's in you, all the way down to your bones."

Andrew shook his head: "And you want to leave all that... your dream job... behind?"

"I am seriously considering it, you bet." Paul leaned forward. Their senses of humor were clicking, and Paul had a good feeling. "Something like this..." and he swept his hand over the El's blueprint laid across Andrew's desk, "...I figure my brother and me, and a couple of the guys who want to come with us, we could strip this, and paint it, and it could last. For years."

"And once you're done, you'll be out of work," Andrew observed.

"There's always more elevators out there, Mr. Lanquist. You're owned by Barris. I figure, me and my crew do a good job, maybe you could put in a word for us."

"You're used to working in a shut down. That's no good for us here."

"*Partial* shutdown. We could do one tunnel, your A Tunnel maybe, while you keep running the B. But it has to shut down, Mr. Lanquist. You can't have stripping and painting going on while live grain is rolling by, right?"

Nine: Andy Junior

The kid was thinking, Andrew could see. Anticipating. Foreseeing problems.

"How long would you need? To have it shut down?"

"You tell me what you can live with, Mr. Lanquist, and I'll figure out how many guys I need to bring along, to meet it. We're used to working on schedule. Endless rolling deadline. We know how to do what we need to do."

Andrew liked Paul Sorensen, and hoped they could work something out.

"It's late," Andrew said. "What say you come in at seven tomorrow, and get the tour?"

Paul Sorensen smiled. It wasn't a signed contract; it wasn't even a handshake commitment. But he had the job; part of him, deep down inside, knew he had the job.

When Paul left the Head House, he didn't turn onto 262 to head to Sioux Falls, and his motel. He crossed 262 instead, and headed to Herky's Market—which, apart from a few bars, was the social hub of Emery. Other than Eddie Glazer—the infamous Teapot Eddie, who was just hanging out to kill time till his social rounds began—Rachel was the only one there.

She leaned across the counter toward Paul.

"Well," she breathed.

"I think so," Paul said weakly. "I think I can pull it off."

She reached across the counter, grabbed him around the neck, and kissed him.

"You can do it," she told him. "You can make it happen."

"If Donny will come. And maybe some more. It's way too big to handle on my own."

"Donny's your brother. He has to come." Her conviction seemed more born of necessity than reason.

"I guess. I hope. But if he doesn't, I'm going to be in a real mess. It could really set us back. Really mess with our plans."

"One way or another, we'll make it work," she said, tidying the counter. Then she added coyly: "Picked out the dress today."

"Better not show me. Don't wanna be getting ideas."

"You better be getting ideas, mister," she teased him. "Hey. I'm off in ten minutes. Want to celebrate? *Chinatown*'s still showing."

"Sure," he said. *Or the new Charles Bronson movie*, he thought, unable to recall the title *Death Wish*.

* * *

"I'm not sure we should go."

"What the… not go? Why would we not go?" Andrew demanded. He had barely settled into his chair in the living room.

"Andy hasn't been feeling that well in the mornings. You know that," Joanie told him, as if, in fact, he did know that.

"Andy doesn't like going to summer school," Andrew explained as though it were obvious. "This is a vacation. He will miraculously recover from his malaise, once he hits the Mississippi."

"It's not fair exposing Arlene and Ted and their kids to something. He could have something contagious."

"What he's got *is* contagious. It's an attitude. But Arlene and Ted know about it already, and they're willing to expose their kids. Andy! Get your butt down here!"

There ensued a brief silence, probably while Andy considered the possibilities of what he might have done now, versus the likelihood of his father having found out. Presently, he tumbled down the steps, delivering himself into their hands—silently, in case it was something major.

From his living room chair, Andrew looked up at his son, saw the stubble that was beginning to regrow, and then looked away before he started them down that path again.

"Andy, do you want to go to Minneapolis?"

"Well, sure. We're going on Friday, aren't we?"

Nine: Andy Junior

"You sure you feel up to it?"

Andy looked puzzled.

"You haven't been feeling well in the mornings," his mother reminded him.

"Oh, Joanie…" he began. But the glare from his father snapped him back. "*Mom*. I'm fine." A stupid slip-up, Andy knew. She would let him call her Joanie, most times. But when *he* was around, forget it. And if he ever heard Andy calling him Andrew? And not just Andrew, but AND-rew the way he did it? Then man, good night.

"OK," Andrew summed up. "Let's see how you feel the rest of the week."

"Dad…."

"We'll see how you feel. You say you're fine? Fine. Just feel fine, and we'll go. Simple."

Andy retreated upstairs, and Joanie turned to Andrew.

"I swear," she said. "If he had an arrow sticking through his neck, you'd say he was fine."

Shades of Thorne Creek

Chapter 10: The Lewee-Bird

"For heaven's sake, Lewee. Why don't you just stay home on Monday mornings?" Annie's question was perhaps two parts sympathy, one part annoyance. And maybe a dash of concern over what the nineteen-year-old had been doing the night before.

Lewee was in no condition to analyze the ratios, or the various sentiments behind them. She merely shrugged—and in the moment she did, she paid for the gesture. The pain to her skin had finished almost as soon as the session had ended last night. But the muscle aches from her tensing during the procedure, those would be with her the rest of the day, and to a lesser degree, the rest of the week. And part of it, she suspected, was from sleeping face down. She didn't sleep well, face down. But before long, she could sleep on her back again.

She gently hefted the plastic bin of parts, and made her way to the man lift belt. Some Monday morning soaring would help ease the pain.

Annie watched her move unsteadily away. Had she been drinking? Her eyes weren't red. And besides, Lewee didn't seem the type. Part of Annie wanted to talk with Lewee's mother about it, but she wouldn't. She had spoken with Mrs. Jorgesson before, and the conversations had usually been strange, often strained. And besides, Annie had access to Lewee's W2; nineteen years old. And a half, as Lewee would often point out.

Lewee approached the man lift belt, walked up till it was right in her face with the rising treads almost clipping her nose. She paused, and then turned around. Reaching down, she let the rising fabric straps of the handgrips brush her left palm one by one, while she held the parts bin to herself with her right. After counting a few cycles, she grabbed one and let it lift her arm, and she stepped back without reservation

Ten: The Lewee-Bird

onto the next tread that came. In a moment the belt had accelerated her, and she was off on her flight.

At once she was in the netherworld above the office, but still far below the gallery floor. With the bin held secure, she leaned back on the belt and eased her grip on the handhold, reaching up higher with her freed left hand as though it were piercing the air for her. The ascending and descending belts of the four elevator legs carried their scoops of grain, faster than the man lift belt was designed to go. From time to time a kernel of pebble-like corn would fall, sometimes clanging near her, sometimes even hitting her. Feeble hailstones, powerless against her eagle-like ascent. Shafts of light snuck in through gaps in the Head House's sheathing. It was a wonderland that she sailed through.

The gallery floor approached, and then passed. Some of the guys spotted her.

"Hey Lewee-bird! Fly away!" one of them called. She sailed on, smiling, her left arm dropping to her side. Time to sharpen up now. The scale floor was here—no time to doodle off in dreamworld. Above, a flashing yellow light reminded her: This was the last exit. The flooring of the scale floor cruised past, and she leapt off the belt, landing with an exaggerated flourish she had learned in high school gymnastics. Her back and her arms and her legs ached as she swept her body out, but she didn't care. Her dismount was perfect.

There was a clapping of hands, and she saw that Ed Libraro had been watching her perform. She blushed slightly, but despite the pain, she re-enacted her last motion in a bow.

"Ah, Lewee, you're quite the thing."

"Thanks Mr. L.," she said, mimicking the Ralph Malph character from *Happy Days*. She handed him the bin of parts. "Anything going down?"

"I've got some reports." He sauntered away, patting dust off his worn coveralls. Lewee wandered among the enormous funnel-shaped scales that received grain to be fed to the galley lanes atop the silos. Grain was roaring into them, filling them, and she laid her hand across one to feel it. Rushing to the window, she looked down at the hopper cars on the off-load siding, dumping their grain. Belts fed it into the Head House, and onto the elevator legs that had been passing her, up to the very top of the Scale Floor, where it fell into the funnels.

Beyond the hopper cars, a train shot past on the main line, so close to the parked hoppers, it seemed to Lewee, that a person on the off-loading hoppers and a person on the rocketing boxcars could almost reach out and touch.

And lose their hands, thought Lewee. Annie had said the trains were moving faster; to Lewee it looked as though she was right.

And the trains were faster. Regulations had been reworked in early 1974 to accommodate increased demands. Upgrades and increased maintenance had been implemented also, all of which meant that the trains that used to travel this line at 40 miles per hour now traveled at 49. The scant nine miles per hour increase in speed had made quite a bit of difference to freight scheduling.

"Here you go," Ed said, handing Lewee a stack of papers.

She waved them at him as if in salute, then returned to the far side of the man lift belt, hopping on for the descent back into the mortal world.

The pain was passing, she noted. What she felt most on her way down, though, was the itching. But scratching was the one thing, above all, she must not do. It could ruin everything, ruin her beauty.

* * *

Lewee took lunch at Herky's Market, buying a sandwich from the vending machine and a Coke from Rachel. She sat at the counter and chatted with Rachel, who, it was generally rumored, was affianced to that young Paul Sorensen who used to live in Mitchell, and who was back in town to try to swing some kind of job at the El.

Would he move back to Mitchell, or even Emery, if things worked out?

Rachel was coy at first, but in time let on that they might settle in Emery. Or in Mitchell. Or even in Sioux Falls. There were so many

Ten: The Lewee-Bird

possibilities, if the contract at the El worked out. But Lewee had to promise not to tell anyone, especially Andrew Lanquist, just how important this deal was for Rachel and Paul. They didn't want to lose their bargaining power.

And Lewee didn't want to lose it for them. She swore herself to silence. She loved secrecy.

Across the street, the man parked in the '71 Chevy Impala, watched her, as best he could, through the Herky's window.

Could that be her? She would be nineteen by now. The age seemed about right. But it was jarring to see her grown up. Part of him always thought of her as the infant she was when last he saw her. Part of him wished she still was that infant. All grown up, now. All grown up. So many years they could have been together, wasted. So many things they could have done, as father and daughter. But she had never known him. And he had never known her, not really.

She emerged from Herky's. For a moment he thought of slumping down, but thought better of it. He might just draw attention to himself. And he was far enough away to not be noticed.

He tried not to stare at her as she crossed back to the El. In the El's lot, she passed by the battered VW that he had watched her arrive in, that morning. It had to be her. She was the right age. And it was the right car; he had checked the plate number. It was the one on which he had been paying the license tabs for years.

Was there still a chance? Might he be able to re-enter her life? There was so much to tell her, so much to explain, so much to share.

But, as always, there was the Dragon Lady.

He started the car and drove off, in search of a pay phone. There was one here, right outside Herky's Market, but it was better to use one farther off; he headed for Mitchell.

Nineteen years old. She was dating, no doubt—only a delusional parent could assume otherwise. And who did Lewee have to guide her through those troubling waters? Her mother? The woman was so twisted inside, she wouldn't know a healthy relationship if it bit her.

Shades of Thorne Creek

He should have been there, through all these years, to guide her and protect her. He could have warned her about boys—about what they wanted, about the games they play, and how to resist them.

He was drawing near to Mitchell now, and as he veered off into the seedier districts, he thought of Lewee making her way through all of that alone, without the counsel he could have provided her. Should have provided her. Would have provided her, if that disturbed woman hadn't seen to it that he was out of Lewee's life.

Could Lewee forgive him, for not being there? He wondered. Could she ever understand the kind of power her mother held over him, the power to destroy him, the power that had kept him away?

In the last few months, he had gotten to where he didn't care anymore. He had to get back into his daughter's life. No matter the risks.

He scanned the street. Two bars boasting competing beer brands in their windows. A tiny place whose neon sign declared it to be "Electric Jesus" (though whatever it was, it was clearly not a church). A pawn shop promising guns, electronics, and check cashing. Yes, this was the sort of neighborhood he needed. Here, he could be on a payphone, and shout and yell at the Dragon. In a neighborhood like this, no one would pay him any mind.

He spotted a payphone in front of a converted storefront. First Assembly of Mitchell, said the sign propped up in an otherwise opaque-sprayed picture window. Assembly of God, he assumed. Fitting. Hellfire and damnation backdrop for a fiery exchange.

Since Lewee was at work, he knew the phone at home would ring many times. On the occasions when he did not know whether Lewee was home, he could always tell by the number of rings. Many rings? She was away. Just one ring? Lewee was there, being guarded by that three headed hell-hound.

Eight rings. Nine. Ten.

"Hello?" The voice sounded so even, so rational. Hard to believe it was the same voice that he knew would soon unravel. "Is anybody there?"

Ten: The Lewee-Bird

"I'm here."

A stream of muttered profanities. The descent was faster than usual.

"Where the hell are you calling from?"

"I'm not in town," he said, proud of his truthfulness, as far as it went. "I'm keeping my word. I'm staying away."

"So how 'bout not calling, huh? How 'bout keeping your word on that?" More profanities, less muffled.

"I'm not calling my daughter, I'm calling you."

"*Your* daughter? You don't have any god-damn daughter, can't you get that through your thick skull?"

But he would always have a daughter. Nothing could change that. No matter what lies the Dragon had told Lewee, he would make it right soon. He would let her know the truth. And things would be the way they always should have been, like they were so many years ago. She would be his daughter, and he would be her father. There was so much time to make up for.

"This is the last time," he told her. "I'm just saying... I'm not going to be calling anymore. You win."

He heard something that he had not heard from his wife in the seventeen years since her terrible threats had driven him into the night: Silence.

* * *

During the course of the afternoon, two separate personal calls were placed from the offices of the El, calls to two different men of the cloth.

The first, by Annie Dale, was to make another appointment for Wednesday night with the Reverend Ackermann.

The second, late in the day, was a call by Lewee Jorgesson to the Pastor of the First Assembly of God, Mitchell, South Dakota, using a number on the back of a crumpled business card. She set up a meeting, also for Wednesday night.

* * *

That evening, Lewee and Mother sat silently watching television, in a post-supper laze of digestion. The broadcast was a local news station, but the coverage was national. President Nixon had tapes he wanted to protect; the court wanted the President to turn them over. The experts spoke, the reporter speculated, and Mother silently rose and lumbered to the set, cursing under her breath.

Although Lewee did not like agreeing with Mother, she had heard enough of it as well. She didn't care how the court case ended; she just wished it would end.

Mother flipped to another local news program. Their coverage was the same, and Mother issued more curses. She turned the knob to a more distant station whose reception was slightly grainy and definitely ghosted, but whose news story was decidedly different. In neighboring Minnesota, the State Fair was gearing up. The reporter discussed the foods that would be available, some new exhibits that were planned, and then shifted to an old reliable: A story about the carnival midway. The reporter explained how the midway exhibits moved from place to place about the country; he told of the difficulty in assembling and disassembling, of the travails of transporting, and of the lives of the carnies and the freaks. At one point, the story touched upon a house of mirrors. The televised image of reflecting walkways struck something within Lewee.

Mother had returned to her chair, but now Lewee arose, and approached the set.

"Don't go changing it again, child. Nothing on anywhere but Watergate. Leave it be."

Lewee did not acknowledge Mother, did not really hear her words at all. Her hand laid upon the set, and in that moment the image of the mirrors was gone, like a bubble burst by an injudicious touch.

Ten: The Lewee-Bird

The house of mirrors had tripped some unspecific memory, a sense of being lost and confused. It was something she wanted to express, needed to express, but Mother was not the proper one to hear it. She turned and headed for the stairs. She had to write.

At the top of the stairs she stopped, gazing vacantly down the second floor hallway. By happenstance all the doors—the bedrooms, the closet, the bathroom—all were closed. At the end of the hall a full length mirror duplicated everything—a double-length hallway, with a tiny Lewee in the distance. A tiny Lewee, like a child, standing alone.

She felt as though she were in the house of mirrors she had just seen. Ahead of her was a path, straight and true—or perhaps an illusion of mirrors, arranged to look as though a straight path existed. She had to write this.

In her room she took a notebook, and, after hunting for a pencil, sat at her tiny desk to write. She was stymied. Looking around, her eyes fell on the copy of *Inferno* on her bed. She began to write her sensations as a poem. She had never written poetry, except when commanded to do so in school—and then always in fractured verse. But now, like the reading of Dante, it seemed to come to her. Perhaps it came to her because it was not commanded. It came without rhyme. Didn't poetry have to rhyme? Dante didn't rhyme. She didn't have to rhyme either… not now. Not for this.

She drew on some vocabulary near the limits of her grasp, but knew she could check on the words later. After some minor reworkings, rewordings, and line break adjustments, she came up with something she only partly understood, but fully knew was right:

Hall of Mirrors
Is the pathway straight,
With mere distractions, reflected, refracted,
Playing to the left and right?
Or is the path I see the allusion,
The only route from here to there
To be learned in inches,
By sight and touch,

Shades of Thorne Creek

Winding in ways unimagined at my journey's start?
Or, worse yet,
Is the straight line before me
But the cruelest allusion of all?
A destination unattainable--
A fiction of both light and shade?

    All of her works—her drawings, her stories, her poems—seemed to be written by someone else. Someone more talented, more articulate, in every definable way "better" than herself. She reveled in this secret, other Lewee—with whom she could visit and commune anytime simply by sliding pen or pencil or chalk across paper. She enjoyed talking to Rachel, and to Annie, and even to some of the girls from high school who had not found her unacceptably odd. But with each of these there were some kinds of barriers, some kinds of things that could not be discussed (even though with each of them, the topics not broached were different.) There was only one person from whom there were no secrets, and with whom she had no fears of being perceived to be "putting on airs". With this other Lewee, in the pages of her secret notebooks, she could be and say whatever she wanted, whatever she needed.

    Tearing the sheet from the notebook, she folded it. She had a place for it, a secure place, a place far away from the eyes of Mother. But she could not go there now; that was a daytime place. Besides, she thought, the poem was innocuous enough. Maybe she would keep it closer at hand.

    She placed the paper randomly within Dante's pages. A seedling among ancient oaks— a seedling which perhaps would draw from their strength. Later, in checking her spelling and her usage, she found one repeating error. But thinking it over, she liked it. She let it stand.

Shades of Thorne Creek

Chapter 11: First Meetings

*H**ey kids, plug into the faithless.*
Maybe they're blinded,
But Bennie makes them ageless.
We shall survive, let us take ourselves along
Where we fight our parents out in the streets
To find who's right and who's wrong....

Lewee's hair blew wildly as her VW Bug accelerated out of Emery, toward Mitchell and into darkness, and the words on the radio conjured for her the image of her and her mother with broadswords, swinging away in the street. Elton John switched to falsetto:

Say, Candy and Ronnie, have you seen them yet?
Oh but they're so spaced out.
Bu-Bu-Bu-Bennie and the Jetsssss.
Oh but they're weird and they're wonderful...

She smiled at the words as she flew up 262. Elton was singing to *her*. She *was* weird, and she *was* wonderful. But just how much of that would she reveal tonight? Who, really, was this preacher that Jimmy had been pushing on her? Could she trust him? Not so much as she trusted Jimmy, of course. But how much?

In the glow of her dashboard lighting, she saw that a button on the cuff of her right sleeve had come unbuttoned. Again. She left it.

Ahead, on her left, she saw that she was creeping up on a train. Cutting the music, she sped up, rolled down her window, and listened

Eleven: First Meetings

to the rhythmic sound of the steel wheels as she pulled alongside. She matched the train's speed, and she drank in the night air, and the steady beat of the wheels on the track's imperfections:

Double-click/double-click/pause.

Double-click/double-click/pause.

Double-click/double-click… it seemed faster than she remembered. She checked her speedometer.

Annie had been right; they were going faster. Lewee used to clock them at about forty. This one was almost doing fifty. She sped up, until she approached a stretch with shorter cars. The *pause* of the double-click/double-click/pause was even shorter here.

She sped up even faster, as if racing the train into Mitchell.

* * *

"I'm sorry, Reverend," said Annie, sitting down across the desk from him. "I don't want to make myself into a pest."

"Annie," he said, in his best avuncular tone. "You are not and never will be a pest. Can I get you some coffee?"

She declined. And Reverend Ackermann sat. He gave a moment's pause, to see if she would begin on her own—a fair measure of the urgency of such visits.

"It's the same thing we talked about before, I'm afraid. But I maybe have a better handle on it now."

Reverend Ackermann nodded, helpfully. Fingers, steepled. He prepared to absorb every word, to divine what was within her mind.

"It's not…" she began hesitantly, and then decided to soften her certainty: "…I don't think it's that I'm tired of this world, and that I want to move on to the next.…"

The Reverend went through a minor palpitation. Had he misread her before? Could she be suicidal? Annie Dale?

"It's more like, more like I'm feeling that the eternal is here, and now, around us."

Shades of Thorne Creek

Not suicidal. But delusional? Still... *Annie Dale?*

"The other night," she continued, "I was out driving, in the middle of nowhere. And I pulled over, in the dark. And I looked up. I literally just laid myself out on the hood of my car, and looked up. And there were no clouds. No moon. Just the stars...."

And in a flash, Reverend Ackermann's concerns slipped away. Non-directive religious euphoria. He nodded, and smiled reassuringly.

"I feel like there's something here, around me, that I should be... connected to. Experiencing, in some deeper way."

His nod deepened, as he quickly flashed through ideas of how to direct this, channel it, into something useful, and productive. Unconsciously, his steepled fingers pressed more tightly against each other as he listened.

"It reminds me of something that I felt a long time ago. When I was a little girl."

The Reverend was grateful for the extra time, to pool his thoughts.

"I was a Campfire Girl, and we were on a campout. An overnight. There was another girl there. I hadn't met her before, but she and I were becoming friends. She attended some Pentecostal church somewhere."

The Reverend's right eyebrow arched, in an expression he would not have wanted to show, had he been aware of it. Annie did not notice.

"She talked a lot about God. About Jesus, about the Holy Spirit. 'Holy Ghost' were the words she used, but it's all the same thing, right?"

Fortunately for Reverend Ackermann, it was a rhetorical question which did not need to interrupt his analyzing, and Annie went on:

"She just seemed to be so... in touch. So connected. Everything around her—the stars, the sparks from the campfire, the crickets—in her mind, it was like they were all connected, all a part of God. And she was, too. For her, God was right there with us, around the fire. And not some weird, everything-is-God kind of Buddha thing. But like God was a person. Not just someone she could pray to. Someone she could *talk* to. And I guess, while I was with her that night, God seemed right there with me, too. I've been thinking about that feeling. A lot, lately."

Eleven: First Meetings

By now, the Reverend's fingers were comfortably interlaced.

"I'm sure, Annie, that you had a lovely experience, a beautiful experience, that night with your little friend." He winced internally at the word 'little'; too condescending. He pushed on: "But that's just the sort of problem, in some circles, with this idea of children proselytizing children. I'm sure your friend had had some great experiences, some great feelings, herself. But she wasn't old enough, wasn't mature enough, to have any proper framework for sharing those feelings."

Annie cocked her head.

Losing her, thought the Reverend.

"Pentecostalism," he said, "has only been around for about fifty years. Oh, Pentecostals will try to trace their practices all the way back to the Bible. But those practices ended centuries upon centuries ago, at the time of the early church itself. The euphoria of the modern 'Pentecostal' experience only goes back to the 1900's. Religious practice, however—formalized Christian teaching—has developed over a much longer time, gaining the wisdom of far many more adherents...."

* * *

Goodbye, Papa, please pray for me,
I was the black sheep of the family.

Terry Jacks always made Lewee cry with that song. She hated him, and hated the song. Even so, she turned up the volume on the VW's tinny AM radio.

Goodbye, Papa, it's hard to die
When all the birds are singing in the sky...

She felt heat building behind her eyes, and cranked the Bug's window wider. What was it that hit her the most? Was it the young singer's strange, unspecified death looming ever nearer? Or was it, really, that his Papa would have to go on without him?

What if, she wondered. What if she died without ever getting to meet her father? Without ever getting to know him? Without him ever getting to know her?

And why was she thinking about dying? Some of the girls back in high school had said thinking about dying was perfectly normal, that everybody thought about dying. And some of the girls said it was a sign that there was something wrong with you. That you think about dying before you think about killing yourself, and that you think about killing yourself before you actually try it, and that once you try it, really really try to do it, that means you're going to try it again someday, until you do it for good. Unless you get help.

She rolled the window the rest of the way down.

At least she wouldn't be short on things to talk about, tonight. The song entered its final stage, the recap of all the choruses:

We had joy, we had fun, we had seasons in the sun.
But the hills that we climbed
Were just seasons out of time.

We had joy, we had fun, we had seasons in the sun.
But the wine and the song,
Like the seasons, all have gone.

She *did* like thinking about death, it seemed to her. But at the same time, she was sure that it was not because she wanted to die. Nope—no shortage of things to talk about, at all.

* * *

"Is anything I'm saying here making sense, Annie?"

Eleven: First Meetings

"Yes, I think it is, Reverend." Though 'making sense' and 'being right' need not be the same thing—a sentiment she discretely kept to herself.

They exchanged the expected pleasantries; she offered her thanks, which he graciously received, then to the door and Annie was once again free in the night—a restless spirit in search of a spiritual *something*.

She began to drive, southeast again, as she had Sunday night, but she exited almost at once, turning left into Thorne Creek Cemetery. The sense that it might be a strange choice never brushed her mind; what better place to contemplate the eternal?

She parked, and began to wander the grounds. What light spilled over from the town would suffice; she had no need to read stones. She wanted a place with a view of the sky, between the trees, because she wanted to see the stars again, as she had Sunday. And she needed a place not actually occupied; lying across an active grave was a bit too much for her, even in her current, surreal mood.

Finding a spot, she knelt and then lay down, flat on her back—owing to her jeans and casual top, unconcerned about grass stains. The grass was slightly wet already. No matter.

By the time her attention settled upon the sky, her eyes were well adjusted to the dark. The Big Dipper was blocked by trees to the North. Orion was six months away. But there was something she vaguely knew—a skewed 'W'—Cassiopeia?

Presently her vision adjusted further, and she saw the trail of the Milky Way meandering across the sky. The densest part of the galaxy, if she recalled her high school science correctly. The region of the sky most tightly packed with stars, so many and so distant that they blurred into a haze.

What were they? Merely balls of gas like the sun, with tiny worlds orbiting them, and upon those, young women lying looking up at her? Or some heavenly markers—sign posts, signals? Or somehow, both?

She prayed before every meal, often before bed, always, faithfully, in church. Those were a certain kind of prayer. A good kind of prayer, she was sure. But somehow, inadequate to this moment.

Shades of Thorne Creek

She swallowed, and smiled. Then, with no idea how to start, or what would follow, Annie did the best her understanding would allow: "Hello."

* * *

"Hello?" Lewee called. The word echoed back from the darkness inside the storefront which had been hastily labeled 'First Assembly of Mitchell'.

In a moment, a door swung open, revealing an island of light across the dark chasm.

"I *am* sorry," a voice said, and fluorescent lights flickered on at the sweep of the Pastor's hand across the wall. "I meant to leave these on for you." He strode across to her, his hand outstretched.

She approached him, more tentatively than he was moving toward her, and counted the half-circles of chairs around the podium to her left. Fifty chairs, maybe. One part in twenty of what the room could accommodate, in a squeeze.

"Pastor Zack Hennessey," he announced, taking her hand as she extended it. "Pastor Zack, to most. And I assume you're the young lady who called Monday...." He was directing them back to the doorway from which he had just emerged.

"Margaret" she said, only partly lying. She had not thought of a last name, and so she offered none. If he insisted on knowing a last name, well, that would be a good sign to end things right there.

"Margaret," he echoed, with a tone suggesting he was committing it to memory. "Can I get you some coffee?"

They chatted casually across a long folding table, much like the ones Lewee used to sort mail at the El, in a room with empty metal shelving that had evidently been used for storage by whatever business had previously occupied the space. The room was a little musty, but not overpoweringly so, nor even unpleasantly so.

Eleven: First Meetings

Lewee studied him as they talked. He wore no clerical garb, not even the traditional stiff white clerical collar (or 'priest's collar' as she thought of it). Just a dark sport jacket, pants, clean shirt.

He seemed in his mid-thirties, with tousled thick brown hair, and a roundish face that seemed to smile easily. His eyes were brown, and just a trifle bloodshot. His face was not weathered, but had a certain ruggedness that suggested he had descended from farmers. Local boy.

Twice she thought of surreptitiously rebuttoning her sleeve, but twice she resolved not to. *You're here, girl. Do something with the time you've got.*

"Jimmy thought I should see you, thought I should talk with you."

"Jimmy?"

Lewee nodded. "Jimmy Turner. He said you were a good man. A good man to talk to about things."

"Jimmy Turner?" he echoed vacantly. Then Pastor Zack smiled. "Jimmy, from down at 'Electric Jesus'?"

"Yeah. I guess you know him, huh? Seems like he knows you."

"Jimmy's a..." he paused in search of the word: "...a semi-regular."

"At your church? I thought the shop name was kind of a gag. I didn't think Jimmy was the 'going-to-church' type."

"There's lots of types out there in the world. I've pretty much given up trying to peg 'em," Pastor Zack said. "So. Jimmy thought we should talk, did he?"

Lewee nodded, looking at the space of table between them. *This isn't how it's supposed to be*, she thought. *This is supposed to be easy....*

The pastor could see that she had jumped right up to the edge of telling him something, something important. But obviously, she wasn't ready yet.

He stalled for her: "So how do you know Jimmy?"

Her eyes snapped up to him, filled with tears but not yet overflowing. She had been going to be *proud*. She had been going to show him *defiantly*. So why was she feeling ashamed? Is this what it would be like when she showed Mother some day? Only a hundred times worse?

It took the pastor just seconds to piece part of her story together. Jimmy was not coincidental to all of this; this girl knew Jimmy *because* of why she was here tonight. And unless he had greatly misread Jimmy Turner these last few months, the part of Jimmy's connection to her that troubled her was professional, not personal. For the first time, he became conscious of her high buttoned collar, and the long buttoned sleeves. One sleeve, anyway. Did that loosened button mean something? Notably, the one concern that should occur to any counselor when confronted with a client concealing their wrists, the possibility of cutting, did not occur to him. Without even realizing it, he was not allowing himself to consider that.

"I… I *hate* my mother," she said, hoping to justify what she had been doing to herself. "I had a boyfriend. Not a real serious, gonna-get-married kind of boyfriend. But a nice boy."

The anger that her face had shown when she mentioned her mother now changed when she mentioned the boy.

"What was his name," the pastor asked. "Just his first name?"

She hesitated a moment, perhaps almost coyly.

"Billy," she admitted, and her face softened further. "His name was Billy."

"And I guess your mother, she didn't like Billy too much."

Lewee shrugged. "It wasn't that, really. She didn't *like* him, exactly. But she didn't *not* like him, either. At first."

She seemed to be gathering herself, and Pastor Zack let her.

Tilting her head a little to the right, she said: "One day Billy asked me to do something."

Pastor Zack tried to not let his face change, but he imagined the unifying scenario playing out in one of its thousands of permutations. He braced himself for the 'if you really love me' that he figured would be recounted soon. But this girl surprised him.

Eleven: First Meetings

"We came into town, to Electric Jesus. And we looked at Jimmy's work. And Billy, he wanted me to get a tattoo."

The pastor remembered the tightly buttoned shirt; he had forgotten that for a moment. *Just let her tell it*, he admonished himself.

"And I did. I got this cute little butterfly." She tipped her head to her left, and he imagined it was on the back of her shoulder. "And I liked it. Hurt like hell... 'scuse me, Pastor... hurt like the dickens getting it, but it was worth it. I liked it. It was pretty, and kind of dainty. Real feminine."

"And then your mother found out."

"Lord a-mighty. What a stink. 'Grounded for life' she said. Like that meant something. Like it meant *anything*. I'm nineteen and a half, Pastor Zack. Well, more like nineteen, back then. She couldn't *ground* me. I could come and go as I please."

"Except you were living in her house." He had the sense to use a tone suggesting he understood Mother's position, while not necessarily agreeing with it. His actual feelings were another matter. But the girl read him the way he wanted, the way that allowed her to continue the story.

"But she laid down the law real good. If I was gonna keep coming home, sleeping, eating, using my car..." *Her* car, Lewee knew, but she refused to say it: "...then it was 'no more Billy'. And she made it clear to him, too. Very next day she came into town here in Mitchell, talked with some judge friend of hers. They both knew I was nineteen. But she got him to look the other way. Got him to agree she didn't need to produce any birth certificate to prove my age, and agreed with her when she said I was seventeen. Got a restraining order on Billy. And she served it on him herself. Scared the..." but this time she caught herself in time, "...scared the bejeebees out of him. I haven't seen him since. I don't know if he's even around. Maybe left town. Maybe went to Sioux Falls. Maybe Fargo. Maybe Russia, for all I know."

"Sounds like a raw deal. And I suppose Jimmy Turner felt pretty bad, being the one that gave you the tattoo that made it all come down."

Lewee's tongue slipped quickly across her lips. She felt better, stronger, for having said it all. She thought maybe she was ready.

"That's not why Jimmy wanted me to see you."

"Oh?"

"She didn't have any right, interfering in my life like that. And I wasn't going to let her. I was going to get tattooed. Some more."

"I see."

"But she played right into my hand," Lewee said, like an eager conspirator. "When she was going on about Billy, she accused him, accused us, of doing all kinds of things. Some things we'd done, kind of. But some other things, Pastor Zack, I swear I've never done. With anybody, ever. But she... she kept going on about it, about how I'd done this with him, and that with him. And you know what I did? Without even thinking about it? I started pulling my shirt in around me, real tight. Covering myself, like I was ashamed. Ashamed for things, even, that I hadn't done. And that night, I was thinking about it. She *liked* the way I was covering myself, like I was all ashamed. So I kept it up. And that made her happy. Made her think she had guilt-ed me into behaving 'more modestly'. So when I came back to Electric Jesus, I was all set. She thought I was dressing the way I was because I was guilty about all those filthy things she said I'd done. But I was dressing that way so she wouldn't see."

"And how long did this go on?"

She swirled a figure eight on the tabletop with her forefinger: "Still is."

"But all this was six months ago, you said."

"Started, yeah. About that. Six months."

He looked at her puzzled, honestly not understanding.

She played with the one unsecured button on her right sleeve, and then released the one that went with it. She slid the sleeve back about two inches.

He did not understand the tattoo at first. There were two irregular shapes near the wrist, which morphed into sticks, or rods, continuing up the arm. He looked at her quizzically.

Eleven: First Meetings

Sighing, she worked the additional button that was farther up, the one that needed to be released for the sleeve to pull up freely. With the sleeve pulled halfway up her forearm, he saw that this was not some small bit of body art, but a massive work that seemed to fill her forearm. It did not seem feminine, but neither was it masculine. But it did seem familiar. The two shafts continued up as far as she had revealed. They were parallel, mostly, and quite artistically shaded.

"I'm not sure what...."

She began rolling the cuff, back, back, till it folded over the elbow. The two rods continued, until they widened and then changed into knobs below the elbow. Now he saw it. He even remembered the names, from college. Radius, and ulna. The bones of the forearm.

Looking at her upper arm, he asked: "How far?"

A slight tilt of her head to the right, which he read as a shrug.

"I don't think you should show me anymore," he told her. "Would you mind... would it be OK if I spoke with Jimmy, got a better idea of just how much is involved?"

"Sure. I'll tell him it's OK. He's even got a sketch he works from; you could look at. Best not to have that leave the shop, though."

"No. No, I agree." The pastor sat, trying to absorb it all. "Margaret?"

She looked at him. *Margaret. That's me.* "Yes?" she said.

"I think maybe that's all we should cover for tonight."

"Yeah. I think we covered quite a bit, huh?"

"I'd say so. OK if we close in prayer?"

"I dunno, Pastor," she said, re-securing her sleeve. "I know you're a man of the cloth. But I'm not into all that 'Jesus' stuff, and 'getting saved' and everything. I mainly just need somebody to talk to. Is that OK?"

In the tiny little storeroom of a smallish storefront in Mitchell, the man Zack Hennessey suddenly felt his true size in the world, and in the circumstances surrounding him. *This* was the case that God had brought him, in response to his prayers? *This* was the case God had chosen, for his return to counseling? Clearly, God's view of what Zack Hennessey was ready to handle was more expansive than his own. She buttoned another button. How deep did this run? How troubled might she be? He wondered: *Am I ready for this? Is it just too soon?*

She didn't want prayer. That was OK. It made no sense to force it on her. But that was not the end of the matter:

"Yeah," he said. "That's OK. But Margaret?" She looked at him as she finished the last button. "Could we close in prayer anyway? Prayer for me?"

Shades of Thorne Creek

Chapter 12: Final Touches

Andrew started Thursday, the last day of his shortened work week, with the air scrubber's external bin—although that wasn't what he called it, exactly. He had a variable string of adjectives that he added before "scrubber", as if the bin were some ostentatious, petty little dictator. The number of words in the string was dependent on his mood. Five, today. Not good.

The external gauge read seventy percent, more or less. He didn't trust it. And he knew Hector wasn't checking it every day. It wasn't that Hector was a slacker. But there were enough people off, between vacations and sick days, that the workload was piling up on him. And checking the gauge every day wasn't high on his priorities list; Andrew had understood that when they had talked about it last week.

The exhaust vent was blowing out mostly clean, and that was good. That, plus the fact that the air back in the scrubber room had been clean, meant everything was flowing through properly. Nothing was backing up. But that wasn't enough for Andrew.

Climbing the ladder built into the side of the huge cylindrical bin, he felt the vibration of the engine as it labored to pump the air through. And, out here, it was relatively quiet. Not a bad bit of engineering—on the whole, that is. But there was still that gauge, which was why he was climbing.

The ladder ended at the edge of the conical roof, into which was built a sliding door large enough for a man to crawl through, if one were so inclined. Releasing the safeties, Andrew slid the door aside.

It was the fullest 70% full he had ever seen. He slid the hammer out of his tool belt, reached in, and banged on the portion of the sensor still exposed above the fine powdered grain dust. The impacts caused dust from all over the bin to spring up. Andrew choked as he slid the

Twelve: Final Touches

door shut and re-secured it. With his hammer back in place, he returned to the ground. The gauge read just shy of 80% now.

"Every day," Andrew muttered. He shook his head. Hector wasn't even doing it every other day; that must've been two or three days' worth of buildup. He'd have to ream Hector out about it.

Within an hour, Hector approached the bin without having crossed paths with Andrew all day. The gauge surprised him, being at 80%. It had been down at 70% two days back. But the exhaust air was still coming out clean, which was good. He climbed the ladder and inspected the sensor, and it seemed to be reading true.

Hector decided to check the scrubber room, and when he found the air there mostly clean, and the exhaust air still coming out clean, he was satisfied. He knew Andrew wanted the bin inspected, manually inspected, every day. He resolved to monitor the gauge, externally, every day. And, when he could, to do a manual check as well.

Andrew's adjustment, which had reset the gauge to 80%, hadn't done the whole job; at the time, the bin was just over 85%, in fact. During the course of the day, with the gauge holding steady at 80%, the level of dust stored in the bin crept up from 85% to 91%. And although Harkin would not acknowledge the fact for some time, this entire unit began to clog up around 90%.

Two factors seemed to minimize the significance of this. One was that the Harkin manuals recommended emptying the bin at 85% anyway. The other was that the condition of the air being exhausted, and the air in the engine room, gave a failsafe check to confirm air was still being filtered.

It was somewhere around noon that Thursday when the scrubber ceased effectively cleaning the air, due to the levels in the bin. Dust-choked air filled the scrubber room. And then, as had happened so many times in the past, with the air pressure raised due to the constricted flow into the bin, the air backed up along one of the vents to the unused Tunnel C, passing the point where the one-way vent had never been installed. Dust-laden air poured into Tunnel C, once again depositing layer upon layer as it circulated toward the point of least resistance, near the Head House, where all the tunnels converged.

Shades of Thorne Creek

Tunnel C, like Tunnel D, lay beneath proposed future silos. These tunnels had no conveyor belts, no official equipment of any kind. They were used, pending the someday completion of the added silos, as storage places for old shelving, disused parts, and all manner of odds and ends.

Before they could ever be used for their original intent, all such stored items would need to be moved out. Other things would need to be done as well, including safety upgrades. The overhead bare-bulb light fixtures, for example, would need to be fitted with enclosing wire cages; the bulbs needed to be protected. A shattered bulb, of course, could be a fire hazard. But that was for the future. There was no grain handling in Tunnels C and D. There was thus no need for safety features like bulb cages in C and D, or even any need to check the disused tunnels for dust build-up

As the air circulated out through Tunnel C, dropping dust into Tunnel D, and to a lesser extent Tunnel B, this tumbler aligned with others—from the many times that dust had been thus delivered, and thus dropped, and thus accumulated. Together these tumblers fell into place, masked by the noise of the rumbling air scrubber engine, churning away. Circumstances had turned several of the tunnels, particularly Tunnel D, into storehouses for grain dust.

* * *

"Annie! Have you seen Hector?" Andrew was leaning into the office from out on the work floor. With the office door open, and with all the belts running in the Head House behind him, the noise was too loud for casual conversation, and so Annie simply shrugged.

"Lewee!" he called.

But Lewee was lost in her filing, tuning out the intruding noise, and she didn't hear him. He called to her louder, startling her.

"Hector?" Andrew called to her. Then, realizing the silliness of keeping the office door open, he stepped in and closed it behind him. "Have you seen Hector?"

Twelve: Final Touches

"He went to Berenger's," Lewee told him, referring to the contractor hardware outlet in Mitchell. "Not gone for the day though. Maybe an hour?"

Andrew shook his head, then crossed to Annie.

"Annie, I'm taking off. Gonna try to get an early start for Minneapolis. You all set for tomorrow?"

"Should be no problem," she told him. They had already reviewed his daily procedures. He would be back Monday morning.

"When Hector gets back, get on his case, will you? He hasn't been checking that gauge on the dust collection bin. Tell him: *Every day.* OK?"

"Will do."

When Andrew left for lunch, Lewee rode the man lift belt up to the Gallery floor. From one of the small windows that faced Emery, she watched Andrew walk across the highway, then follow the road northwest, and saw him enter the Dew Drop Inn.

By the time she had ridden the belt back down, she reckoned, enough time had passed. She could take a casual stroll to the Dew Drop, and not look like she was following him.

She stepped out into the midday heat of the El's parking lot. *Stalking, it's called,* she thought to herself. *But it's not really stalking, if you don't mean anything by it. If you're not doing anything wrong.*

At the counter, she ordered a ham and cheese, to go. As she waited, she began a casual turn about the restaurant, during which she could happen to see Andrew. He got her attention first; with his burger in one hand, he motioned her over to join him. He seemed pleased that they had stumbled into each other, and they chatted idly, until Lewee's sandwich came.

Taking her first bite, she wound up her courage. *If you're going to do it, then do it.*

"Andrew? You've got kids. Any of them girls?"

"My youngest. Julie."

"I'll bet you're a good father."

"World's finest. No doubt about it. I remind my kids of that, every day."

She smiled. "I'm serious, Andrew. You really love your kids, don't you?" It was more a statement that a question.

Andrew still held his burger, but he stopped taking bites.

"Yeah, Lewee. I do. What is it? What's on your mind, kiddo?"

"It's just... Andrew Junior, he was your first, right? Your oldest?"

"Yeah."

"He's your son. And your first. I mean, I know you love them both, but isn't it special with him? Because he's a boy, and all?"

Andrew took another bite while he worked that over in his mind.

"Lewee? Are you asking me if I love him more, because he's a boy?"

"Well, kind of. That's not wrong, or anything. But isn't it special, because you're a guy, and he's your son?"

He had always tried to stay out of Lewee's personal life, but he knew enough to have a sense of where this was headed.

"I'll tell you, Lewee. It's... different. A relationship a father has with his son is different from what he has with his daughter. It's not more, or less. Or better, or worse. But it is... different."

She did not meet his eyes as he said this, but focused on her sandwich.

Silently, Andrew cursed all those of his gender. *What is it with men?* he wondered. *Stonebridge, badgering Annie. Jorgesson, abandoning his daughter. Alright, so don't treat them like goddesses. But how about like human beings?*

Twelve: Final Touches

"Lewee?" She did not look up, but made a noise of acknowledgement around her mouthful. With her failure to look at him, Andrew knew that he was right; he had to say what he was going to say. "Lewee. I'm gonna tell you something. And it's something I ought not to say. It's something I've got no business sticking my nose into. And if you want to get up and leave, that's fine and I understand, because I've got no business saying this."

She was no longer chewing, but she wasn't looking up. She was staring into her plate.

Andrew set down his burger, knowing he wouldn't be finishing. *What have I got myself into*, he thought. But at the same time, he knew his preamble had left him no way out. Every second he waited would make this harder.

"Lewee? It wasn't right. Your father. He never should have left. And whatever it was that happened, it wasn't you that made him go." *Good God almighty*, thought Andrew. *Did I just say that to her? Is she gonna bust out into tears?*

Lewee nodded. "Thanks, Andrew," she whispered. "You're sweet." With a fork, she poked at her sandwich on the plate. "But you don't know. You never even met him. Who knows why he left."

Andrew had no answer to that. They sat in silence. He became aware of the overhead fan, almost silent as it cooled them. A fly was struggling against the plate glass of the front window, trying to get out. Trying to head in the direction of the El.

"So what're you gonna tell me, Lewee? That he left because of you?" He let the question hang a while, and debated with himself the dangers of what he was about to say: "I always thought you were more honest than that." At once he drew from her a physical response, a lean back, and then forward. A laugh, or a cry?

She looked up, with tearless eyes and a slight smile. "Thanks, Andrew." She pushed away from the table, and left half her sandwich. "Thanks for sharing the table. I'll see you at the office."

Shades of Thorne Creek

Andrew nodded, and she left him. He hoped that the smile had been real, and that she wouldn't burst into tears after leaving. She paused in the restaurant doorway, looking back to him. And then, in a voice not overly loud, but not meant to be concealed from any of the patrons on the stools, she said:

"You are, you know. You really are." And she was gone.

He sat puzzled by it. He thought over the things they had discussed. In a minute, he hit upon it. "I'll bet you're good father," she had said at the outset.

He stared at the remains of his burger. Now he had to hope that *he* wouldn't burst into tears. He wished Frank Jorgesson were across the table now, so he could reach over and beat him to a bloody pulp.

* * *

"She's really something, ain't she?" Jimmy said, as he cleaned his tattooing pens.

"She is that," the pastor said. "Have you ever done one like this? This extensive?" He was looking over the drawing Jimmy had laid out. It was a simple line drawing of an unclothed adult, of unspecifiable gender, facing away. The legs were together in a normal, comfortable stance. The arms were held straight out from the sides. It was a generic drawing, a template, that seemed to have been mass produced. But where the body was only an outline, Jimmy had added the fine details of the tattooing job.

Wiping a pen, he stood beside the Pastor.

"Never done one like this before," he said. "Heck, Pastor Zack. I've never even *seen* one like this, not on a regular person. Circus freaks maybe. But not on a regular person."

He turned to Jimmy: "Did it occur to you to turn her down?"

"You gotta believe me, Pastor. I tried. Usually, we just work off of samples, something from one of the books. But this? I told her I'd have to sketch out the whole thing. And I took my time. Figured by the

Twelve: Final Touches

time I finished the plans, she'd have cooled to the whole thing. But no dice. She was still full bore ahead. In fact, she did most of the layout herself, brought in pages of drawings. So I figured she would've just gone somewhere else. Maybe wound up with someone who wasn't so careful. I tried to get her to go see you, right from the start. And I started with the stuff that wouldn't matter so much, if she changed her mind."

The tattoos were a stylized version of the human skeleton. With a few drastic exceptions, they were mostly technically correct in terms of their basic shape and function. But she had stylized them to be thinner, making them almost wispy, and in some cases adding curves as if they were undulating. Jimmy's use of detailed shading and an occasional touch of color infused them with a strange realism, as if one were looking through transparent skin and muscles at the actual bones of some strange human-like, yet not altogether human, creature.

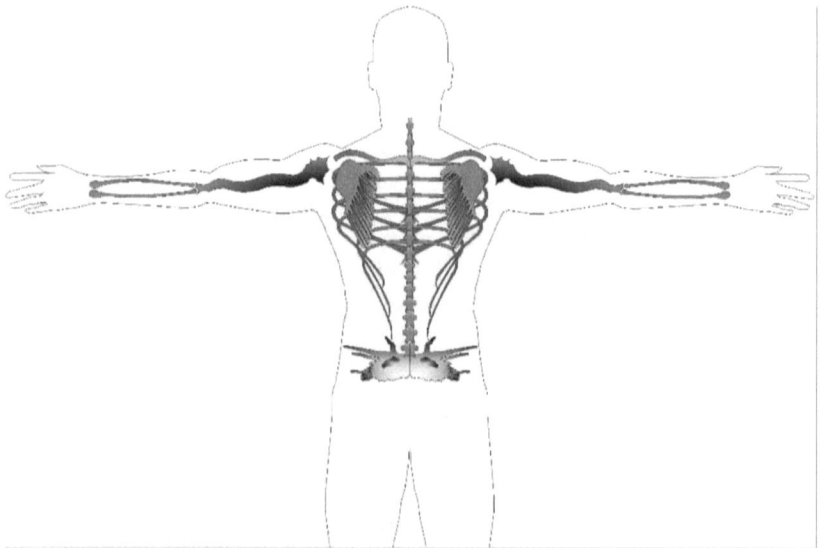

Jimmy pointed to the shoulder area: "Kinda wild, huh?" The scapulas, while smaller than actual shoulder blades, had been changed into feathered wings. The narrow ribs, as they moved outward from the spine, moved down. When they neared the figure's side, they turned and moved back in, as though one were looking through the body as they wrapped around to the front. And as they turned, they continued downward. Rather than rejoining at a sternum, they ended like a fan of swords spread over the lower back.

"How much of this is you," Pastor Zack asked, referring to the design.

"The shading work," Jimmy said, "is all me. But the ideas? They're all her, Pastor. I didn't think up any of this stuff. She brought me her own drawings, and I traced off 'em."

The vertebrae, while seeming to be compressed to about half their normal width, seemed to Zack Hennessey to be fairly accurate in height and in number.

"How far along are you? How close to done?"

"With this? Pretty much all done. She's gonna want the same thing done for her legs, I think. But first we've got to finish the shading on this." Jimmy pointed to the bizarre, high-riding pelvis.

Jimmy laid down a drawing of a dinosaur, a four-legged creature with a skull frill—like a triceratops, but with a more elaborate border.

"I don't understand," the pastor said.

"She left me this. It was her inspiration, the pattern, for the pelvis. It's a stacky-something."

A label at the bottom read *Styrachosaurus*.

"But I don't get it."

"It's a kind of a model, a concept. For what she wanted on the pelvis."

He began to see it. The pelvis was a highly stylized stretching of the dinosaur's skull, flattened, widened, but still more resembling the dinosaur's skull than a set of bird's wings, which it could easily have morphed into.

"I'm supposed to have the shading plans ready by Sunday night. That's when we start the finish work on this."

What, Zack Hennessey wondered, *have I stumbled into?* He thought of the way she had kept her wrists covered, as well as her neck. It all made sense now. But there was the other explanation, the one that had not occurred to him until well after their session. Why had that

Twelve: Final Touches

other explanation not occurred to him at the time? Why had it not occurred to him that she might be a cutter, and that her wrists were scarred? He shook the question off. The only answer to that would suggest he was not ready to return to counseling. He couldn't risk failing this girl Margaret, like he had failed before, but he could not simply turn her away. After all, she was *not* a cutter; he knew that now. His thoughts returned to the drawing.

"I can see why you kept pressing her to see me."

Jimmy shifted uncomfortably.

"Well, it wasn't really this, the art work. This didn't faze me. I guess the whole thing is looking almost normal to me, now. It was what she said. Made me think it was time she talked to somebody. She's been real careful all this time, keeping herself covered, you know? So no one would find out. But it turns out that lately she's been slipping up. Making mistakes. Leaving things unbuttoned, doors unlocked, that kinda thing. She's been talking about it, while I work on her. I figured, maybe she's trying to let it out, trying to let people know. And she just doesn't know it yet. You know?"

* * *

After dinner, and the clearing of the dishes, and the loading of the dishwasher, but before she could settle herself onto the couch, Annie Dale's doorbell rang. The face that greeted her at the door was at once familiar, and quite unexpected.

"Eddie! Come in, come in." She stepped aside to make a path for him.

Teapot Eddie glided in, beaming.

"Ah, Mizz Dale. Been too long. Too long since I was a-callin'."

"It has, that, Eddie dear. Join me in the kitchen?".

With a tip of his head to one side, he said "Thank ye kindly, ma'am." Annie moved quickly down the main hall, past the end table, and past the stairs that led to the second floor. Removing her apron, she busied herself with cleaning off the kitchen table, and placing chairs, and generally tidying things for company. She was busy enough that she did not notice—Eddie was not immediately behind her.

Teapot Eddie had been distracted, in the hallway, by the end table with its curious display. This was a new feature of the household. But no, he thought, as his fingers brushed the worn cloth liner—not new, only new to him. It must have been kept elsewhere in the house when he had last visited, so long ago. And now it had been brought out.

Fishing his fingers about the stones, he explored. He had not the slightest intention of taking anything; he was no petty thief. He was merely intrigued by it, and by what its presence here meant—this added feature to such a central location.

Yet something more than curiosity drove his fingers as they slid forth, then back, among the crude rocks. It was something he did not understand, even as he performed his next curious action.

Her preparations complete, Annie stepped back from the kitchen table, and turned to him. "There," she declared.

Leaning against the doorframe between the kitchen and hall, and looking for all the world as if he had been right behind her all along, Eddie smiled and then advanced to take a seat.

"Would you like some tea?" Annie asked, as if there might be some doubt as to his answer.

"Oh, splendid, splendid, ma'am. And here… I have some sugar cookies, if you are of a mind?" He set his parcel on the kitchen table. It was a towel, loaded with cookies, with its four corners tied to make it into a bundle.

"I would be delighted, Eddie."

She gathered the makings of tea; he untied his delivery. So began the evening's dance.

Teapot Eddie was a fixture of Emery. Retired from farming some years back, widowed without children, Eddie was an intensely social creature who bided his time during the days, but lived for the evenings, just after supper, when he would make his rounds to the homes of those amenable. He would bring some snack or trinket, drink their tea, and maintain the give and take of gossip that formed Emery's social life.

Twelve: Final Touches

All news of note, and much that was not, passed through Eddie; every visit was filled with transactions. A few cookies for a few cups of tea. Some news about the relatives in exchange for the latest scuttlebutt. There was never any discussion of it in terms of barter. But those without much information (new information, for freshness was paramount in his line much as it was with the milkman of yore) would find themselves out of Eddie's loop of visitation for a time.

Annie, while enjoying the sociability of the arrangement, had found Eddie's wares tending toward the tawdry for a while, and thus she had elected to offer him little—in the hopes he would focus elsewhere. And he had.

But now he was back. To Annie's mind, this meant one of several things. First, that the other sources of information were, for the moment, running thin. Second, that he had some interesting bit of kibble that applied directly to her. Or third, and most likely, he thought she might be the source of further details on some morsel he had found—some choice truffle he had rooted out.

Eddie drew gently from the cup she had poured him.

"I understand Andrew Lanquist left town early," he said, making no effort to conceal his eagerness. "Unplanned extra day off from work. Most unusual for the Lanquist clan. Most."

Annie smiled. She said nothing.

"Probably needs a bit of rest, I expect though," Eddie went on, charitably filling her silence. "Busy days, these days. Lots of pressures. Lots of strains."

"Oh, I don't know. No more than usual, I would suppose."

Eddie slid the opened towel of cookies an inch closer to her, and she took one.

"Minneapolis," he said.

"I'm sorry?"

"The Lanquist clan. Going to Minneapolis, I understand. Visiting relatives, I suppose."

"Friends, I think. The woman's name is Arlene, if I recall."

Shades of Thorne Creek

Nothing new, and Eddie kept drawing from the surface of the tea. He had been testing her with the 'relatives' reference. He was sure she knew they were visiting this "Ted and Arlene" he had heard of; he wanted to see if she would feign ignorance.

"They have some kids about the same age," Annie said. "Three, I think."

"Ah, that's nice," Eddie said casually. He had hit the mother lode. This was the best stuff. Nothing salacious; that tended to put people off. But simply information about other people's friends—the sorts of things people like to know. The ever-unseen Ted and Arlene have three children, Eddie filed.

So the evening progressed. Eddie's information was refined, tweaked, expanded ever so slightly. Annie learned things she didn't really need to know, but that were all harmless enough, and were mostly true.

A few patently false rumors were squelched. Some precursors of rumors failed to gain any strength, as Annie had nothing to add to them: A Chevy Impala had been seen around… perhaps someone had had out-of-town guests these last few days? But Annie, like the others on Eddie's route, knew nothing of it.

* * *

The Impala was parked for the night in Mitchell, where enough cars granted a reasonable assurance of anonymity. Father Jorgesson stretched out across the front seat, sleeping. Dreaming, as he often did, of 1941.

"Wh-wh-when's it gonna come, J-Jorggy?" The same words he dreamed, over and over.

The USS Colorado had been in Puget Sound on December 7th. When news of Pearl Harbor came, their orders were close behind, and they steamed out into the Pacific at full bore. The weather was rough, and everything was confusion and haste. And when Jorgesson and three

Twelve: Final Touches

of his mates were washed overboard, it was hours before they were missed. The area that the local ships searched was wide.

Two of the men had been drawn through the propellers. Their body parts refused to drift away, but rather seemed to gravitate toward the two slowly freezing survivors. The waters off of Washington State, even in December, were not cold enough to kill quickly. But they were cold enough to kill slowly, draining off body heat—degree by degree by degree. The ocean swells even calmed for them, ensuring a more protracted death.

"They'll come," Jorgesson had kept telling him. "Just wait. They'll come." But the sailor kept asking 'when', 'when', 'when', the stuttered question emphasizing the cold that was sapping them.

"Wh-wh-when's it gonna come, J-Jorggy?" the question came again, and again. Until, even in his dream, he did not answer it any more.

Jorgesson woke with a start, shivering uncontrollably. He could feel the warmth of the August night. He *knew* it was warm out. But his body was still submerged in that cold, cold Pacific, and he could not make himself stop shivering.

"Two-thirty," he muttered, after glancing at his watch. Cupping his hands over his mouth, he directed the warmth of his exhaled breath down onto his sweaty chest, and waited to sleep again. Even though sleep would likely bring dreams. And even though, once he started to dream that stuttered question, the dreams always led to the same end. Even with that, he had to sleep. A man could only go just so long without sleep, no matter what dreams it brought.

But the dreams did not bother him the way they once did, nor did the memories that inspired them. He was not the same man, who had tumbled into the ocean with his ship mates that December day.

Chapter 13: Thursday's Prayers

I've been thinking a lot about my brother Bob." Annie paced along the side aisle, heading, for the moment, away from Reverend Ackermann, toward the rear of the sanctuary. He sat in a front pew, turned sideways in order to watch her.

"I've been thinking," she said, stopping abruptly and facing him, "about what would happen if I died."

"Do you have a will?" he asked.

She nodded, then turned and continued away from him. It was her request that they not meet in his office this time. *Too much nervous energy*, he thought. *She's pacing like a caged animal.*

"The will is in place, and technically Bob's provided for, by the county, anyway," she said. Reaching the rear of the sanctuary, she turned and headed toward the front. *His office is too much like an office*, she had thought. *I need to feel like I'm in Church.* "It's not a question of money, or of care-giving," she mused, trying to figure it out for herself as she spoke. *This is working*, she thought. *I'm focusing where I need to.* She stopped short. "It's about Bob. It's about him, being alone in the world."

Reverend Ackermann studied her, framed as she was by the night-darkened stained glass window behind her.

"Well, as you say, if there are provisions for his care, he won't really be alone."

"There will be staff to tend to his needs," she said, reaching the first pew, touching it—almost like a relay racer taking a baton—and heading once again to the back: "But he won't have a friend. Someone who cares *about* him, not just *for* him. Someone who will watch scary movies with him, and go to Church with him. And make counterfeit coins with him."

Thirteen: Thursday's Prayers

Reverend Ackermann let that one go, trusting it made some kind of sense. "Because you're the last of his family," the Reverend said.

Annie stopped, still faced away from him. She reached a hand out to the window frame to steady herself, and her fingertips brushed the stained glass. The Reverend cocked his head unconsciously.

"I am the last of the family," she agreed, moving again to the rear of the sanctuary.

"Annie?"

She did not stop, or respond.

"Annie, could this be about something that goes... farther back?"

Reaching her mark at the back, she returned, more slowly now.

"I guess it is," Annie admitted.

Reverend Ackermann waited, counting the stained glass windows that she passed. Three... two... one....

She stopped, and he tried not to smile; he recognized, now, the pattern to her pacings.

"I guess this has been building up, ever since our parents died."

A delayed grief, he surmised. Or a simmering bitterness. Either was predictable with an untimely death of a parent. Doubly so, in this sad case. No real mystery as to the cause, or the best route to talk it through.

The only real mystery to Reverend Ackermann was the one he didn't feel it was appropriate to discuss with her, because of its relative triviality. It was her fixation—why every time she chose to stop, it was always in front of the stained glass image: John the Baptist, with Christ at the Jordan. The one with the Holy Spirit as a dove.

* * *

"But are you sure, Margaret," Pastor Zack pressed, "that you really want to keep it hidden?"

Shades of Thorne Creek

Lewee struggled to hold back an impolite laugh. "Oh, yeah, Pastor. I'm sure. Lordy, lordy. If Mother found out. About all these." She nervously slid her right hand along her left arm.

"But what you're doing, the whole tattooing process, you agree it is a kind of lashing out, against your mother."

"Yeah...."

"I just wonder how much of a lashing out it is, if she doesn't know."

"Why're you saying this?" Lewee asked.

"Well, it was something Jimmy said. He thought you were getting a little careless sometimes, about keeping yourself covered."

"Sometimes..." she admitted, thinking of the times she had told Jimmy about, about her being careless. And about the other times, the times that Jimmy knew nothing about.

"But I think careless is just careless," Lewee said.

"Well, maybe it is. So you tell me, Margaret. What *are* we here to talk about?"

"The tattoos, I guess."

"And what about them?"

"I'm sure Jimmy told you. He doesn't think it's 'healthy'."

"I'm sure Jimmy can speak to the health effects of tattooing better than I can."

"Not that kind of healthy. More like 'is this girl going crazy' kind of healthy."

The pastor swallowed, hard, as he thought of the implications. "And? Is she? Is this girl going crazy, Margaret?"

"I don't know. I don't think so. It's just like I need to feel something. And the more I get tattooed, the more I feel it."

"And what is that, Margaret?" Each time the pastor used the name, it stung her a little more. "What is it that getting tattoos makes you feel?"

Glorious, thought Lewee. *Wonderful*, she thought.

Thirteen: Thursday's Prayers

"Margaret?"

"Loved," she whispered. Her eyes, filling with tears, fixed on the empty space of desk between them. Continuing to whisper, softer now, she added: "Louise. My name is Louise. But I go by Lewee."

* * *

Annie sat in a front pew, across the center aisle from Reverend Ackermann. She was turned to face him, as he was turned to her. Each had an arm draped across the back of a pew.

"But I don't *feel* angry toward God," she said.

"Which, I suspect, is why these feelings are having such a hard time working their way out. It's hard to deal with a feeling, when you don't even know you have it. But it's perfectly normal, Annie."

She thought back to what she had felt, staring up at the stars—on the roadside, and in Thorne Creek. It didn't feel like anger. Not at all. It felt like wonder. And it even felt like love.

"Could it be," said Reverend Ackermann, knowing it was best not to lead, but not knowing how else to move things along, "that all your life you trusted God? You believed in God? Believed he wanted what was best for you? And then one day something terrible happened. Your parents died. God took them away."

All the pieces seemed right, Annie knew, by themselves. They just didn't seem to fit together this way.

"When a child has a terrible disillusionment with a parent, it can be very disruptive. Very unsettling. Discovering a mother is an alcoholic. Discovering that a father is a thief. The trust which that child grew up with is suddenly swept away."

None of this was anything Annie could dispute, even though on some level she thought she should.

"In that moment, the trust a child has had in the goodness of the parent is crushed. Now, Annie, it is a normal part of the maturing process for a child to withdraw from the parent's influence, to become independent. But children who experience things such as this, they go through that withdrawal far too fast, far too early."

"I... suppose so...."

"A dozen people in Mitchell pray for sunshine," the Reverend said, "because it's time for a weekend parade. And a dozen people in Emery pray for rain; the crops are parched. An adult faith, a mature faith, understands that it will either rain or it will not, and that some prayers, no matter how heartfelt, will have to be ignored. A mature faith understands."

Annie arose slowly, thoughtfully. She felt as though his words had stirred a question in her, but it was a question she did not know.

"But a faith that is not mature sees the rain, or the drought, as a betrayal," he spoke after her, as she slowly moved along the side aisle. "And anger, or perhaps the denial of anger, is the result." He was flailing now, but he did not let his voice betray it. *Maintain a tone of confidence* he told himself. He counted her progress, as measured by pews, approaching *Baptism at the Jordon*. "Anger, when it cannot be expressed, and dealt with, can manifest itself in other ways." Three... two... one....

Annie stopped. She laid her hands on the sill. Her fingertips played along the glass.

"Other ways," she echoed. "Like... fear?"

Reverend Ackermann confirmed his assent by way of silence.

The glass was cold, yet comforting, as Annie's fingers moved along it. A sensation, an urge came over her. Had she needed to put it into words, the words would have sounded as if they were, in fact, spurred by fear. But that was not the sense of it. Not fearful, but orderly. Had she been compelled to put the sensation into words, the words would have been *"run away"*.

"Thank you Reverend. You've given me a lot to think about."

* * *

Thirteen: Thursday's Prayers

"Dear Lord," Pastor Zack prayed, his hands upon Lewee's head as she rested it on his desktop, "reveal your love for this girl, this lady, this child of yours. Touch her now, and let her feel your compassion. May your grace be upon her."

Lewee sighed.

"Thanks Pastor." She did not lift her head. "But I... I just don't want you forgetting."

"What's that, Mar.... Lewee?"

"You can pray if you want." Her head remained on the desk. "It's just that.... All that glory-hallelujah stuff, and Jesus, and gettin' saved. All of that. It's not where I'm at. You know?"

He smiled at her honesty. Slowly she lifted her head. She left a small puddle of tears behind.

"I mean, I'm not here because this is a church, and you're a priest and all. It's just that Jimmy, he said you were a good one to talk to. About getting my head on straight, and all."

"I understand." His smile changed to mischievous. "As long as you don't mind my praying for you to get saved, anyway."

She laughed: "Shoot, no. Who knows? Pray long enough, maybe it'll 'take' somehow."

"OK, then. I think we understand each other. But you know, Lewee? I've got to tell you, after all the talking is done, I think I know what's at the heart of all of this."

"Some kind of God thing, huh?"

"Yeah. Each one of us has needs, Lewee. All kinds of needs. Some are needs we all share. Food. Water. Shelter. Another human being, somewhere, somehow, to love us, to care about us. And God. That's the one that a lot of people try to do without, to explain away, or just plain ignore. But I think... I believe... that each one of us needs God. And when we try to fill that need with something else, it all just goes haywire."

"So, we're at some kind of a crossroads, huh? You think I need God. I think I need something else, even if I'm not sure what it is. So how can you help me, if I don't want to go down that road?"

Shades of Thorne Creek

The pastor leaned back in his chair.

"Well, Lewee. Like I said, each person has many needs. I think one of your needs is God. But I think you have others. Other needs, that probably aren't getting met either. If we work on those, then we'll get to a point where you're doing better, and better, and pretty soon one of two things will happen."

She smiled at him. She liked the way he laid things out.

He continued: "Either you'll be perfect, and all your needs will be met. Or."

"Or...."

"Or, after all those things are fulfilled in your life, there will still be something missing. But it won't be like now, where it's like a jigsaw puzzle with a bunch of big gaps. There will just be one piece left. And you'll be able to tell the shape of it pretty well by then, because everything else will be in place."

"God, huh?"

"I think so, Lewee. But I'm willing to wait and see. And I'll trust you to be honest about it when you get to that point."

"Sounds fair, I guess. But you really think there's all those different things messed up about me? All those different 'needs'?"

"I think it's pretty much true about everybody. It's just that with most of us, it doesn't wind up getting drawn all over us, in tattoos."

"Kinda weird, I guess, huh?"

"Let's say 'unusual'. You've mentioned your mother a number of times. Where does your father fit into things?"

"I never knew him."

"Sorry, Lewee. He died?"

"Nah. Just left. I guess. I was too little to remember him. My mother doesn't talk about him. And I've learned not to ask. About all I know is, he was on a ship in World War Two."

A sailor, the pastor thought. *I wonder if he had any tattoos?* But there was no way to ask the question, without implicitly suggesting the answer. He would have to dance carefully around it, and see if she

Thirteen: Thursday's Prayers

mentioned it on her own. A long shot, anyway. But stay on the tattoos. He was getting somewhere, he felt. He was helping her. The fears he had in the beginning all seemed miles away now.

"You said how the tattoos made you feel. You said getting them made you feel loved."

"I think so. Maybe getting them. Maybe having them."

"You don't feel loved? Without the tattoos, I mean?"

"I suppose my mother loves me. In her own, screwed up kinda way."

"But that's not enough."

"Billy loved me. I know he did. He really did. But now he's gone."

"But that wasn't really his choice. He didn't want to go, right?" Pastor Zack said no more; he wanted to focus on Billy's not wanting to go, not on her mother's forcing him to go. It was a fine line—emphasizing that Billy didn't want to desert her, without focusing blame on the mother for the fact that he did go.

Lewee nodded. She knew Billy didn't *want* to abandon her.

"But still," she said. "He did go. He's gone, and it hurts."

The Pastor knew where this was going. *My father left me. Then Billy left me. Every man who loves me, leaves me.* He wanted to explain it to her, explain about the one who would never leave her. But if he were just a little off in the nuances, he would steamroller the truth. She might even accept his version, and make *it* the truth. She needed to see it for herself. He needed to draw it out of her.

"And after Billy left, you started the tattoos?"

"Well, I did the first one because Billy asked me to. The butterfly." She smiled as she said it.

"And after Billy was gone?"

"That's when I started the rest." She looked at him for a time, thinking. "So you're saying I did all this, all this tattooing, for Billy? Like it would bring him back?"

"I don't know, Lewee. That's something you'll have to think through. Something we'll have to talk through. It's an idea. Does it make sense to you?"

"Parts of it. Maybe. I don't know."

"Why the bones?" he asked her.

"I don't know."

"The one you got for Billy was a butterfly. Was a butterfly his idea?"

"No. The butterfly was my idea. He wanted me to pick something I liked. I like butterflies."

"Did Billy have any tattoos of bones?"

"No. No, he had an eagle."

"So why the bones, do you suppose?"

"I don't know."

I don't know. The three deadliest words, his seminary professor had told him, when they covered counseling.

"Well, let's come back to that."

"It's all my mother," she said, for no reason he could discern. He waited. "She's the reason Billy left. She's the reason my father left."

Anger towards the mother, he thought, *or abandonment by the father—what road to pursue?*

"What do you remember about your father?" he asked.

"Nothin'. He was gone before I was old enough to remember. Except maybe *yelling*. I remember yelling. I think it was between Mother and Father. I don't know. I remember I was scared when I heard them yelling."

"Were they yelling at you?"

Lewee shook her head; she clearly had words to speak, but she wasn't able to speak them. Again, he waited.

"I...." Nowhere. Waiting.

Her mouth moved. Nothing.

Waiting.

Thirteen: Thursday's Prayers

He wanted to jump in. To tell her it was alright to say it, whatever it was. If he could only help her say it. But there was one word, above all others, that had been emphasized in his counseling classes. The golden word, that had been hammered home. He had trusted it before. But he had never before needed to trust it to fight off his impulses quite like he needed to trust it now. The word was *wait*.

"I think…" she said. "I *don't* think…" she corrected. "I don't think they were yelling at me." She was not looking at him now, but rather at the tiny tear pool she had left on the desk. "I don't think they were yelling *at* me. I think they were yelling *about* me." She had said the first part, and now the rest poured out. "I think I must have done something really, really bad. I think I must have been a really bad little kid."

* * *

Annie lay across her fully made bed, pondering her ceiling and all the wonders beyond it. When she prayed at Church it was on her knees, or at least with head bowed. Always with hands folded in supplication. But praying alone lately, she never folded her hands, never bowed her head, certainly never kneeled.

Prayer, when she was alone, was more like talking with a friend. Not an idle chat—more the kind of quiet but intense conversation one has with a best friend one hasn't talked to in years, filled with the kind of reserved urgency that accompanies discussions of matters simultaneously small and urgent.

Was the church experience—were the church prayers—more valid, more real, because of those differences? Or was the opposite true? Was the experience she was having right now the truer one?

"I don't want to go back," she said, an observation that sounded at once to her more like a plea of desperation. "To talk to the Reverend, I mean. I'd still like to go on Sundays. But can you show me what I need to know, here? Like this?"

She rolled onto her side.

"I don't think I'm angry. Help me to see it, if I am, but I don't think that's it."

Her head rolled back, and she looked again toward the ceiling.

"Maybe I was, when you first took Mom and Dad. I don't really remember. But...." She searched herself for meaning, within the concept of death. "Everybody dies. It wasn't going to be pleasant, no matter how, or when. I would have liked for them to have been around longer," she admitted. "But it's not all about that, is it? It's not all about us getting everything we want, and everything being perfect."

Her eyes closed, almost involuntarily.

"I don't know what it's all about. But I know that it's about more than that." She thought of Lewee, growing up without a dad. She thought of families where children died before their parents, like Mr. Tommerson, years ago, the widower who had lost his only daughter. Annie wondered if her own parents could have endured such a thing. Parents should never, ever have to bury their children. But sometimes they do.

It was better—not perfect, but better—for the children to bury their parents. Even if it forced the children to grow up a little sooner than they were ready to.

She tensed. She was getting to it, now. She knew that.

"But what if it's a child that can't ever grow up?" she asked. Her brother, she knew, had become her son. She was his only family, his only parent. And he would never be ready to stand on his own. He would never be complete, without her. She had been ready, even glad, to assume the role of parent. But now it was dawning on her that she might not always be able to fulfill that role. That was it. That was what was really at the core of all of this.

"Oh, God," she prayed. "I don't want him to be alone. But I'm all he's got left." The cold arithmetic of it settled over her, and what entered her heart terrified her. Sliding off the bed, she knelt. This was not the time to draw close to a long-absent friend. It was the time to approach the throne of the living God. And the prayer in her heart terrified her, sickened her.

Thirteen: Thursday's Prayers

"Oh, please don't let me pray this. Let there be another way. Let there be another way...."

She continued in this manner for some time, repeating the request until it almost became a chant. But the chant lost its power, and she knew what was her task, her duty, to pray. She wept.

"When the time comes," she said, the back of her throat aching as she tried to cobble together a compromise, a halfway measure, "when the time comes, please take us together."

But she knew that wasn't right, that it wasn't the thing she had to ask. The image of Bob sitting alone at Redeeming Love, waiting on Friday nights for a sister who would never again come, weighed on her.

"Oh God, forgive me for this. But if we can't go together...." The pain in her throat choked her off. "Please don't leave him alone. If we can't go together. Oh, dear God. If we can't go together, please take my Bobby first."

Shades of Thorne Creek

Chapter 14: Catastrophe

The pre-noon sun shimmering off the Mississippi, the sounds of powerboats towing skiers up and down, a light and variable breeze, a cold beer in hand; for Andrew, it was the perfect day.

Andrew settled back in his chair and quaffed from the dark brown bottle. It was five minutes from the pivotal moment— what would become the focal point, the pole star in Andrew's existence. Everything in his life could be viewed as circling around that moment, a few hundred heartbeats away. Andrew drew deeply, and swallowed the beer.

"You let me know when you finish that," Arlene said, passing by in her sundress, starting down the railroad-tie stairs that led to their short dock on the river.

"Heaven," said Andrew. "Absolute freakin' heaven."

In the chaise lounge next to him, Ted sighed. "Hard to argue. We could've taken a property higher up the bank. Better view, see more of the river. But we like it down close to the water, for the kids."

Andy waved as he skied by, and Andrew waved back. Ted's oldest was driving the boat. Eighteen. A little young, maybe. But Joanie was in the boat, spotting. He let the thought go.

"I'll tell ya, And, it's a whole lot better," Ted said, speaking upwards through the hat that covered his face, "spending a Friday like this, than it is spending a Saturday."

Andrew kept his eyes on the river. Did they see that other boat? OK, making a turn, they had to swing wide, but still. Then he let it go. "Hmm," Andrew intoned. "How's that?"

"Because," Ted explained. "Saturday you're *supposed* to be off. But Friday? Hell, it's like playing hooky."

Fourteen: Catastrophe

"Humph." *Hooky*, thought Andrew. That would appeal to Andy. They were moving from left to right, approaching the dock. What were they doing so close in? Let it go, he thought. But this time he couldn't.

"Hey!" he yelled out, and Ted jumped up in surprise from his repose, his hat tumbling down into his lap. "Hey!" Andrew yelled again, as if his voice could somehow carry over the engine noise and be heard by Ted's boy, and by Andy. "Not so close to the dock!"

"Hey, And, it's OK," said Ted. "He's just coming in for a beach landing. It's cool. Watch him."

Andrew did watch, his mind calculating out the numbers: Speed, drag, distance. Andy was coming in a little too fast to stop right at the beach, but that wasn't what worried him. What worried him, as Andy released the tow rope and began his glide in to his right, was that something might go wrong—something Andrew didn't know, couldn't think of, couldn't calculate. Just the sort of thing that happened then before him, at that very moment.

Andy's left ski caught in the water, and was pulled off of his foot. Had Andy gone down then, a lot of things might have been different—but somehow, using the strength and agility of youth, he managed to stay up on one ski, his left leg dangling behind him. And, with all his attention focused on the heroic deed of staying up, he didn't notice that his gyrations changed his course, parallel to shore rather than in towards it.

Andrew leapt up, cursing as Andy plowed into the dock. Andrew reached the shore just as the boat finished its loop back to the dock. In two feet of water, Andy was hopping unsteadily on his right leg, now freed from its ski as well. But it wasn't that which held Andrew's attention, nor the scrapes on Andy's chest and arms.

As Andy issued a pained and whimsical chuckle, what held everyone's eyes was his dangling left leg, and the slight but definite angle that it took, mid-tibia.

"Oh man, Pop," Andy called up, forcing a smile. "Think I busted it."

Shades of Thorne Creek

* * *

Ted assured them that the short trip to Hennepin County Medical would be faster in the back of his station wagon than waiting for an ambulance, and indeed it would have been hard to imagine getting there faster than they did.

Once Andy had been wheeled in, Andrew and Joanie and Ted all had a chance to collect themselves.

Joanie was still wearing her one-piece and hadn't stopped to grab a towel, but she didn't seem to notice or care. After Ted called Arlene from the ER lobby, Arlene left the kids with the neighbor, borrowed the neighbor's car, and was enroute with towels and changes of clothes for everybody. She had not yet arrived when the awkwardly young intern came out to speak with them. He spoke with Andrew and Joanie, while Ted prowled anxiously, uncomfortably, across the room.

The leg was OK, the intern told them. Nice, clean break, as these things go. No reason it shouldn't set properly. It took no genius of interpretive skills to read the "however" behind all that he was saying.

Did Andy Jr. have any health issues? Any chronic problems?

Without knowing what he was fishing for, all Andrew and Joanie could do was shake their heads.

Andy seemed to be bleeding a lot, internally, around the break.

"It was a bad break," Joanie said. "Just terrible. I mean, you could see it. All... crooked. Isn't it normal for there to be bleeding?"

"Some," conceded the intern. "But what we are seeing is more than usual. More than we expect in a case like this. We ran some preliminary blood tests, and the results came back very strange. We are running some more tests, more definitive tests, and should have results soon...."

Andrew could only latch onto, and echo, that one word: "Strange?"

The intern nodded, reluctant to press on with only a preliminary result.

Fourteen: Catastrophe

"Strange how?" Andrew demanded softly.

The intern knew he was stuck. He had used the preliminary results in the hopes of drawing out some information that the parents were, perhaps unintentionally in the confusion of the moment, withholding. But they knew nothing, and now that he had spoken, he could not very well undo what he had started.

"I assume young Andy has no history of... hemophilia."

"Hemo..." said Joanie. "What?"

"Hemophilia. It's a blood disorder connected with excessive bleeding."

"He *is* a bleeder," Joanie said, which elicited a flurry of questions until they clarified that she only meant Andy tended to bleed a lot, and heal slowly.

"All his life?" the intern asked.

No, they explained, thinking it over. More just over the summer. Nothing serious. He was always getting injured. Active boy, and all.

In late afternoon, with everyone's clothes changed, and everyone managing to convince themselves the day was all just some terrible mistake, the intern returned—with the additional, more definitive test results in hand. He spoke the words they would hear many times over the next few days, from ever-escalating figures of authority:

"We are concerned."

* * *

Friday night, or more properly, Saturday morning, Bob Dale was asleep on the couch, his coffee having successfully seen him through *Bride of Frankenstein*, but absolutely no further.

Annie, rather than going upstairs to bed, was heading outside. She would have liked to have gone somewhere far away—maybe Thorne Creek, maybe farther, but with Bob, that wouldn't work. Besides, she thought, maybe the back yard was as good a place as any for the conversation she wanted to continue. As she stepped out onto the porch, the phone rang. She rushed for it, to answer it before Bob was awakened. What time was it, she wondered as she picked it up. Two AM? Who would be calling?

"Hello?" she said, more perplexed than annoyed. There was no response. "Hello?" she said, this time more concerned than annoyed.

There was a sound, like a raspy voice, saying one word. She couldn't make it out. Her name?

"Hello," she repeated, very quietly.

"Annie? This is... this is Andrew."

"Andrew?" She had no idea what the call was about, but she knew something was very, very wrong.

"Annie, I'm not coming in. On Monday. I can't come in."

She nodded for a moment, before realizing that a nod meant nothing to Andrew over the phone.

"OK, that's fine," she said. "I can cover things. Andrew? Can you tell me... what's happened?"

There was a long pause.

"I'll... I'll tell you later. We've gotta go. They're going by ambulance, to Rochester. Ted and I are driving. I'll call you from Rochester."

The line went dead. Annie set down the receiver. Presently, the only sound was her pulse, which she could hear somewhere deep in her ears.

Rochester. To her, under these circumstances, that could only mean one thing: the Mayo Clinic. Like a sleepwalker, she moved out onto the porch, out into the yard. She found her place at random. She had planned to lie out on her back, but kneeling seemed a better choice just now.

"Dear God. Dear Jesus." She clasped her hands before her. For a fleeting moment she wondered if any of her neighbors might stir in the night, and shuffle past their windows and see Annie Dale praying in her back yard. Just as quickly, the response came from within her: *Fine.*

Fourteen: Catastrophe

"I don't know what's happened, God. But please help Andrew. And Joan. And their kids." Andy was the only one she remembered by name, and she felt odd about singling him out, if it wasn't him.

But, she thought, *who am I kidding? Who else could it be?*

"Oh Lord, please bless Andy this night. Please protect him from... from whatever has happened."

As she prayed, the evening wore on. She prayed simple prayers for protection—prayed unaware of what was transpiring in-flight between Minneapolis and Rochester.

In time, she prayed inquiring prayers, asking for understanding of the great fundamental truths of life and existence and meaning—prayed unaware that the great thinkers of Western thought had with confidence pretty much already nailed down everything of importance.

She prayed questioning prayers, about her parents' deaths, and her brother's condition, and political turmoil in Washington, and the tragedy of war unfolding halfway around the world—prayed unaware of the burning presence all about her, eager to share with her each step of understanding as she would become able to receive it.

"Help me to understand. Why they died." She was asking about their parents. Immediately she amended the inquiry: "*When* they died." For she knew everyone died. But for them, it had been too soon. No answer came to her, but the question seemed to change. It lost some of its edge. She realized that initially it had had the tinge of accusation. Now it seemed more inquisitive. Perhaps, she thought, more like a question that might, in time, be answered.

* * *

"The platelet count is extraordinarily low," the doctor at the Mayo Clinic told them. "That's why he's been bleeding."

"What's this got to do," Andrew asked, "with his broken leg?"

"Probably nothing, in fact. Although the break may have caused this condition to manifest itself sooner than it otherwise would have."

Shades of Thorne Creek

"Condition?" Joanie asked. "What... condition?"

"Aplastic anemia," the doctor said, slowly, evenly. It seemed to them as if the doctor were speaking in a tone specifically geared not to frighten, as if he expected the words themselves to terrify. They had never heard the term, however; it washed over them like just one more wave.

"A-plastic?" Joanie said.

"His bone marrow, the part of his body that produces new blood cells, is suffering from an aplasia. It is unable to function properly, unable to produce red blood cells, white blood cells, platelets."

"So his blood doesn't clot," Andrew said. "That's why he's been bleeding."

"That is part of his problem. He needs all three types of cells. The shutdown is so complete, we're being forced to consider a very narrow range of treatment options, and quickly."

"Can we give him transfusions? Fresh blood?" Joanie asked.

"He is receiving them, now. Quite frankly, that's the only reason he is alive right now."

Joanie's hand tightened around Andrew's. She focused on him, and on the pulse she felt in digging into his skin, to keep herself conscious. She was floating now, right on the edge. She could feel that. Focus on Andrew....

"The transfusions cannot go on indefinitely. We need to go with a more effective strategy. A more aggressive strategy."

"And that would be?" Andrew led.

"Our first choice would be a transplant of bone marrow...."

"Transplant," Joanie said. "Bone marrow? You can do that?"

"We've been doing it for some time now. It doesn't get the headlines that heart transplants get, but yes. We can definitely do it. The biggest problem would be finding a suitable donor on such short notice. We've checked the blood types of everyone in your family. I'm afraid none of you are candidates. Andy has a rather rare typing, a rare combining of your blood types. And as I say, time is very critical here."

Fourteen: Catastrophe

To Joanie and Andrew, it sounded as if the doctor were closing off each door just as he allowed them to peek in. Joanie's eyes welled with tears, but she held them back. Her son was dying, she knew, slipping away, as they sat talking.

"We have him on a number of medications. They could yet take effect. But if we are not seeing a substantial change by the end of the day today, or at the latest tomorrow, we need to look at a very aggressive approach to buying more time."

"And that... 'aggressive' approach?" Andrew asked.

"The spleen. Its primary function is to remove old blood cells from the system, as they are being replaced. In Andy's case, of course, the cells are not being replaced. If we remove his spleen, the blood we are giving him will stay longer, last longer."

"Remove his *spleen*," Joanie said, and her tears spilled over beyond control. "Doesn't he *need* that? Why does he *have* it if he doesn't *need* it?"

"It would mean," the doctor conceded, "that he would have to remain on certain medications, probably for the rest of his life. But it would give him a chance, to hang on until a transplant could be arranged. I think we need to plan to move ahead with the procedure. Tonight, or tomorrow."

Although Andrew had no medical training, the doctor's next words came as no surprise to him whatsoever:

"However, in Andy's case, there is a problem...."

Shades of Thorne Creek

Chapter 15: Business Deals

When Lewee had left the house, Father had followed at a safe, discreet distance. But when she pulled into Herky's Market, he looped back and found a spot from which to watch the house. She would return here with her groceries, he was reasonably sure. The less he was physically following her, the better.

And while she was away, he could watch the movements of the Dragon.

There was no sign of life for five minutes, then ten, then fifteen. Eventually his lack of sleep caught up with him, and he nodded off. He soon found himself floating in the North Pacific.

"Wh-wh-when's it gonna come, J-Jorggy?"

"Soon, Swanny. Soon. Just be still." The ocean had settled into slight swells, across which no wind played. He closed his eyes, and imagined the comforting feeling of dying.

"C-c-cold, Jorggy."

Jorgesson's eyes opened, narrowly, on Seaman Swan. He thought over the options.

"Swan."

Swan looked at him, blue lips shaking.

"Swan, it's no good. We're not gonna make it like this."

"You said. You said they were g-g-g-gonna come J-J-Jorggy! You said!"

Jorgesson steeled himself, waiting until he could speak without shivering: "They'll come. But we'll be dead by then, rate we're going."

Swan was too exhausted to argue. Jorgesson reached out a hand.

"Come here."

Fifteen: Business Deals

Swan complied. Jorgesson turned him, so Swan was facing away, straight in front of him.

"Gotta hold in our heat." Jorgesson drew Swan in close, so Swan's back was against Jorgesson's life jacket. Jorgesson wrapped his legs around Swan's waist.

"Be still. Keep in the heat."

There was silence for about five minutes. It didn't feel like they were any warmer, but it did feel, maybe, like they were losing their heat more slowly. Jorgesson began to feel a flicker, just a flicker, of hope.

"Wh-wh-when's it gonna come, J-Jorggy?"

The stuttered words sapped the hope from him faster than the sea was sapping his life. Jorgesson shut his eyes. In that moment, the dream ended. Lewee's Bug was in the driveway. She was carrying in groceries.

* * *

In the clean, modern, very business-like office of a well-established company in Mitchell, South Dakota, the owner said goodbye to a pair of clients he had just signed on. It was late in the day Saturday, and it had been a good day, as far as his line of work went. He slipped off his suit coat, loosened his tie, re-assembled and reorganized the brochures that had been laid out, and settled in to finish off the paperwork that the arrangement with the couple required. As he did, the phone rang.

"Anderson-Miller," he said, in a studiously even and pleasant voice.

"Mr. Miller please."

"This is Robert Miller."

A sigh. Miller waited. This sort of thing was not uncommon. He was a patient man.

"Mr. Miller, this is Andrew Lanquist."

Shades of Thorne Creek

"Yes, Mr. Lanquist..." and like lightning he was silently flipping through his quick reference index card list. He remembered the name. A family plan, he was sure....

"Mr. Miller...." Another expected pause. Miller found the card, confirming his recollection. The voice continued: "I'm afraid... we're going to need your services."

"Oh, Mr. Lanquist, I am so sorry to hear that. But rest assured, Andersen-Miller is prepared to do everything we can to ease this process."

"Thank you," Andrew whispered.

Miller swallowed. The toughest part, when it hasn't been volunteered up front: "I am sorry to ask, but who has passed?"

Another long, expected pause.

"The arrangements are for my oldest."

Miller scanned the card: "Andrew Junior. I see. Again, Mr. Lanquist, my deepest regrets."

"Thank you. We're out of town. Rochester, Minnesota. Are we covered for that?"

"Indeed, Mr. Lanquist," he said, scanning the card. "We can contact one of our associated facilities there, if that's your preference. Or we can have your son transported here. The arrangements you made cover either option, and Rochester is certainly within our range."

"Home," said Andrew. "We want things handled at home."

"I understand. Can we send someone now? Is he... ready for transport?"

"No," came the response, with an unusual firmness, considering the tone that had preceded it. "He's not. He's not... ready yet."

Autopsy, most likely, thought Miller. The thought of an autopsy can be very disturbing for the family.

"It'll be a while yet," said Andrew, softer now. "Tonight, or maybe Sunday. I'll have to let you know."

Miller made a note in his pad: Monday pickup—no Medical Examiner was going to do an autopsy on Saturday or Sunday.

Fifteen: Business Deals

"Will you want the visitation here in Mitchell, at our facility, or at the church... in Emery, Holy Redeemer?"

"No. Your facility," said Andrew. He didn't want Holy Redeemer Lutheran, or Ackermann, involved any more than they had to be. A quick service, the burial, and done. Holy Redeemer hadn't done squat for them over the years, and Andy's condition proved they weren't doing them any good now. That service would likely be the last time Andrew would be through their door.

"Very well sir. Is there anything else we can do for you at this time? Any way we can ease your burden?"

Andrew thought of the long walk he needed to make to the chapel to be with Joanie, and the long walk back to Andy's room again. He hung up the phone without answering. Should he explain it to the boy? *Could* he explain it to the boy? How do you explain a choice that is no choice? How do you pick just which way you want to die? There was nothing anyone could do to make this any better. The doctors were making that clear enough.

Hardening himself for the tasks ahead, he headed for Joan.

Andrew slipped silently into the chapel. Joanie was alone, in the third pew. She seemed to be kneeling. As he approached he saw there was a kneel bench, which was extended into the use position. That was a Catholic thing, he thought. Inter-denominational chapel. Joanie just figured she might as well make use of it. He slid in next to her, and knelt.

Thankfully, she didn't ask him where he had been.

"Aren't we supposed to get credit, somehow?" she asked, looking ahead.

He turned to her.

"I mean, for everything. Everything we've done. We've led good lives. Andy's a good boy." She winced slightly; this was hardly the time to lie. "I mean, he's gotten into trouble. But nothing really serious. Nothing really *bad*. Nothing to deserve...."

Shades of Thorne Creek

"Andy never did anything to deserve this. It just... happened." Andrew had fallen into the odd spot of defending God. The words rang hollow.

"And we come from good stock, too," Joanie said, though whether she was talking to him or to God, Andrew couldn't say. "I mean, we're descended from missionaries. The first missionaries in Minnesota, direct line. That counts for something, doesn't it? We go to Church, most Sundays, anyway...."

Christmas, Easter, Thanksgiving at least, thought Andrew. The truth of their attendance was somewhere in between.

"Oh, God. Don't let my boy die," Joanie pleaded. "Don't let him die. Please, please, please...."

Hearing her grovel, hearing her debase herself, the vacillation Andrew had been feeling between helplessness and anger now slipped into the red. But he would not call curses down on God. What was the point? Why make God any angrier? Assuming God was even listening, which seemed pretty doubtful anyway. All those wasted Sundays in Church. The prayers before holiday meals. He felt like a sap, as he imagined those scenes. Joanie was right; they had invested for years, for no return. Like ferreting money away in the bank every week, only to find the bank doors locked and the windows boarded, once you needed some cash. Once there was an emergency.

But what do you do? Stand out there on the sidewalk, ranting? Letting the whole town see that you'd been taken in?

No. He was too smart for that. He had made the investments? All right. His dues had been paid? OK. Now you go for it. Joanie was calling in her markers. He would make his deal.

Silently, so Joanie would not hear, so she would not think him even more foolish—or worse, get some false hope—he spun his deal.

OK God. I don't know if you care about this. If it'll make a difference. But here it is. Spare his life, let him live through this... he thought for a moment, considering loopholes and double-crosses... *and let him live to be grown up, let him live to at least...twenty-five. And healthy. And here's what I'm going to do. Sunday, every Sunday, at Church. Grace before supper every night.* He had heard that some of

Fifteen: Business Deals

the more far-out groups said you were supposed to give ten percent of everything to the Church. That was a lot. But he probably wouldn't have to pay up anyway. And if he did, if he got Andy back, wouldn't it be worth a little blood money? *And ten percent, God. I'll give ten percent of every paycheck... after taxes... to the Church. Not Holy Redeemer. But somewhere. Some Church. And not just to a charity. To a Church. Starting with every check I get from now on.* He paused to ponder the reasonableness of the deal. Wasn't this all the stuff that God was supposed to care about? Going to Church, praying, giving money? God might get a better offer somewhere, but not from somebody who would actually follow through. *That's it, God. Just let him live. Amen.*

Andrew wasn't offering much. Truth be told, if he knew that God was listening, and if he knew that it would help, Andrew would have offered much more. But Andrew knew, from his own experience, that that would *not* help—that it would only make things worse.

He had had first-hand experience with "being God". That's what being Head of Operations was, after all. The power to hire; the power to fire. It was very much like the power of life and death. Andrew had wielded that power—and had learned its lessons.

A year ago he held four lives in his hands. He had done what had to be done—and had shown mercy where he could. And time had shown the wisdom of his choices. Andrew knew God was at least as smart as the Head of Operations of a South Dakota grain elevator. If Andrew knew when a scared employee was over-promising to try to keep his job, wouldn't God recognize a man scared witless over losing his son? Wouldn't God dismiss wild promises made by a man who would, in truth, say anything to keep his first-born son alive?

The only promises that would matter to God were the ones that could be believed. Andrew made his choices, and drew his lines. His deal stood.

He looked over to Joanie. She was lost in prayer. She had always been more religious than him. He wasn't sure she believed in God any more than he did, but she acted more like it, on the outside.

Noiselessly, he arose and slipped out, and headed for the elevators.

Shades of Thorne Creek

Andy's was a semi-private room, but there was no roommate. Andy was alone. No doctors, no nurses. He was asleep, and Andrew did not have the heart to wake him. Not for this discussion. They had to choose, and choose soon. If they were going to operate, it would have to be early tomorrow.

Had the circumstances been different, Andrew and Joanie would have made the decision for him. They were the parents; he was the minor. But this... this was different. He wanted Andy to know, and be involved in the decision. How can you be concerned your child will make the wrong choice, Andrew knew, when every choice is wrong?

Andrew decided to wait an hour, then wake him if he had to. He left, and returned to the bank of pay phones. There was no reason, really, why Annie needed to know. But maybe he could make more sense of it, if he tried to explain it to someone else.

"Andrew," she said to him, and then had no idea what more to say.

"Listen, Annie. I'm sorry about last night. Calling you so late like that."

"Andrew," she said softly, "forget that." She collected herself, and then said the words: "What's happened?"

He ran through the basics, the knowns, and the unknowns. Andy hadn't been well for a while, the water skiing accident, the blood tests, the diagnosis. They still had no idea what had brought it on—radiation? Certain chemicals? A handful of drugs, no longer in use now that their dangers were understood? But the whys mattered little, now.

And then he came to it—the choice. He explained the splenectomy.

"It does sound drastic," she admitted after weighing it. "But if it's the only way...."

"There's a problem," Andrew said, almost dizzy from the reversal of his role: The explainer, rather than the receiver, of insanity.

"The condition..." he said, "...his bleeding. It's so advanced. This 'splenectomy'. It's a *surgical* procedure, Annie. They have to cut him open, on an operating table. And in his condition...." Andrew steeled

Fifteen: Business Deals

himself. "He'll bleed to death, even before they cut it out of him. Just getting in, getting to it. He'll bleed to death."

Annie wanted to comfort him. To say anything. Even his name. No words came. Andrew understood.

"So Annie, it comes down to this. We pick. He can die, probably sometime Sunday night, with Joanie and me at his bedside. Or he can die, on the operating table, Sunday morning." He waited, for either himself or Annie to be able to speak. He was ready first. "So what we're figuring out right now is, which way do we want him to die. I'm sorry, Annie. It's not right for me to dump this on you. There's nothing you can do. I think I just needed to talk to somebody. Explain it to somebody, so maybe it would make some kind of sense to me. I'm sorry. I'm sorry, Annie."

He paused, in case she might be able to speak. When she wasn't, he said: "We're OK. We'll be in touch. I'm really sorry." And mercifully, he hung up.

Annie listened to the tone, the dial tone, the steady, rational, reassuringly endless dial tone. In the living room Bob was playing the radio. It was a song she knew. Billy Joel. *Piano Man*. That song always made her cry. And so she did.

Chapter 16: Sunday

Annie, who almost always went to Church, did not on that Sunday. She phoned Lewee's house, and, after one of the typically short and strange conversations with Mrs. Jorgesson that always began such calls, Annie explained to Lewee what was happening. And Lewee, who almost never went to Church, chose that Sunday to take Jimmy's advice and attend Pastor Zack's church in Mitchell.

And both of them, on their diverging-from-pattern courses, prayed as they had never prayed in their lives.

In Rochester, Andrew had held himself mostly together, explained the situation as best he could, and elicited from Andy what it was the boy wanted. Although Andy's mother was opposed, she conceded to their decision. The surgery was scheduled.

Joan Lanquist dedicated herself to the chapel, pleading for mercy for her son, her family, herself, and calling up whatever debts their heritage and deeds could warrant.

At just after nine o'clock, a very young nurse's aide came to Andy's room to prep him for surgery. She brought with her a small plastic dish, mercurochrome, cotton swabs, a safety razor, and a small capped can whose label Andrew could not read. She was barely older than Andy, it seemed to him. But Andrew acceded to her request that he leave the room.

Andy smiled at her; she was cute. She smiled back, and explained her task:

"We have to shave the area where they're going to operate. Get it disinfected, and shaved, and ready to go."

Sixteen: Sunday

She had him reposition his hospital gown while she prepared her things, and pulled a chair beside his bed. He shifted the gown so the left side of his abdomen, around the bottom of the ribcage, was exposed. She wiped the area in broad strokes with mercurochrome-laden cotton pads, and then dropped them into her plastic tray. The mercurochrome left broad swaths of orange on his skin. Removing the cap from the bottle, she shook it and sprayed out a foamy disinfecting shaving cream onto the area. It was cold, and Andy joked about it, and they laughed. She adjusted the razor, and made her first, gentle sweep.

As the razor's head moved, it cleared away the foam, and the thin shafts of hair it had shorn. And almost as soon as the razor had passed, Andy's skin began to bleed. Not from any specific cut. Simply from the abrasion of the razor.

The aide froze at the end of that first stroke, watching the whole area slowly ooze blood. She looked up to Andy. He wanted to smile, but couldn't. He managed to shrug, as if to say *It's okay.*

Her eyes filled with tears, as she looked back to what she had done.

"It's normal, for me," Andy said, as comforting as he could muster. "Last few days, I've been a real bleeder."

"Oh, lordy," she whispered. Fresh cotton pad in hand, she tentatively wiped the blood away. More blood replaced it. She looked up to him again, this time with fear mixed in her eyes.

Andy couldn't think of what to say to her.

The plastic tray slipped from her lap; the bottle of mercurochrome shattered on the floor, and she leapt up and ran from the room. Almost running into Andrew, she stopped short. Then she turned and ran blindly down the hall.

Andrew inhaled, and straightened, and walked into the room. Andy was gently maneuvering the razor about the area, wiping the blood that followed it.

With a strength Andrew had no idea he possessed, he said simply: "It's OK, son. Just leave it."

* * *

Shades of Thorne Creek

Lewee's father was worried at first. What could it mean, that she had come to Mitchell and gone to this church? This same storefront church by the payphone he had been using the other day? In time he convinced himself that it might be just a coincidence. And so, with a heightened sense of awareness of all that was around him, he waited—and with mixed feelings, he pondered what her presence here might mean.

He had always been uncomfortable with the outward trappings of religion, especially the more raucous variants; he cringed at the thought of her yelling "Glory hallelujah!" and handling snakes and all. But it need not be like that, necessarily. And church-going might have kept her path straight and true, might have helped her avoid the pitfalls of boys, and what boys wanted.

But of course, religionists had their problems, too. They hated all sex, deep down, really. They thought of it as evil, and would try to convince her that her own body was an evil, unclean thing. But he knew better. He had seen her walking around town. She had flowered into the glory of young womanhood. That was the tragedy of his absence. He could have made her see her beauty, helped her experience it. He could have made her comfortable with her body, and with the changes she had gone through. He would have loved her, and she would have loved him. And he would have prepared her, paved the way for her, made sure her body was ready to receive a boy, once she felt the time was right. And until that time, he could have fulfilled all of her needs.

As long as they were discreet. And as long as there was no sexually-deranged Dragon Lady peeking around every corner, trying to make perversion out of any little thing.

She had been a baby, a complete innocent. He wasn't hurting her. She was enjoying his touch; he was certain of it. But the Dragon had seen, and had assumed, in her own, internally twisted way, that his touching her in that way was somehow for his gratification, not his dear little daughter's. And the Dragon had exploded, and lashed out, and tried to destroy everything.

Sixteen: Sunday

And so it had been all more of the same. The same tired rants, the sick tirades he had heard over and over. From his first wife, about their step-daughter. From his parents, about his sister. The whole world was caught up in a psycho-sexual tornado. That was how the therapists phrased it, always unknowingly pointing at themselves when they tried to stick labels on others.

He would not be returning to them, not if he could help it. When it came time to let Lewee know he was back in her life, for good, he would be sure that everything was safe. The Impala had been a good move; it was largely untraceable to him. But there were further steps he could take. In case anything went wrong, he would make sure he had no ID on him before making his move. There were always fingerprints, if some committed deputy wanted to take things that far, and if his smooth talk were to fail him. But talk had stopped things short of that, many times. Of lesser concern was his forearm; so many men had served on the USS Colorado over the years, that it was only marginally useful in identifying him—his old ship's name tattooed in scrolled letters, above the bold skull and crossbones.

People were beginning to filter out of the church, but slowly, unevenly. Churches like this sometimes dispersed in fits, he figured.

He had waited all these years. He would wait a little time more. She was a prize well worth it.

* * *

Feeling out of place among the crowd of worshippers—prayer warriors, Pastor Zack called them—Lewee stood in their midst near the podium, and felt herself awash in the strange energetic praying.

At the service's conclusion, Pastor Zack had invited anyone who wanted prayer to come forward. A handful came forward for prayer, and most everyone else folded in around to pray for them. Lewee wanted to offer Andy's name into the petitions that were being explained to the crowd, but she was unsure of herself, of the protocol for adding a name, and of just how much to explain. Before she wrenched up her courage, the praying had begun.

She was surprised that she did not feel uncomfortable with the process. They mostly prayed one at a time—that is, with one person praying loud enough for all to hear. But usually several others were also praying aloud, much more quietly, and apparently independently of whomever was "leading" at the moment. Sometimes those quieter prayers, which she could occasionally isolate and follow, were an odd gibberish-like stream.

Snake-handlers, Mother had declared all Assemblies attendees. But nothing here seemed as scary as Mother had made it sound. Strange, yes, but not scary. And not even strange, really, the longer it went.

The prayers were different from what she was used to. There was a... a tone, perhaps. These were no 'now I lay me down to sleep' recitations. These were heartfelt, and confident. Almost bossy, it seemed to her—treading the line between confidence and assertiveness. *She* could never talk to God that way. There was something else in the tone, though; a pleading humility. She kept listening. It was as though they were pleading for God to help them, all the while knowing that he would.

The prayers seemed to wind down, and Pastor Zack led a closing prayer to wrap things up.

She stayed behind as the last worshippers left, and helped Pastor Zack tidy the room. It was then, when it was just the two of them, that she told him of Andy.

The pastor wanted to say something comforting, but in the face of these circumstances, of Andy's diagnosis, he found his own faith wavering. Although it bothered him, he felt he could only speak honestly by offering the temporal, earthly assurances that anyone might offer:

"He's in good hands. Mayo is the best," he told her. "When are they going to operate?"

"I'm not sure," Lewee told him. "Annie said it would be soon. Real soon. How soon do you suppose they could do it?"

(Even as Lewee spoke the question, Andy was being wheeled down to a Mayo operating room. And Andrew was standing alone, not

Sixteen: Sunday

knowing of the distant prayers of strangers in Mitchell. Had he known of them, he would not have wanted them, anyway; he had made his deal with God, and his deal would stand.)

"If it's really that pressing," the pastor speculated, "they'll probably re-arrange the surgery schedule. Probably get him in first thing Monday morning. We have an evening service tonight, Lewee. We'll be sure to pray for him then."

"The way you guys pray. It's like you're not talking to God. It's like you're talking to.... I don't know."

As Pastor Zack realigned a row of chairs, he struggled with himself. It seemed artless and harsh, given the girl's circumstances. All his training said this was not the way to bring up the issue. And still he spoke the words: "Bible says that God's like our father in heaven. Maybe it seems more like we're talking to a father. More like that, than talking to some distant, unapproachable God."

"Talking to your father, huh?" Lewee shrugged: "I guess I wouldn't know about that."

The impulse to pursue the matter left him. He chided himself internally: *What kind of counselor are you? Taking random shots on a whim? You owe her better*. He wanted to suggest that they pray about the issue—that somehow, Lewee's dad could get back into her life. Zack Hennessey's faith felt so small just now, in the face of Andy Lanquist's troubles; Lewee's father returning seemed like something more reachable to pray for.

He felt a tingling burn of shame flush across his face. The God to whom he prayed was the God of Abraham and Isaac, the God who guided the Israelites in the desert, the God who raised the dead at the touch of his son's hand. The pastor felt miserable and petty for not trusting God to heal the Lanquist boy.

And somewhere, in the mix of his emotions, and guilt, and re-arising faith, the idea of praying for Lewee's father to re-enter her life got lost in the shuffle.

Outside, the pastor and Lewee parted ways, under a pair of watchful eyes. The Impala followed Lewee's Bug, but at a discreet distance. He had thought today might be the day, but now felt it would be better to wait. For a while. Just for a little while. Besides, there were a few more preparations to be made, first.

* * *

In the basement of the Dale house, in dim light admitted by hopper windows, and in cool moist air too seldom circulated, the home's fuse box door stood open. A single fuse lay, business-end up, atop the adjoining cabinet.

Up in the world of light, Bob Dale sat on the porch. The transistor radio distracted him for a time from the unease of a disrupted routine; Sunday morning was time for Church, and it was Sunday morning *now*, and they weren't *at* Church, and that was *wrong*.... But the radio—that had an allure which, for the moment, engrossed him. Often he could not wait for a song to end before working the tuning again—up, up the dial, then stepping back down, station by station, always in search of some perfect song. One more bit of treasure.

Farther up, in the second floor bathroom, Annie removed the screws holding the cover plates of three adjoining switches. The rewiring task before her was daunting, but it was better than having nothing to hold her attention—better than simply waiting for the phone to ring. Her eyes stole to the clock. Andy Jr. might be going into surgery, even now.

She wanted to pray for Andy again, but she could not. It was too much to contemplate—that her words might turn the will of God, and save Andy's life. For if that were true, then her lack of words might let Andy die. How could she believe such a thing? How could she believe either one?

Andrew had told her—Andy Jr. was going to die. There was no question, no option. The only question was how, and when. How could she pray against that? Against the wisdom and training of *doctors*?

Sixteen: Sunday

Reverend Ackermann's words came back to her: *A mature faith understands that some prayers, no matter how heartfelt, will have to be ignored.*

The words that had eluded her before came to her now, and she spoke them without thinking: "So, then? Do I *not pray at all*?"

And in that moment, as she set her mind that she would pray despite the wealth of reasons against it, another thought occurred to her. If she prayed yet again for a miracle, what would she do when Andy did, in fact, die—as Andrew told her he had to? What would she do then? Could she experience again the things she had been experiencing? Could she believe God was present, and with her, and communicating with her? Communing with her? She looked to the now exposed boxes of switches, and wire, and conduit. She used them, as she had all morning, to draw her mind away from such thoughts.

The switches had been added by her father, one by one, over the years as he had added more lights, and then a fan, to the bathroom. He had added each in its own separate electrical box, rather than replacing the whole thing with a single box, a triple-width box.

Each separate box had been mounted slightly askew, and each had its own cover plate. But with the boxes so close, the cover plates interfered with each other, and her father had had to trim them, and he had inevitably trimmed them imperfectly.

Almost a year ago she had purchased the triple-wide box, with an extra wide cover plate to handle all three switches. And the parts had sat in storage under the vanity, because her dread of the job always outweighed her dislike of the old switches' uneven, cobbled-together appearance.

She had been in attendance when her father had added the last switch, the fan switch, and she remembered what he had said about how complex it was to wire off all three together "from a single feed". He was no electrician, but he had worked it out. A little knowledge, a little trial and error. But if he was no electrician, she was certainly not one. To remove the three boxes and reset the switches all into one big box meant undoing all of the wiring. And that meant that, during the reassembly, she would have to learn all that he had struggled through before.

But that was precisely the point, just now: It would hold her mind, hold her thoughts. That was the most important thing. It would keep her from thinking of Andy, of thinking....

She loosened the next set of screws, the ones that held the switches into the boxes. Pulling the switches out, as far as each one's coiled wire would allow, she made a discovery. Someone (her father, she realized, for who else could it have been?) had put a masking-tape flag on each of the wires, and written on each flag a single word to note its function. Line. Load. Ground. These were all words Hector had taught her, in their little impromptu tutorial on the phone that morning. And as she thought of what Hector had said about them, and as she traced where each of the labeled wires went, it all made sense. It was confusing, the way the switches interconnected, but it did make sense. It all seemed... possible.

For an hour she struggled, removing wires from the switches, snaking the wires back out of the old boxes and into the new box, reattaching them where they belonged. There were points of confusion where the process was not as linear, as step-by-step, as she had hoped. But it seemed to come together.

With the triple box still hanging outside of the wall, and the switches still hanging outside of the box, everything was wired in place. With all switches flicked off, she went to the basement and put the fuse back in place. Back upstairs, she paused.

Andy's situation was huge—too huge for her to address again in prayer. But this—this seemed more in proportion to her faith.

"Please, Lord, let it work."

She flipped the fan switch. The fan spun to life. She flicked the switch—off, on, off—and the fan obeyed. She thanked God, and she thanked her father for adding the labels years before.

She flipped the light switch, and nothing happened. The other light switch—again, nothing. She beat down the brief surge of helplessness,

Sixteen: Sunday

and looked over the wiring. The labels on the wires, the colors of the wires, the words stamped into the switches, everything seemed to be right. She thought of the prayer she had just spoken for the wiring—a failed, unanswered prayer. The Reverend Ackermann had been right; obviously, it could not work like some magic incantation, yielding guaranteed results. Yet surely, prayer must mean *something*; it must be more than just empty hopes, echoing in the void.

Three times reviewing the labels of Line and Load, and comparing them to the labels on the switches, revealed no problems. She blanked her mind, as if she were flipping over and shaking an Etch-a-Sketch, and she looked at it afresh, just in terms of the logic of how the wiring ran from switch to switch. And something occurred to her. Something odd. She was sure she had transferred all the connections, one by one, from what they had been in the old boxes to the same places running through the new box—but still…. The way things were connected, it *shouldn't* work. At least, it shouldn't work *right*. The way it was wired, the light switches should only work if the fan was "On". She flipped the fan switch on, and once again it obeyed. Leaving it on, she flipped the next switch. And there was light. And the next switch after. Light again. Flicking off the fan, the lights died with it.

Though she did not know how, she had brought the connections forward incorrectly. A trip to the basement, fuse out, a trip upstairs, switches rewired, a trip to the basement, fuse in, a trip upstairs… and then a moment to reflect.

"Lord, thank you for helping me see this. And please. Let it work."

Fan switch on, fan running. Switch off.

Light switch on, and light. She tried all the permutations. Everything worked.

And it occurred to her: She had prayed it would work, and it had worked. The first prayer, the one that had not been answered, was an implicit one: "Please make this work *right now*."

Another thought occurred to her. Not a vision, exactly. But not exactly a memory, either—although it was couched in the terms of a memory. She thought of herself, riding a bicycle. Or learning to ride a bicycle, anyway, with her father to one side and behind. Without looking back, she called out, in her imagining: "Make it work, Daddy! Make it work *this time*!" And it might work that time, or the next, or some time a dozen down the line. What her father would do, as long as she wanted him to, was to stay with her, and help her, until it *did* work. The image faded from her imagination.

Her attention returned to the wiring, protruding from the still-hanging triple box. Wiring like some rat's nest. Wiring that she had worked out. With prayer. She did not know if her spotting the wiring error was a divine intervention and revelation, or if it was the result of a sort of cleverness God had given her, or if it was the result of a cleverness that was her birthright by virtue of being her parents' child. It did not seem to matter. She had asked that the wiring work. And God had stayed beside her and behind, steadying her until it worked.

And as she had traveled from the second floor to the basement and back, time and again that day, and as she passed along the main hallway many other times, she always passed by her basket of stones without seeing the curious message that had been left there. Had she seen it, she might well have not noticed it. Had she noticed it, she could hardly have understood it. Hardly understood, for that matter, that it even was a message, any more than Teapot Eddie had understood it to be a message when he arranged it. Such things cannot be seen, much less understood, until their time has come.

* * *

Andrew waited alone in the post-surgical waiting room. Joanie maintained her vigil—and virtual residency status—in the chapel. Andrew had asked Ted to return to his hotel room for now; Andrew wanted to be alone when the word came from Surgery. No other families waited; it was Sunday, and only extraordinary circumstances led to Sunday operations.

Sixteen: Sunday

Hearing a stirring down the long, long hall, Andrew looked up to see two doctors approaching. This was it. It was over. Andrew stood.

The doctors stopped, stood facing each other, talking. The one put his arm on the shoulder of the other, who waited for a moment, exchanging a few more words, and then turned and left by a side door.

The first doctor turned, saw Andrew standing in the waiting area, and then did something Andrew did not expect. He reached an arm out to the nearest wall, as if bracing himself. After a moment, he seemed to shake his head.

"Come on, Doc," Andrew muttered. "Buck up. For God's sake." Andrew needed the doctor to be strong, emotionless, and clinical. Any show of emotionality—from the doctor of all people—and Andrew would fold. *These people lose patients all the time. Don't they train these guys how to....*

The doctor was approaching. Andrew took a few steps, but then stopped. Not that he wanted to stop. His legs just wouldn't move. They would not take him any closer, any sooner, to the news for which he had prepared himself.

"Mr. Lanquist," the doctor said, as soon as he was near enough to be heard without raising his voice. He spoke from behind a bland, almost colorless mask of a face. "He's in post-op. He's... he's alright."

Andrew responded with a gesture of his head that was a random mix of a cocking and a shaking; his jaw moved without sound. The doctor spoke again:

"I... cannot explain what happened."

"You didn't perform the operation?"

"No, Mr. Lanquist, we did. We did perform the operation. Please. Let's sit." The doctor gestured to some chairs.

"What happened?" Andrew asked, refusing to move.

"I do not have an adequate answer for you, Mr. Lanquist. I made the incision. I made the incision myself. And... and your boy bled. Profusely. And then. And then, he didn't. The bleeding stopped. We proceeded. We removed the spleen. We closed. It was an altogether normal operation. An absolutely, extraordinary, normal operation."

Shades of Thorne Creek

"The drugs? The medications? Did they start to work? Is that what did it?"

"Mr. Lanquist, may we sit?"

"I'm okay, Doc."

"No, Mr. Lanquist. For me. May we sit?"

Andrew realized then that the doctor's pallor was not his normal shade. They sat.

"In my professional capacity, I do not know what to tell you. In weeks, perhaps a month, the drugs might have gradually curtailed his bleeding. You may choose to believe that they had their effect sooner. Sooner than has ever been reported for this sort of situation. But as to the manner of the change. This, Mr. Lanquist, this was as if a faucet were simply turned closed. In all honesty, I know of no medical reason why the bleeding stopped."

The doctor looked away, down the hallway.

"Might I ask, Mr. Lanquist? Are you a religious man?"

Under other conditions, Andrew might have found the question intrusive, even offensive. Under other conditions, the doctor would never have asked it.

"I guess so," Andrew said. "Sometimes. Not much, really."

"I, myself, am Jewish." And here the doctor let his head bobble a bit: "Sometimes. Not much, as you put it. But I know the... what would you call them... the *big stories*, of the Torah? And of the Christian Bible? I know of the Israelites in Egypt, and the Passover, and of leaving Egypt. And of crossing... the Red Sea." The doctor turned toward him, but not completely. He spoke now, almost to Andrew.

"To believe that the medications worked so soon, and so thoroughly—and so abruptly—in a case of aplastic anemia so advanced, is to tread into believing something in the realm of the miraculous. But. In my professional opinion, and the opinion of others in attendance in surgery, the miraculous, in one respect or another, may be all that we are left with to understand this."

Chapter 17: Pretenders

Andrew spent Monday shuttling between the hotel, where Joanie was spending the day mostly in bed—a physical, emotional, and spiritual wreck—and the hospital. Most of his hospital time was spent with Andy, talking with him, watching TV with him, sometimes just watching him sleep. The balance of the hospital time was spent either with doctors or in the chapel.

With the doctors, he learned the endless regimen of medications that would be needed for Andy, and their various side-effects. There was a good chance that his hair growth would be prodigious. A somewhat lesser chance that his fertility might be lessened. And on, and on. He learned of the appointments that had to be scheduled, some with Andy's doctor at home and some that would require trips back to the Clinic in Rochester. And there were discussions of ways to try to track down the mysterious triggering event; things to investigate, questions to ask.

At the chapel, Andrew came to feel the weight of the commitment he had made. Sitting silently and prayerlessly in a back pew, his promises settled on him the way a wet, heavy snow settles on a flat roof—moment by moment growing heavier, pressing down against the specification limits of materials ill-chosen and ill configured for the unexpected turn of weather.

Church attendance had never been terribly onerous to Andrew, but that was mostly because it was in some measure voluntary. Joanie would not have sat still for his *never* going, but any given Sunday had a sense of possibility, of compromise. That sense was gone now. But Andrew tried, and mostly succeeded, in not thinking of the balance of his life as a prison sentence—time being served Sundays, 9:45 AM to 11AM.

Seventeen: Pretenders

Finances added to his fitful ill ease. What would ten percent translate into, in the real, practical world? A shorter, less expensive vacation? No vacation? An extra year between new cars? Two years? Three? Buying used? It was like the days after his back injury, relived.

He was becoming acutely aware, now, of the pattern of foundering hopes which was his life. Of how circumstances kept dangling the promise of a secure and comfortable life before him, putting him at ease. But circumstances, or Circumstances, always yanked things away.

He shook off the thought. It didn't matter. He was committed.

Not that God would strike Andy down if Andrew failed to uphold his end of the deal (though Andrew figured God would be within his rights, in such a case). No, something more basic was at play here. One of two things had happened here on Sunday, in these very pews.

The first possibility was that God had heard his prayers, and his commitments, and had acted to save Andy's life. If that had happened, then it would be wrong to renege, regardless of whether there were consequences. A deal was a deal. If you sign a pact with the devil, thought Andrew—without the slightest recognition of irony or humor—then you've got to pay up.

The second possibility was that he and Joanie had been alone, and no one had been here in this chapel to hear him. His prayers had simply bounced around inside his skull till they were lost, like fading echoes in a canyon. Some turn of chance, as yet not understood by the doctors (if it ever would be) had changed Andy's fate. And it would have done so, no matter how much or how little Andrew had offered. And if that is what had happened, then Andrew's sentence now was due punishment for his foolishness.

Either way, his course was set, and he was prepared to take his lumps. Because along with everything else in the plus column, he had managed to keep his integrity; he had managed to not promise away the one thing he could not give: He had not promised that any of it would mean anything to him.

He had spent some time in the chapel on Sunday, but had no idea how much. And so, on Monday, between meetings with the doctors and visiting Andy and checking on Joanie, he put in yesterday's full hour and fifteen.

* * *

In Andrew's office, Annie fought gamely to wade through the items in Andrew's voluminous inbox, separating the pressing from the can-wait.

"Miss Annie?" asked Hector, standing in the doorway to Andrew's office. Annie felt suddenly embarrassed, caught sitting in Andrew's chair, her hands in Andrew's papers. She knew her rightful place, and how deep her knowledge of the El operations went. But did others? Did old-timers like Hector understand that she wasn't just a pretender, posturing in Andrew's absence? She had to act as if he understood, that much she knew.

"Hector. Yes. Come in."

Stepping in, Hector shut the door to close off most of the noise leaking in from the work floor.

"Miss Lewee said you wanted to see me?"

"Yes, Hector. Andrew was concerned about the air scrubber system."

"Yes, ma'am. The bin. He doesn't trust the gauge they put on the outside. But I've been checking it, and it seems to be OK."

"You have? Oh. Andrew thought maybe you hadn't been getting the chance to do it."

Hector smiled. "It's been a little crazy out on the floor." Then a more serious expression came over him. "But I know Mr. Andrew was worried about it. That's a major safety system. And I've been checking it, just like he asked me to."

And there was, in fact, no real deception on Hector's part, in this. As he was speaking them, the words "just like he asked me to" meant, to Hector, that he had been checking the bin in precisely the manner Andrew had asked for—namely, climbing the ladder, opening the door,

Seventeen: Pretenders

and visually comparing the level with the gauge. For Annie, who knew nothing of the particulars of how the bin was checked, the words "just like he asked me to" had only one meaning, the meaning Andrew had impressed on her before leaving on vacation—that the vital concern was that the bin be checked every day, not every two or three. And thus, with one set of words, and two sets of meanings, the issue was settled amicably and satisfactorily for them both.

As Hector left, Lewee slipped in past him.

"Annie! It's Andrew on line one! And it sounds like good news!"

Annie motioned her to stay as she began talking with Andrew, and it did not take long for Lewee's impression to be confirmed.

Annie had cried at the news Andrew had given her before, the news of Andy's doom. She cried with him now, at the news of Andy's deliverance. And, confronted with Annie's joy, and with her certainty of the hand of God, Andrew felt his own inclination toward the second of his two explanations, toward the rationality of the inexplicable, beginning to waver.

Between the stone blocks of monumental news, both Annie and Andrew filled in with the mortar of day-to-day reports and questions.

In time, Lewee floated out, and back to her tasks in the main office. She knew Annie would give her the particulars later. For now, she had all she needed. Andy Lanquist Junior had been rescued from the edge of certain death. A small group in Mitchell had prayed, and a young boy had lived. She wondered about her tattoos, and what had driven her to seek out Pastor Zack Hennessey; she wondered if she had been delivered to him for an altogether different, and more wonderful, reason.

As Annie and Andrew talked, Annie watched rail cars being offloaded on the siding, with clouds of grain dust rising into the air and being blown harmlessly across the prairie beyond. Between the cars, she watched a train rocketing past, on the main line. She wondered if any coins or electrical box knockouts had been left on the rails—freshly minted currency, for a day on which all things seemed new.

Shades of Thorne Creek

Andrew was talking about returning to work. Though Annie assured him she could handle things, Andrew promised to return on Tuesday.

"I've gotta get to work, Annie. Gotta clear my head. I'll drive back tonight, to stay."

"And Joan?"

"Our friends, Ted and Arlene... they'll drive Joan back home later in the week, to pick up some things, and then they'll take her back to Rochester. She's gonna stay down here till Andy's released."

By the time the conversation had wrapped up, Annie had lost the thought she had had about writing up the conversation with Hector. Hector had no plans to discuss it further, having gotten tacit approval for his actions from Andrew's surrogate, Annie Dale. And Andrew, upon his return, would need several days for the emotional battering of his 'vacation' to wear off, before returning his thoughts to such things.

The time was too short; the air scrubber bin would never be checked again, until it was inspected by the investigators while it lay as just one more tangled piece of wreckage in the debris that had once been the Emery El's Head House.

* * *

Late Monday afternoon, Hector showed the eager young paint bidder the layout of the tunnels. Paul wanted to review the inventory he had taken earlier of all the dimensions, features, and fixtures—and of every unexpected surprise he might encounter. This job had to work out right; it had to come out on budget.

The conveyor was rumbling past them, carrying grain to the elevator legs in the Head House. There was dust, and so both Hector and Paul wore masks, but most of the dust was being sucked up into the overhead vent.

"You won't be painting in here!" Hector reminded him, shouting over the din. "Just down at the end! After the end of the belt!" Hector

Seventeen: Pretenders

motioned him to follow, toward the outer end of Tunnel B, but Paul held up his hand:

"More tunnels?" he shouted. "The other way?"

"Two more! Not in use! You won't be painting those!"

"OK if I look in there, after here? I want to scope it out, make it an option on the bid!"

Hector shrugged. "Sure! When we're done, you just come all the way back to here! Then through there…" he pointed to a door in the foundational structure of the Head House, "…all the way through! Sign says 'Tunnel D'! Just go through! Same layout on the other set of tunnels!" And here he pointed to a large vault-like door, propped open, on the wall that divided the active Tunnels A and B. There was writing stenciled on the door, which Paul noted but did not mention, preferring to wait for the quieter environs of the disused end of Tunnel B.

They walked past the noisy, dusty downspouts from Silos Two, Four and Six, passing two more of the large doors along the way, although these others were not propped open. It was at Silo Six that the continuous conveyor belt began its long journey to the Head House and back. But beyond the downspout for Six, Tunnel B continued. There was a framework for a conveyor, but no belt was running. They removed their masks as they neared the end of the tunnel, where the downspout for the someday-anticipated Silo Eight would be.

"You can put up some kind of tarp, I guess," Hector said, "back at the start of the belt, to keep paint away from the grain. And to keep dust away from the paint. You'll want to tarp over this too," he added, pointing to the conveyor frame.

"Every bulb have a cage?" Paul asked, pointing to the exposed-bulb light fixture above them, shielded in its wire framework.

"You bet. Broken bulb can flare. Explosion hazard."

"Not much dust down here, though," Paul observed.

"Not much. But maybe enough. Or maybe not. Better safe than sorry. Any bulb in a dust area has a cage. Both tunnels. We'll mount 'em in C and D, too, before we even start building those silos."

Shades of Thorne Creek

Before Hector went back, leaving Paul to his measuring and note taking, Paul remembered to ask him about the big door between the tunnels.

Hector smiled: "Great thing, those doors. Didn't used to be there. You were in here, and needed to get over to Tunnel A?" He pointed at the dividing wall, indicating the tunnel that lay beyond. "You had to go all the way back, to the freakin' Head House, go up the stairs, over, back down, and walk the whole length of the tunnel. Just to get over there." He gestured through the wall again. "These doors were a big improvement."

"I was wondering about the warning."

Hector looked at him puzzled. "Warning?"

"It's stenciled. Right on the door. 'Keep Door Closed When Not In Use'."

Hector had to think, but then he recalled it. "You know, you look at those stupid doors every day, and after a while, you don't read it any more. Yeah. They say that. I guess we're cheatin'. But I figure, that one down there? It's always 'in use'. You feel how hot it is down here?"

Sweat was beginning to bead on Paul's forehead, and he nodded.

"Sometimes, we get conditions just right, we get a breeze blowin' through. Tunnel A to Tunnel B. So we leave the door open, and it makes things a lot cooler."

Paul nodded, knowingly. He had seen a lot of things, a lot of rule-bending, in the refinery. This was no worse than what he had seen elsewhere.

Hector was about to leave, when Paul thought of a question, an unimportant, idle question. He asked it anyway.

"Hey Hector. That breeze? Where does it come from?"

Hector thought about it, then shrugged. "Tunnel A, man. What can I tell you?"

* * *

Seventeen: Pretenders

When he was finished, Paul traipsed all the way back to the Head House foundation, and then followed Hector's instructions to enter Tunnel D. Just inside the entry door to Tunnel D, he found light switches. The first one had no effect, but the second and third brought light. He found it pretty much as Hector had described it, except for two things.

First, Hector had not mentioned the piles of junk and storage shelving stored there. Paul decided not to make clearing the area part of his quote, but rather to specify that the El personnel would have to empty the tunnel themselves; quicker just to quote it that way. Besides, the whole Tunnel C and D thing was just a shot in the dark anyway. The tunnels had not been in use, and were only in minimal need of painting. No point wasting too much time quoting it.

The second thing was that Hector had said there was no dust. Which was partly true. The air was less dusty than in Tunnel A. But the floor, and the shelves, and all the junk piled up—all of it had a layer, a quarter inch in places, a half an inch in others. At first Paul assumed it was sand, or plain dust. But it looked and felt to him more like grain dust. He couldn't be sure. He was careful when he was walking around, though, not to stir it up too much. He understood grain dust was dangerous when it was floating. No point in taking any chances.

As he left, he switched off the lights with a single sweep of his hand. He missed, however, the first switch—the switch that had had no effect. And since that switch had not turned on any light, the tunnel returned to darkness. Paul never noticed it.

The switch was properly wired, and the light socket it fed was functional, but the bulb within that socket was burned out. And now there was power to the socket, and power reaching up into the bulb, at least up until the point where it reached the broken filament. But the gap across the filament break was too far for the current to jump, and even if it did jump, the spark would be securely contained within the glass bulb.

And one day, if all went according to plan, the additional silos would be built. And then the glass bulb would get a protective wire cage. And the tottering shelving nearby would be moved out. One day, if all went according to plan, there would be no danger of falling objects breaking the glass, and pushing the filament, and creating a spark in the live circuit.

* * *

After Rachel's shift ended at Herky's, they hung around while Paul worked up the numbers.

"The job's not as big as I thought," he said absently, scribbling some notes. "The tunnels, the part of the tunnels they want painted, are pretty short."

She looked at him, trying not to show the disappointment in her eyes. "Not gonna bring in much?" she said.

Paul cocked his head: "Oh, it'll bring in enough. Just not enough for me to try to pull together a whole crew. And that's a good thing. Fewer people means a smaller payroll, and less wildcards. More predictability. I think Donnie and me, we can do it ourselves."

"Have you heard from him yet?"

Paul set down his pencil, and looked at her squarely. "No. No I haven't. And I really need to know. I've got to have him."

She smiled, reassuringly. "He's Donnie. If he knows you've got to have him, he'll come."

He smiled back at her, a Cheshire cat smile. They were engaged. She was family, almost. It was time for her to know the one secret black mark on reliable, trustworthy Donnie Sorensen's past.

A quick scan of Herky's revealed Teapot Eddie lurking about, preparing for his evening rounds.

"Come on," Paul said, scooping up his papers. They walked the darkening streets of Emery.

"When Donnie and I were still living at home, in the place outside of Mitchell..." and here he looked about, and then shifted into a reasonable Boris Karloff impression: "...on a night very much like this one, my dear..."

Seventeen: Pretenders

Rachel punched his shoulder, and he went on in normal voice:

"There was a construction project going on just down the street. It was summer, and most days we'd hang around and watch them plowing, moving dirt, you know. They had this bulldozer. Great big honkin' bulldozer. And Donnie and me, we were always talking about how cool it would be to drive it. But we never asked any of the guys on the crew; we knew they'd say 'no'.

"But it was out in the country. Small town. And a while back. At night, they didn't lock things up like crews do now. They just shut 'em down and left 'em. I mean, who's gonna steal a bulldozer?"

"Oh, Paul...."

"Don't 'Oh Paul' me," he said with a laugh. "I didn't do anything. So it's late. Almost midnight. And Donnie and me, we're just lying in our beds, half laying across the bedside table between us to look out the window, and we can see all that equipment in the moonlight. It's just like two blocks away. And then Donnie, he can't take it anymore, and he gets up and gets dressed and out we go."

"We?"

"Yeah, well. But I didn't start it up. I didn't even climb up. But Donnie, Mr. Heroic. There's no key, just a big Start button, and he pushes it, and *vroom*! That baby's purring like a kitten. Well, like a lion kitten, or a tiger kitten. But he's careful. He tries out all the controls, and figures out how things work. Before he starts going anywhere."

"*Going* anywhere? Where did he go?"

"Not out in the street or anything. Just on the lot. Just where things were chewed up already. The moon was out, so he could see pretty well. So there was Donnie, tooling around like Lieutenant Tank Commander."

"Lord have mercy."

"A little too much like Lieutenant Tank Commander. He started to think he really was in a tank, and he tried to run it across a ditch." Paul waited for her to prod him. But she said nothing, and just waited. "So he rams headlong into the ditch, and *bam*, he's stuck. He tries to go back; he tries to go forward. He tries to lift and drop the blade, but he can't make it happen. And it's in some kind of a slow-forward idle, so the treads are creeping along, just digging deeper into the dirt."

"So what did you do?"

"Nothing to do. We figured we'd just have to shut it down and leave it there. Except for one thing. We couldn't figure out how to shut it down."

"Oh, no. Couldn't you just turn..." but then she stopped herself.

"The key?" Paul asked.

"No key," Rachel remembered. "Just a button to push, to start it."

"And facing the way it was, and angled into the ditch, the moonlight wasn't on the console. We tried punching a bunch of buttons. Found some kind of a horn, and realized hitting random buttons wasn't such a hot idea. So we just took off running for home. And all night, we laid in bed, just listening to that big 'dozer's engine idling away: 'Rowr... rowr... rowr... rowr...' all night long."

"Didn't it run out of gas?"

"Not the whole night long. Maybe they had just filled it. Maybe it doesn't draw much in idle. We didn't sleep all night."

"Donnie."

"Big brother Donnie. Reliable, mature, responsible Donnie."

"Hey," she said, stopping their walk. "Maybe I should call him up. Threaten to tell your folks, if he doesn't go ahead and commit to helping you."

"Oh," he said, resuming their walk, "you're gonna make a great Sorensen, alright."

"Hey," she said, stopping them again. "See where we are?"

Paul looked around in the darkness. They had gotten beyond the town proper. There was a driveway, and a sign he couldn't read in the darkness, but whose shape he knew.

"Thorne Creek," he said.

She snuggled into him. "Wanna find a place, and neck?"

Seventeen: Pretenders

He sighed. He had neither the will nor the inclination to decline. With a gentle touch from his forefinger, he lifted her chin.

"Just a little while," he said. "And just some necking. Five minutes."

"Deal," she said, leading him by the hand.

In five minutes neither was prepared to stop, but they came up for air. Barely seeing her face in the shadowed moonlight, Paul stroked the hair away from her eyes as they leaned back against a cool headstone, as if it were the back to a chair.

The crickets stopped—a response to some small creature moving in the brush surrounding the grounds—and then started again.

"That wedding dress," Paul said, with trepidation.

"Yeah?"

"You really like it."

"Don't you?" She shifted slightly, to speak to him more directly.

"Oh, it's... a nice dress. Yeah. I like it. I'm just wondering. Do you have your heart set on it?"

She thought about it a moment.

"It's just a dress. Why?"

Leaning his head back on the stone, he spoke out into the night: "If I get this job, and if everything goes well, we'll be set. Not set for life or anything. But we'll have enough to get started. A cushion, a little security."

"But you're wondering, what if the deal falls through."

"Yeah. Or worse. What if I get the job, and it all goes haywire? What if it costs more than I bid?"

She thought again. "Sometimes bad stuff happens. It just does."

"I know. But we've been putting this off for so long. We were gonna get married this summer, and now look at us."

"December is nice. My grandparents were married in December, remember? December the fourth is OK with me."

"Have you put anything down? On the dress? A down payment?"

"No. I'm just looking. Just dreaming."

"Rach, I want you to have that dress. But if this whole thing blows up in my face, could you skip it? Skip the dress?"

Her fingers played along the contour of his nose, and touched his lips.

"I have some old jeans, with patches on the knees. They'll do fine," she whispered.

"I love you so much," he said. "I'm just aching. I don't want anything to stop us. No delays. Not again."

"Dress or no dress. Cushion or no cushion." She kissed him lightly. "For richer, for poorer. December four."

He pulled back, rather than falling into a deeper kiss.

"Rachel, we gotta go."

She knew he was right. It was late and it was dark, and they were too alone. They were slow-stepping too close to the dance that awaited them.

* * *

As Lewee pulled into the driveway, she saw the drape in Mother's second-floor bedroom window shifting. She was waiting for Lewee again; watching. Lewee felt as if she were in that Hitchcock movie. As if Lewee were Tony Perkins, looking up to that house on the hill, looking for Mother's movement at the window. She pulled the keys from the Bug. Better to be Tony Perkins, than Janet Leigh.

As she approached the house, she did not see, could not see, the figure that discreetly watched her from a block away, mostly hidden by an old oak tree. Father had parked his car yet another block farther. There was nothing to connect the car to him, but it was still better to be safe. As she entered the house, he approached. He wouldn't enter the yard; he would just pass by. Just an unrecognizable neighbor, out for an evening's walk. He would pass by once... maybe twice. Maybe more. And if he did enter the yard, he would not go to the door. Maybe

Seventeen: Pretenders

just pass by a window or two, to see what one might see. He wouldn't see much of his little girl, though; he had learned that much over the last few days, when he had taken the unconscionable risk of climbing the tree near her window. At night her shade was always drawn. Very private. Very modest. His good little girl.

Inside Lewee stood waiting for a time, to see if Mother would come down, to see if she had an interrogation prepared. Nothing stirred, so Lewee headed for the kitchen. On the way, something caught her eye. Not what she saw, but what she did not see. The phone was missing from the end table beside the couch. She went to the table, and leaned over, looking for the cord. She saw nothing. Kneeling on the seat of the couch, she leaned over it, looking down between the couch and the wall. She spotted the four-pronged phone outlet; empty. Mother had taken the phone. Lewee looked toward the stairs, her expression tight.

Blustering into the kitchen, Lewee found the wall-mounted phone gone from there as well; the four-pronged wall outlet was askew, and the screws were not set in all the way. Taking a screwdriver from the kitchen drawer, she ran the screws out. The wires connecting to the phone outlet had been cut. Even if she got another phone, and a wall connector from the hardware store, she still couldn't use it. And Mother had done the same to the jack behind the couch, Lewee was sure.

There were only two phones in the house. And only two jacks? Or was there a third, in Mother's room? Was she maintaining one line of contact, just for herself?

Nineteen and a half, Lewee thought. Of legal age, and she could prove it if she had to, phony restraining order or no. But was she really free to leave home? Or was this all more like the Hitchcock movie than she dared think?

Maybe, Lewee thought, she would have to get her own court order, to make the crazy old woman leave her alone—to let Lewee move out, if Mother tried to stop her. Turnabout, she reminded herself, is fair play. For now, though, Lewee had never felt so unsafe in her own home.

Shades of Thorne Creek

Chapter 18: Final Arrangements

Andrew's return to work on Tuesday, the 6th of August, was as uneventful as he could make it. There had to be explanations, and storytelling, and with all of that there had to be tears.

Annie felt she was the most grievous offender in that regard, and did her best to not let Andrew see how moved she was by Andy's story—because she knew that every tear-swollen eye that Andrew saw made it harder for him to maintain his own composure. Annie knew him, knew that maintaining his composure now was important.

Most of Tuesday, between the tellings of the tale, Andrew spent closed off in his office. He emerged around noon, holding a folded paper in his hands, and he motioned Annie over to him. He handed it to her, still folded.

"This needs an envelope. It's for Ed Gulleif. Standard mail."

She nodded as she took it from him. Outgoing mail was Lewee's realm, and although Andrew was off peak form, she knew he wasn't that confused. He wanted Annie to handle this. She had an idea why, and tested it.

"You want the letter typed up?" she asked.

"No. Just like that's fine."

"Right away," she promised him, with another nod.

"Thanks, Annie."

As she turned, she caught a glimpse of his desk. The In and Out baskets remained as they had been before he arrived. The handwritten pages she held had occupied his whole morning.

Lewee was out on the floor somewhere on an errand, which was nice because it eliminated any possible questions. Annie slid into place

Eighteen: Final Arrangements

at Lewee's desk and prepped an envelope, addressing it to Ed in Flagstaff.

Lewee wasn't a snoop, but Annie understood. Ed Gulleif had been like a father to Andrew, had promoted him to Foreman, and had exited the scene with a recommendation that Andrew become Head of Operations. Andrew had spent the morning pouring his heart out to Ed, no doubt telling him everything that had happened, and telling Ed things he hadn't even shared with his closest office personnel. Even though Lewee wasn't a snoop by nature, Andrew didn't want to risk some unexpected pique of curiosity leading her, or anyone, to unfold those sheets before they got sealed into the envelope.

Annie slid them in, and sealed them for their journey. One first class stamp, and she set it on top of the outgoing mail pile. No need to slip it lower in the stack; this wasn't espionage. The envelope's seal was enough.

Annie went home for lunch, pulling from the refrigerator a sandwich and an orange, items that she easily could have, and normally would have, simply brought with her to the El that morning. But she wanted to have lunch at home. She wanted to keep up on the latest TV news, and it was news that no one wanted blaring around the office. The President of the United States was embattled, with Congress and with the courts, over Watergate and over secret tapes. None of it was pleasant, for Republicans or for Democrats. No matter how you felt about the political parties or the personalities involved, it was a dark time, maybe even a dangerous time, for the nation.

Hunched over her sandwich, in the darkened living room surrounded by drawn shades and unlit lamps, she sat before the television oblivious to the grim setting she had unconsciously created.

Andy. Life and death. Political upheaval. The passing of time.

She thought about the horrid, wicked thing she had prayed before, about Bob. She had not meant it to be evil. She had meant it for Bob's good, that he wouldn't be left alone. But no matter the reason, she had prayed he would die. *And wouldn't that be convenient*, she chastised herself. Obligation gone, she could move to Kansas City. Better pay. New career. Had any of that been in the back of her mind?

Shades of Thorne Creek

With her plate laden with crumbs and orange peels, she headed for the kitchen. In the hall she passed the end table, and her basket of stones. As she did, she felt a notion to look at it, but she shrugged it off. Too much to get done, she thought. And it's not like there was anything to see, there. Just reliving old memories. Time, instead, to focus on the "now".

She called Mrs. Finney next door, and reviewed what they had discussed some days before. Confirming things. Moving ideas from the offhand idea stage to the solid plan stage. When she was done, she called Redeeming Love Convalescent, and spoke at length with Annabel at the front desk.

Then, with every required light turned green, she asked for Bob to be put on the line.

"Who's this," he said rather than asked, with a tone edging between suspicion and annoyance.

"Hey, Bob ole boy. It's Annie girl."

"Annie girl! Annie, A-A-Annie, what you calling for? Not Friday yet, it's not."

Always the creature of habit.

"Well, Bob. I was wondering if you'd like to come over to my house, tomorrow. When it isn't even a weekend!"

"No!" he said, with a forcefulness near anger. "Come on the weekend I do! Watch movies. I wanna come on Friday."

Adaptability, thought Annie with an inward smile, was not Bob's long suit. "You can still come Friday, Bobby. This would be extra. Like a vacation."

"Vacation? V-v-v-vacation at your house? When Annie? When would we take a vacation?" Vacation. The very word had wiped the distress of disruption from him like some chant of deep magic.

"How about we start tomorrow?"

* * *

Eighteen: Final Arrangements

Wednesday began very early for Annie—a special trip to Mitchell, to RLC, and then back again. Breakfast at home. Herself, Bob, and Mrs. Finney as a special guest.

"Now Bob," Annie intoned, passing the plate of pancakes to him. "While I'm at work, and you're with Mrs. Finney, you have to do everything she says. Just like it was me, right?"

"Right," said Bob, ignoring the serving fork and grabbing a handful of cakes. Annie winced, and Mrs. Finney smiled; Bob had grown up next door to her. She knew all of his subtle charms.

"Whatever Miss Finney says," Bob echoed.

"And I'll be home for lunch," Annie said, taking the syrup pitcher and pouring for him, to maintain at least the illusion of decorum. "We'll all eat together."

"W-w-what am I gonna do, Annie? While you're at work? What'll I do? Gotta pass the time."

Got to pass the time, Annie thought. Not something she had taught him. They were good people at RLC, but they weren't really geared to dealing with the retarded. *Got to pass the time* was no doubt an idea he had picked up from the staff.

"Oh, Bobbie," said Mrs. Finney. "We've got lots to do. We'll go for walks. And you can help me grocery shop. And we can play board games, and card games."

"Don't like card games, I don't. Don't like 'em!" There was a decided edge to his tone. The face cards looked too much alike, and he never trusted the numbered cards to match up with the numbers of diamonds or hearts or clubs or spades shown. He always spent his time counting and recounting them, to the point where the rules of any given game just washed over him.

Many of Bob's limitations were quite sharply defined. Some small conceptual leaps were like stone walls—either because he really could not process them, or because he had convinced himself he could not. In the end, the distinction was probably meaningless; the result was the same.

"Well, board games it is. We'll play *Sorry!*"

Shades of Thorne Creek

"Bam! Land on you, make you go back. Sorry, Miss Finney!"

Mrs. Finney laughed good-naturedly. "Oh, Bob. I don't think you'll be sorry at all, when you send me back."

"Send you back, I will. Send you back."

* * *

Annie got to the El after Andrew, which was unusual. Had she lost track of time, getting Bob settled? Was she late?

"Got a big afternoon coming," Andrew said, holding the door for her. Her eyes swept over the clock; she was still early. "We're going to empty Silo Two. Truck it up to Mitchell. I've made arrangements with three elevators there, to take it."

"And I assume there's some good reason," Annie said, "to let the Mitchell elevators take the contract on the grain we already have?"

"Welcome to the seventies, Annie my girl. We're not into grain *storage*. We're into grain *moving*. The whole world is in motion. And Barris has signed a big deal, to handle one mother lode of grain."

"For which the rate had better be pretty good, to offset the handling of clearing out all the corn from Silo Two."

"Oh, it's a pretty sweet deal," Andrew admitted. "But you haven't asked the $64,000 question yet, Annie."

She cocked her head playfully.

"You haven't asked me," Andrew said coyly, showing as much humor as he had ever since his return. "How much is coming in."

"So how many tons are we talking?"

Andrew smiled wider. "This job isn't measured in tons, Annie. It's measured in *silos*."

Her eyes narrowed, unsure if maybe Andrew was ribbing her. "You're not talking about *filling* Silo Two."

Eighteen: Final Arrangements

"Indeed I am not talking about that," Andrew said. "I am talking about filling Silo Two *and* filling Silo *Five*." Silo Five had been standing empty for over a month.

"Oh, Andrew. Andrew, Andrew, Andrew." She ran some numbers through her head, and her smile dimmed. "Busy afternoon? You can't offload Silo Two in just one afternoon. And the incoming grain—it's coming in by rail? How long do we have the rail cars? Can we unload two silos-full fast enough?"

"Hector's calling in some day workers. We've got trucks rolling in here starting at noon."

So much for lunch at home, thought Annie. *I hope the morning goes well for Mrs. Finney.*

* * *

But lunch proceeded as planned. At home, Annie explained to Mrs. Finney what was supposed to happen, and then what *did* happen:

"Everything was lined up on our end. The incoming grain is arriving by rail first thing in the morning. But the elevators in Mitchell aren't ready yet to receive what we're offloading. And they won't be, not till tomorrow."

"But isn't one of your silos already empty? Haven't you been saying… it's been empty for just ages and ages? Can't you start filling that one, once the train pulls in?"

Bob said nothing; he just ate, and his eyes moved back and forth between the two women as they spoke.

"The infamous Silo Five. We will. We'll fill it as fast as we can. But once we get number Five filled, we'll just be idling. And the clock will be ticking on getting the rest of those rail cars unloaded. We've got to get the grain out of Silo Two. If we could have done all that today, then we could have loaded both Two and Five at the same time. Now we'll have to be onloading one set of cars and offloading another, at the same time."

"It all sounds crazy," Mrs. Finney said. "It's all the same, isn't it? You folks don't keep this person's corn and that person's corn in separate places, do you? Doesn't all the corn get piled together in the silos?"

"It does," Annie said. Bob's eyes moved, as if he were watching a tennis match.

"Then why not just load this new corn straight into your silo Two? Take the right amount out, later on. Move it to Mitchell when they're good and ready."

"Just one hitch," Annie said. "Silo Two does have corn. But what's coming in is wheat."

"Wheat?" That gave Mrs. Finney pause. "Don't get much of that around here."

"That's the thing. I don't think it is. From anywhere around here, I mean. Contracts," Annie told her. "Connections. This wheat? I don't know whose it is, and Andrew doesn't know whose it is…. Whoever owns it probably doesn't know that there are Mitchell elevators with space. If they knew, maybe they'd contract directly with the Mitchell boys."

"All sounds pretty sneaky. Pretty 'CIA'."

"Just business. Truth is, Andrew doesn't want to know. If anything goes wrong, if the deal falls apart, and the wheat goes to Mitchell, he doesn't want Barris thinking that maybe he was talking to somebody."

"Oh, Annie Dale. Just look at you. The queen bee, with the whole hive bustling around you. And you understand it all. You're on top of it all."

Annie laughed. "Not a queen bee. Just a worker bee."

"A Do-Bee," Bob said.

The women stopped short in their conversation, and turned to him.

"'*Do* be a *Do*-Bee,'" Bob recited. "'*Don't* be a *Don't*-Bee'."

Mrs. Finney tried, without success, to stifle a laugh: "We were watching a little *Romper Room* this morning on TV."

"Are you a Do-Bee, Annie? Are you?"

Eighteen: Final Arrangements

Mrs. Finney cut in before Annie had a chance: "Your sister's a Do-Bee alright, Bobby. From the day she was born, through and through."

"Day she was born, day she was born," Bob echoed. "I was born first, I was. I'm a *Don't* Bee, sometimes."

Annie patted his food-smeared hand, but the debris smears she picked up didn't bother her: "No, Bobby-boy. You're a Do-Bee, too."

But Bob's mind was back on 'born first'. Birth order. Family. "Go to the cemetery. Thorne Creek Cemetery."

Again, the conversation was abruptly halted, but this time Mrs. Finney was unable to jump in with any handy explanation of the conversational shift. 'Do-Bee' she had figured out, but she had no idea what had gotten him on to the cemetery.

"Can we, Annie? Cemetery? Visit Mom and Dad? They're dead, they are. Dead and buried. In Thorne Creek."

Twenty-plus years of life-with-Bob had inured her to such transitions, and such declarations. She was surprised, but not disturbed.

"We did visit them, Bob. In April. Just like last year. Just like every year."

"See 'em again."

There was an uncomfortable silence. Mrs. Finney did not want to offer to take him, without knowing how Annie felt about it. Annie did not want to suggest Mrs. Finney take him, without knowing how Mrs. Finney felt about it. Bob's mouth was full of food again.

"Why so soon, Bob ole boy?" Annie asked.

Bob thought while he chewed, and then he swallowed, loudly. "Don't know."

"Annie?" Mrs. Finney began, tentatively.

Annie looked to her, read the willingness in her eyes, and smiled. Mrs. Finney ran with it:

"There should be some time, after the grocery shopping."

"Mrs. Finney, you're too sweet."

Shades of Thorne Creek

Now Mrs. Finney patted Annie's hand. "It's nothing, child. Been awhile since I've been out there. Some people I haven't visited in quite a while, myself." She smiled wryly. "Maybe we'll make an afternoon of it."

It was after Mrs. Finney had left with Bob, starting on their errands and adventures, that Annie noticed it—the curious change in her display basket. She almost passed by without seeing it, almost continued down the hall about her business. Almost. Standing over the basket, looking down into the collection of rocks, she puzzled over what she saw. All of her rocks gathered over the years had been rough, jagged affairs. All except the first five, the five that had started it all, the five from the dry bed of Thorne Creek, the five that were buried down at the bottom of all of the rest. Except they were not buried. The five now lay across the top of the others, piled together in the center.

Who would have disturbed them, rearranged them? Bob seemed a likely candidate, but only for a moment. This curious act required too much focus, too much deliberation. Mrs. Finney had just been here—but it was too nonsensical of a deed. And too strange of a liberty, rearranging another's display, in another's house. Besides which, Mrs. Finney would have had no time; Annie had been with her. Had Annie thought back to Teapot Eddie, she would have dismissed him on similar grounds.

She put the mystery aside; she had things to do. She would ponder it some other time, she told herself. In fact, she would not. When next she thought of those five smooth stones, enough would have changed in her life that she would care less about the 'how' of the stones, and more about the 'why'. More about the meaning of it. The 'how' would seem to her a triviality.

* * *

At Herky's, Rachel busied herself with cleaning and straightening behind the counter. Lewee sat on a stool. She wasn't hungry.

Eighteen: Final Arrangements

"Rachel, when you and Paul get married, you're getting a place of your own, right?"

Rachel smiled. As amicable as all of the in-law-to-be relationships were, living with either set of parents was a no-go concept.

"Yeah. We'll get a place."

"What if you can't afford it?"

"We'll get someplace cheaper," Rachel said with a shrug. "There's always someplace cheaper. I know we can find something."

"But I mean, what if you pick a place, and move in, and then things change? What if you can't afford it after you move in?"

Rachel stopped tending to her chores, and came to the counter. She smiled, and waited till Lewee met her eye.

"Lewee, I appreciate your concern. But this isn't really about Paul and me, is it?"

Lewee looked down, and leaned back slightly on her stool. Rachel removed her apron, tossed it onto the back counter, and came around to sit next to her.

She did the closest her vocal range would allow to a Bogart: "Come on, kid. Spit it out."

Lewee smiled, as she always did for Rachel's imitations. The men were the funniest.

In her own voice, Rachel prodded: "Come on, Lewee. What's up? You thinking about moving out?"

Lewee's gaze rose to the empty space behind the counter.

"Thinking about it. Yeah."

Rachel nodded. She didn't know Mrs. Jorgesson well, but what she had seen of their interactions, Lewee moving out wasn't much of a surprise.

Shades of Thorne Creek

"But Rachel, what if I do it, and then I can't make it? What if I got it figured wrong, or something happens? What if I lose my job or something?"

Rachel thought over her own situation, weighing how to be positive for Lewee, without lying about her own fears.

"Lewee?" She waited for Lewee to look to her. "You look at it like that, and you'll live your whole life in your mother's house." The cold calculation of her own words almost stopped her short. Not *at home*, not *in your mother's home*. But *house*. *Your mother's house*. "If it's time to move out, then it's time to move out. You probably have a little something saved?"

Lewee shrank imperceptibly. Jimmy Turner had given her a good rate, but so much of what she could have saved had gone to Electric Jesus. It wasn't just her comfort she had sacrificed, she knew now. It was her freedom. Her chance to escape. It had all been buried as ink in her skin.

"Some," Lewee said. Even that was perilously close to a lie. "Not much," she said, to redeem herself.

"Well. You start saving. Today. I mean, right now. And you start looking for something on the cheap. Something safe, something clean, but cheap. Don't be afraid to take a step down." Rachel had never been inside the Jorgesson home, but it looked reasonably comfortable from the outside. She knew Lewee might not be able to afford 'reasonably comfortable'. "And then, when you find it, and you're sure it's what you want to do, you do it."

Lewee met her eyes firmly.

"You *do* it," Rachel intoned. "Caution be damned, pardon my French. If everything goes to pieces, say you lose your job, so what? What's gonna happen? You borrow some money from friends while you look for a new job." Bad suggestion, she thought, considering the situation she and Paul were in. What if Lewee came to them? "Or you sell something you own. Or you're late on your rent for one freakin' month, pardon my French again." Her eyes caught a figure approaching

Eighteen: Final Arrangements

from across the street. "The worst, Lewee? The very, very worst? You move back in with your mom."

Lewee rolled her eyes.

Rachel smiled and arose. "Yeah, yeah, I know," she said, moving back behind the counter. "Fate worse than death." She re-secured her apron. "But think about it, Lewee. The off chance that the very worst happens, and you have to end up where you are now? Put that up against the chance to be on your own."

"I guess you're right...."

"Hold that thought." The bell on the door was tripped, and Teapot Eddie came in to bottom-feed. He issued feelers to both of them. Rachel and Lewee shared a smile, knowing they held a nugget they would never give up before its time.

* * *

Once Lewee returned to work, there was no point in Father hanging about the El. Lewee would not emerge until five PM or later, and a persistently-waiting figure could only draw attention. This afternoon, Father killed time in Thorne Creek Cemetery. A couple of other people came, and he stayed clear of them, wandering the headstones, looking for familiar names. He found few.

Swan would have liked a place like this, he mused. But a land burial had not been fated to be. Swan's cold-stuttered 'whens' had been spoken too many times; Jorgesson had resolved that those words not be the last thing he remembered before he died. So with a firm push forward, Swan had been bent forward over Jorgesson's encircling legs. Both men had been exhausted by the cold, and in a fair fight Swan might have taken him, but the position Jorgesson had maneuvered him into had ruled all; in seconds, Swan had stopped struggling. It was finished. The wisest course of action then would have been to cling to Swan's body till the last of its heat was gone, but Jorgesson did not want him around. Slipping Swan from his life vest, Jorgesson had let him slide into the deeps. Then Jorgesson had laid back, and waited for the end to come. In peace. In quiet. He had felt no guilt. He had felt only relief.

The ocean had become almost like glass when he heard the horn—a Coast Guard cutter's horn, sounding again and again. In the end, there had been nothing left to tell the tale. Had two men been sliced by the props? Or had it been three? There were so many body parts, most of which had by then sunk, or been eaten, or dispersed in the untold ways the sea conceals her dead. Seaman Jorgesson wasn't sure who all had gone over, he had told his rescuers. He was the only one who had made it back to the surface, after plunging in.

So. No grave marker for old Swan. He doubted Swan cared—or, if he did care, that he was in any position to complain.

Frank Jorgesson had taken one more major step in his life, back in '41. One more meaningless taboo had fallen away from him, had sunk away from him, while he kept floating peacefully alone. He had not killed often since then. Never for pleasure. Only when circumstance and convenience suggested it.

By now he had wandered closer to the two fellow visitors. Must be the retard, Bob Dale, he thought. It had been years, and he never knew Bob Dale well—but how many retards could there be in a town like Emery? And was that the sister? She hadn't aged well, he thought. Jorgesson moved off.

* * *

Bob stood looking at the double-wide headstone for twenty-five seconds—something of a record for him.

"Rotting away," he said, with no more emotion than he might use to describe the color of a ball, or a TV program he either liked or didn't.

Standing slightly behind him, Mrs. Finney wasn't sure how to respond. But she was sure Annie would want her to say *something*.

"No, Bob. Your parents are in heaven now."

Eighteen: Final Arrangements

He turned to look at her, as if considering it. Then he looked back to the grave.

"Buried them, we did. I helped. I threw in dirt, dirt on the coffins. Annie did too. We buried 'em right here. Right here. Right here."

"But the part that lives on, that's in heaven."

The concept was utterly beyond him.

"I die, I wanna be buried here too. Buried with 'em. In the ground, right here. Right here, I do. Keep 'em company. Always."

Mrs. Finney wanted to speak, but could not. With a gentle hand on Bob's shoulder, she turned him to the main walkway. Together they sought out other graves, other friends long separated.

Shades of Thorne Creek

Chapter 19: August 8th, 1974

Joanie drove herself through the early morning darkness, in Arlene and Ted's car, with the idle chatter of the radio her only company. Arlene and Ted had both insisted they drive her, but she had persisted in her need for time to be alone. She stayed steady on Interstate 90, bypassing Sioux Falls, with the redness of the sky behind hinting at the pursuing dawn.

She would gather more clothes for herself, and for Julie and Eric. And probably some for Andy as well, although it might be a while before he was out of hospital gowns. None of that mattered though. Andy would need the clothes eventually. That was all that mattered.

When she returned to Rochester tomorrow, there would be people around her again. Julie, and Eric. Arlene, and Ted, and their kids. The doctors. The clergy. The nurses. Now was her chance to be alone, really alone.

What had it all meant, she wondered? Why had God put them through all of this, just to turn things around in the end? Was it a warning? To Andy, to straighten out? To Andrew, to trust in God? To her, *not* to trust in her own spiritual heritage? But God had answered her appeals to her heritage; that couldn't be it.

Surely there was some lesson to be learned. She hoped it had been more than just a warning to Andy. She knew her son; if that were God's message, it would not be received.

God, as always, was a mystery. A distant, unknowable enigma. With power over everything, and considering of every detail. A contradiction of infinities. Incomprehensible. Maybe, she thought, it was better that way. It made it easier to maintain a comfortable distance. Still, at times, she wished she could understand, could be drawn into some inner circle of understanding. Like Dorothy

Nineteen: August 8th, 1974

approaching the Great Oz, she sometimes wished to pull back that curtain. Just a corner of that curtain.

Andy had nearly died. One day, she would face death, too. Wouldn't it be better, she wondered, to have a little better idea of what was waiting?

She considered the plots in Thorne Creek Cemetery that Andrew had arranged for, years before. She had always assumed that she and Andrew would lead the way. Andrew first, then herself, and later the children. For a time it looked as though Andy would usurp a place in that arrangement. Now all had returned to its proper order. But it all seemed so much nearer now, so much more plausible that it would all one day happen. After all this was over, Joanie decided, and Andy was home, and life was back to normal, she needed to take some time, and walk on down to Thorne Creek. She wanted to see again the spot Andrew had shown her years before. She felt the need to see it, to know it. Death was somehow more real now, closer now.

* * *

As if in some bizarre military operation, the procession of empty trucks that would deliver corn to Mitchell began arriving just after dawn. It was a cloudless morning. Clouds might have masked the sunrise, or, under the right conditions, have made it glorious. But in their absence the sunrise was unremarkable; an unremarkable start to an unremarkable day.

A train was approaching Emery, up from the southeast. It carried many things—boxcars with assorted commodities, tankers with various chemicals ranging from the mundane to the exotic, and hopper cars with coal and bauxite and various grains. Somewhere in the midst of these sundries was a clustered string of cars dedicated for the Emery siding.

The drop-off at Emery had been duly planned and reported. All information concerning all trains—standard cargoes, dangerous cargoes, planned travel speeds, estimated arrivals and departures, and particularly stoppages along main lines for transfers onto sidings—

Shades of Thorne Creek

were reported well in advance to the Midwest Regional Offices of the Federal Rail Authority. Among other duties, the FRA ensured that no conflicts would arise and no safety limits would be breached.

Around eight AM, the train drew within sight of Emery. It slowed, and began the methodical dance that allowed it to leave a string of fully-loaded, covered hopper cars on the siding.

The revised information for the drop off at the siding at the Emery El had long since been entered into the system. The ambiguous long dash, improperly intended to signify "unknown"—that the specific cargo, be it corn or wheat or soy, was unknown—was improperly interpreted to mean "vacant"—that nothing was being left on the siding. No cars of any kind. It was a small error, a minor miscommunication.

In this curious play of circumstances, an altogether different set of tumblers began to align. On most any other stretch of track, it would not have mattered; the operators of the El would never schedule more rail cars than would fit, anyway.

Owing to the miscommunication, when the engineer for a freight train leaving Pullman, Kansas, was handed a punch-list detailing the maximum and minimum speeds along his route, one item of little intrinsic import was included. Amid the cautions and the sundry reminders, the long stretch by Emery, South Dakota, was listed as a forty-nine miles per hour line. This was exactly what the rules called for, with the siding at Emery being empty. Had all information been passed through correctly, and had the siding thus been listed as occupied, the maximum speed would have been forty. It was a quirk of the layout. When the siding had been laid, there was less room between the main rail and the El than the designers were comfortable with. But since 40 was the limit on the stretch, it met the standards. Just.

But once the speed for that leg was upped to 49, it was just pushing the safety limits too much when the siding was occupied. So a rule was imposed. 40 when the siding was occupied; 49 when it was empty. Occupied versus empty: a nine mile per hour difference.

But nine miles per hour, over a long haul, can have quite a scheduling effect. The load of coal hoppers, and lumber-laden flat cars,

Nineteen: August 8th, 1974

and gasoline tankers, and box cars of machine parts, all plied northward with an extra nine miles per hour trimming its transit time. And that same nine miles per hour had two related, silent, and inescapable effects on the physics of the train; twin effects, inseparable. One effect was stopping distance; the other, kinetic energy. They were effects which, under other conditions, would both have been inconsequential. They were effects which, under other conditions, would have added nothing to the death toll.

Once the grain cars had been moved to the siding, the train at Emery powered north, and the El's switch engine—the rail yard equivalent of a tugboat— began maneuvering the hoppers along the siding; the offloading of wheat was begun.

As each car was in turn pulled up alongside the south side of the Head House it dumped its cargo into the chutes below, which led to the elevator legs. The legs scooped the grain, lifting it to the top of the El, where it was dumped into the giant conical scales. There it was weighed, so the amount arriving could be monitored and confirmed, dropped to the gallery floor, and fed onto a conveyor. The conveyor in turn carried the wheat out along one of the two tunnel-like galleries atop the silos. The belt dumped and dumped, endlessly feeding the hungry Silo Five. In time both belts would be running, filling Silos Five and Two simultaneously. But before Silo Two could be loaded with wheat, its corn had to be removed.

So Silo Two poured its corn down into Tunnel B, for the short conveyor trip back to the basement of the Head House. There, at the same time one set of elevator legs was raising the wheat, another set was raising the corn. Upon reaching the top of the Head House, the corn also was directed into a set of conical scales, so the weight leaving could be monitored as well. But upon leaving the scales, the corn was not dumped onto conveyors. Rather, it was fed into downspouts that protruded from the side of the Head House, downspouts had been positioned and temporarily secured to the trucks that pulled up, two by two, outside the Head House on the north side.

Shades of Thorne Creek

This continued throughout the morning. Wheat came and corn went, and the conveyors never ceased. And as they always did when run extensively, the rollers of the conveyors grew hot. About 10:30 that morning, in Tunnel A, a bearing heated enough to deform. Having lost its shape, it became simple, even inevitable, for it to pop out of its proper place. It fell, unnoticed, and harmless, on the Tunnel floor. In time, it cooled. The roller from which it fell, however, now minus a bearing, ran even hotter.

* * *

Paul Sorensen stood in front of Herky's market, surveying the bustle at the El, and wishing he could count on all the activity, all the rush, to serve to distract Andrew Lanquist. If Lanquist were too busy, he might not notice that Paul's bid had not yet been submitted, might not wonder what was causing the delay, might not wonder if there was a problem.

But Paul knew he couldn't count on that. Lanquist *might* notice, and that could be bad. Paul feared it could be *very* bad. Paul couldn't do the job without Donnie's help—couldn't submit the bid without Donnie committing to the job. And there was still no word from Donnie. In Paul's mind, there was only one thing to do: Go back for more surveying, more measuring, so Andrew Lanquist wouldn't suspect there was a problem. There was too much riding on this to risk Lanquist's looking elsewhere for a bid.

Paul headed for the El, crossing Herky's huge, irregularly-shaped parking lot, which was defined only by the slightly lower curbless roads on all sides of it.

There were only a few cars in the lot at that time of the morning. A few belonged, a few did not. But Emery was not a town of a size that cared much about concepts like "customer-only parking". Thus the '71 Impala drew no one's attention.

Nineteen: August 8th, 1974

Its driver, however, was acutely aware of all that moved around him: the young man that had just passed by heading towards the El, each passing car, the trucks that pulled up to load grain.

It was a busy morning. A busy, busy morning. Was that good, or bad? More eyes, to see and remember him? Or more clutter and confusion, in which he could hide?

No one would remember him after all these years. And if some police car were to chance by, and for some reason take an interest, the borrowed license plates would lead to nowhere; they were from another '71 Impala.

And even if the worst were to happen, and questions were to be raised, nothing in the car could point to him. All of his identification was squirreled away safely, where he could get it later.

Everything was safe. Every contingency accounted for. He was ready to make his move, once the circumstances allowed it. It was today. He was committed. And everything, *everything*, was set. So why was he so nervous? Anticipation. Across Highway 262, in the El's parking lot, he kept watching her VW Bug. She was in the El. She was waiting for him. She didn't even know it yet, but she was waiting for him.

Unable to sit still, he got out of the car. He crossed the lot, crossed the highway, and approached her Bug. No one was watching. No one knew him. No one cared.

He did not dare get into her car. He just laid his hand upon the gentle curve of her roof. It dawned on him suddenly. The VW was a car with almost no straight lines, a vehicle of all curves. What a perfect car for her.

He removed his hand from her roof. *Not yet*, he thought, calming himself. Then, through the driver's window, he saw the book lying on the opposite seat.

Inferno. Dante. He smiled. Primitive, superstition-religion imagery. But if its terrible images warned her away from things, then Dante was a fine stand-in for him, until he could take over the role of tutor, of guide, of moral compass.

Shades of Thorne Creek

He could not stay any longer. With a quick glance around he confirmed no one was watching—then he opened the door, reached across, took the book, and left. He retreated casually to his car. It had been a long time since he perused a classic. Too long.

* * *

"You got the quote?" Andrew called out across the work floor, only half looking up from a clipboard of papers. "'Cause I ain't got time to look at a quote. Not now."

"No-no," said Paul, approaching him. "Soon. But I just wanted to look a few more things over."

Now Andrew looked up.

"Today? Jeez, it's nuts today. I haven't got anybody free to show you around."

"I know my way," Paul offered, trying not to sound too assertive, even as he raised his voice to be heard over the din. "If that's OK?"

Andrew shrugged. "Just watch yourself. Things are really hopping. Don't touch anything."

Paul smiled, and waved, and headed for the stairs that led down to the tunnels.

* * *

Father flipped through the pages of *Inferno*. Here and there his eyes played across lines of text, but it was poetry, and poetry of another era. He could not understand it. This edition did have illustrations, however; reproductions of etchings by Gustave Doré, awesome in their detail, terrible in their content. They amused and troubled him at the same time.

There was a folded paper, a bookmark of sorts. He was about to open the sheet, but the illustration on that page of *Inferno* stopped him.

Nineteen: August 8th, 1974

As the image caught his eye, so at the same time it loosed his tongue: "Good God Almighty." It was the closest he had come to prayer in a long time. The etching on the page was not the tired cliché of sinners tormented in lakes of fire. This was... quite the opposite. Two men—Dante and his guide through Hell, according to the caption—walked upon ice, in which were frozen the living souls of the tormented. The head of one protruded above the ever-frozen lake. The poet grasped him by the hair, and turned his face upward. The poet seemed to be speaking:

"Wh-wh-when's it gonna come, J-Jorggy?"

Jorgesson shut his eyes, but the image in the book stayed.

"Wh-wh-when's it gonna come?" the poet asked him again, as Jorgesson lay frozen in the ocean of ice. He could hear the Coast Guard cutter's horn, as it drew near. He could hear it, again. And again. Louder.

He snapped back. A train horn was blaring as it drew near. Without looking around, Father jumped out of the car, and hurried over to return the book. The shivering would not stop. He tossed the book back in place on the front seat.

That's not what Hell is supposed to be like, he thought. *It's supposed to be fire, not freezing.* It didn't matter; he didn't believe in Hell, anyway. But just now, it did matter. What was wrong with her, reading that kind of crap? He would straighten her out. He wasn't eager now, so much as angry. Returning to the market lot, he recklessly paced alongside of the Impala in a way that could easily draw attention.

With a long, solid blast of the horn, the engine roared by with its load from Pullman.

* * *

"Yeah," the engineer's trainee confirmed. "According to this, that siding's supposed to be empty."

The engineer took back the sheet, scowling as he reviewed it, and then backed off the throttle.

"Does it matter?" the trainee asked. "I mean, as long as the main line is clear?"

"Siding's too close to the main line. They had to create a variance for it. If there's cars on the siding, we have to back off to 40 miles per."

"But we're already here. By the time we slow down, we'll already be past it."

The engineer smiled. "Okay, that's fine. And if something goes wrong, you can explain to the NTSB why we weren't even *trying* to slow down."

The trainee adopted a sickly smile. "I get your point." He watched the last of the siding's cars shoot by. "So what might happen? I mean, I know the siding's close, but we've still got room. So why the slow down?"

"Because," the engineer explained, with the wisdom of years backing him up. "Because of the unexpected. Everything goes the way it should, we could whip by at 80 miles per. But you never know."

Nineteen: August 8th, 1974

"But like what? What kind of 'unexpected' could happen?"

"If I could think ahead and plan for it, I'd have a work-around. You do know what 'unexpected' means, right, kid?"

* * *

The engine had passed beyond the siding, but the cars that followed it still shot along past the grain hoppers. Although the train was slowing, it was a long process. In 70 more seconds, it would still be near 48 miles per hour. How much it might have slowed after that would never matter.

In Tunnel B, a roller short of a bearing continued to heat under the strain of steady use. The roller locked in place, and at once the remaining bearings began to cool. The roller itself, however, once helping the conveyor along, now became a drag upon it. The conveyor dug into the rubber of the roller, melting it.

Paul Sorenson, alone in that stretch of the tunnel, could smell the burning rubber. He did not know much about grain elevator safety, but he knew that burning was bad. He looked around, but there was no one to alert. His first impulse was to seek out the source, so he would know just what to report to the Head House. He began to walk along the conveyor.

Far above, on the scale floor, in the midst of running an errand, Lewee Jorgesson looked out the window, at the train racing past. The yard engine began to creep the row of grain hoppers slowly ahead, to align the next one with the chute.

In the office on the main floor, Annie Dale pondered another glitch in the software that had, in its earlier incarnation, been her creation.

Andrew Lanquist stood outside, taking his first drag off of a cigarette in eight years. He saw his wife pull by in Ken and Arlene's car, though she did not see him, and he watched her pull into the lot at Herky's. She stopped not far from a man, nervously pacing. Andrew could not tell who the man was, at that distance.

Shades of Thorne Creek

When Paul was still ten feet from it, he spotted the problem roller. He headed toward it.

All tumblers, within the El and without, were in place.

The metal staples that joined the segments of the conveyor belt began striking the roller's metal core. Paul stood before it, amazed as it sparked. He knew he had to do something, and he looked around. Across the conveyor, in the wall separating the tunnels, was one of the securely closed blast doors. In the same moment, he had two competing thoughts. He was glad that its stenciled admonition about being kept closed had been obeyed. And he wondered about that other blast door, near the Head House; he wondered if that one were still propped open.

All of these thoughts flashed by in a moment, as the next stapled joint in the conveyor belt approached. Paul turned, to look for some phone, or some alarm that could be pulled. Or some door, through which to flee.

The pentangle was complete. Physics ruled. The first explosion occurred.

Shades of Thorne Creek

Chapter 20: Unplanned Events

Technically, Paul Sorenson survived the moment of the initial explosion. The compression damage to his organs was irreparable, but his heart continued beating for another 15 minutes. For those who draw comfort from such things, he was most certainly unconscious during that time.

The explosion's compression wave, traveling at the speed of sound, had numerous effects. The most profound of these effects was a virtually instantaneous abrupt shake of everything within the El. Dust which had, for months, accumulated on the floor of Tunnels C and D had its surface layer loosened, preparing it for what was to come. A ladder, leaning up against shelving in Tunnel D, fell backward and shattered a single unprotected bulb mounted in the ceiling. Broken filament ends touched, and a spark leapt. But the loosened dust had not aerosolized and climbed far enough, and there was thus insufficient dispersion of fuel for the second pentangle.[2]

Along the ceiling of Tunnel B, a barely-perceptible sheet of flame shot along, burning those particles of dust that had not been consumed in the explosion itself. Behind the concussive shock wave, and ahead of the ceiling-crawling flame, the most deadly aspect of the first explosion manifested itself: A simple but powerful blast of air. Had the emergency doors between the tunnels been secured, as their signage

---

[2] In the investigation that would follow, this alternate path to disaster which did not play out would trouble several investigators. In poorly run facilities, several potential routes to an explosion might be present. However, despite its shortcomings, the Emery El could not be classified as such a facility. Those involved in the investigation were surprised by the presence of two separate sets of circumstances fully capable of leading to an explosion. In private notes, not part of the final report, one investigator mused on fatalistic interpretations of these circumstances.

Twenty: Unplanned Events

demanded, both the blast of air and the thin layer of flame would have been confined to Tunnel B. The death toll would have been two (a worker near the Head House had been hit by the initial impact as well) and there would have three or four serious injuries.

But with those doors open, the path to Tunnels A, C, and D was clear. The air, and much more slowly, the flames, followed the available paths.

As the rush of air flowed into Tunnels C and D, greatly overpowering the backed-up air flow from the clogged scrubber bin, it kicked up the accumulated grain dust that the explosion's shock wave had loosened.

Dispersion was now added to this tunnel's mix of fuel, oxidizer, and confinement. Only ignition was lacking, and that continued to burn its way along the ceilings of the tunnels, drawing closer to its final destination.

Andrew, knocked off his feet by the first blast, knew at once what had happened, and struggled to get up.

Annie sat beside her overturned chair, looking up in confusion at the underside of her desk. She understood, vaguely, that she had been knocked off her chair, and to the floor. But she was uncertain how she had ended up under her desk.

Lewee had been raised off her feet, and landed kneeling. Nausea crept over her, and her ears rang—both effects of the first compression wave that had been channeled and amplified by the peculiarities of the Head House.

Ed Libraro knelt beside her, steadying her, keeping her down. He understood what had happened, and knew it was possible it might not be over.

The ceiling-running flame lapped into Tunnel A, to no effect. But when it reached Tunnel D, it found its ultimate fulfillment; the beginning of what the official report would come to call "the second in a series of unplanned events".

An explosion, far more powerful than the first, caused all of Tunnel D to explode. At the same moment that a blast wave ripped

Shades of Thorne Creek

through all the tunnels, killing all eight men still alive within them, it simultaneously blew up through the ceiling of Tunnel D, blasting a nine-foot hole through the buried concrete roof, exploding upward through the empty trucks that were parked above. The upward blast, channeling the enormous overpressure that even the open safety doors could not disperse, was under the engine block of one of the trucks.

The blast lifted the truck, tossing it backward and into the creeping hopper cars on the railway siding. The hopper that the truck hit, like those immediately ahead and behind, was empty; the truck's mass was enough to begin tipping it, along with the cars to which it was coupled. The hopper leaned far beyond its own balance point, held back from fully flipping only by the cars to which it was joined.

Briefly it hung there; then, with the slight energy imparted by the pushing of the yard engine, whose driver had not yet had time to react, it fell onto its side.

It was now perilously close to the main line's racing cars. Those cars continued to rush by, their speed barely abating, occasionally nicking the hopper that had intruded on their space.

Ten more cars passed, till the hopper was nicked firmly enough to shift it. Thus moved, it caught the next car more firmly, and was dragged in along with the hoppers to which it remained coupled—until the two strings of cars fully engaged.

The twin effects of the train's extra nine miles per hour were about to manifest themselves. The first was the greatly increased stopping distance, an effect which caution and due diligence might accommodate. But the other effect—stopping-distance's deadly twin—was kinetic energy. And for that, there was no accommodation. While a change from forty to forty-nine miles per hour represented just over a twenty percent increase in speed, it represented nearly a fifty percent increase in energy—a fifty percent increase in energy shared by each car on the line, and by all of their cargoes. It was an energy that was about to be expended without reason, without pity, and without remorse.

The train in motion scooped up the chain of linked hoppers until everything—hoppers, box cars, rails—became a hopeless mish-mash.

Twenty: Unplanned Events

The trailing rail cars began piling into the crush alongside the El—a stack of debris that, with each successive impact, pushed farther ahead to the northwest. The cars could have accumulated to the south side of the tracks, where they would have plowed into the heavily damaged Holy Redeemer Lutheran, whose windows had already been blown out by the second blast, and whose siding was pocked by impacts from all manner of shrapnel. But instead, the cars piled up to the north, where Emery's main road crossed both the tracks and the highway. It was here, at the crossing, that the tanker cars began accumulating, smashing into one another. Some began leaking their contents.

Outside Herky's Market, Joanie Lanquist and Father Jorgesson, both unaware of each other, stood beside their cars in stunned disbelief watching the rail cars pile up like toys.

As the gasoline from the tankers poured out and flooded the intersection and Highway 262 itself, and began pouring into Emery's streets, the two had their attention stolen away by the El's Head House. The entire tower, its connections to the adjoining Silos One and Two having been stripped away, shuddered on its weakened foundation.

Like some stricken giant, the entire Head House slid down, collapsing on itself.

Andrew, as he was about to re-enter the structure, saw what was happening and ran from it. Dust and debris passed him, and the larger pieces cast off from the collapse struck him down. His injuries, while serious, were not fatal.

Joanie, never having seen him in the unfolding chaos, knew with certainty that he had been inside, and that he had been killed. She slowly began walking, like the living dead, toward the El.

Although the crashing of rail cars would go on for a while, extending back to the south east, the final impact at the intersection with the highway now took place. A fully loaded boxcar of machine parts, as if drunk on the extra energy of the added nine miles per hour, rammed the middle of a slowly-leaking, jack-knifed tanker, ripping it nearly in two. The gasoline poured from it, washing past the flows that had gone before, nearly washing up the rise of Herky's parking lot, coming close to where Father Jorgesson stood, and rushing on into the streets of Emery.

Dazed by the catastrophe playing out before him, the smell of gasoline returned him to his senses. He backed away. Looking around, he saw the lake of gas was on all sides of him. He fumbled for the door to his car.

Amongst all the debris filtering back down to earth—from the explosions, and from the collapse of the Head House—a few pieces were burning. Several landed in the gasoline pools, and, by chance, extinguished themselves without event.

One burning paper, however, did not extinguish. A quarter inch above the gasoline, the ember ignited aerosolized gas. A path of ignition crept along the edge of the El's silos, following the gasoline path, to the tankers, and out into the roadway. The wall of flame shot upward before Joanie Lanquist had waded into the fuel, and she stopped short at the sensation of the intense heat on her face and her arms. She backed away.

Father had started his car, but was unsure what to do. Could he cross the flames? Could he wait, and ride it out, and let it burn itself out?

The woman who had pulled in near him returned to her car. As she got in and started it, he stepped out to warn her: "Hey! *Hey!*" he yelled through her closed window.

The woman was paying no attention to him. Her expression was glazed; he wondered if she even knew what was happening. The flames were ten to fifteen feet high by now, on all sides. She drove through them, and disappeared. For a moment he wondered if perhaps she had chosen rightly. Then he heard the collision. After that, there was nothing—nothing but the roar of the flames.

The pavement was melting beneath him. *Maybe she made it*, he thought. He had to take his chances, as well. He reached for the car door, and it burned him. Under the influence of the adrenaline rush, he hadn't felt the heat before, but he felt it now, bearing down on all sides. He felt like his clothes would surely ignite.

Twenty: Unplanned Events

Then another sound reached him—beyond the roaring fire, but nearer than the distant siren. Something more pressing, more human. A human voice. A woman, screaming. Out, beyond the flames, in the direction the woman's car had disappeared. A woman, screaming.

At that instant, as the scream shifted from human to animal to death, he recognized where he was. This was the image of Hell he had always nurtured—the simple-minded, religionist Hell. What had just happened? Had he watched the El being destroyed? Or had he already gone into the El, to meet his daughter? Had he been killed with her, along with everyone else? Was he, now, in Hell? The walls of flame surrounding the parking lot reached endlessly to the sky; he was in a cathedral of flame. He dropped to his knees, and his knees began to sink; softened asphalt burned him. He remembered the picture from the book—being forever frozen. Spots on the pavement around him began to spontaneously combust. He had time for one prayer. One prayer. Which kind of Hell should he ask for? The kind of Hell he had floated in years ago—the freezing Hell shown in his daughter's book? Or the Hell he felt crawling on his skin, burning him even now? He had to decide—decide now—what to pray for. It was the last prayer, he was sure, that he would ever pray.

Lewee felt cool on her back, and warm on her face. She awoke, half buried in corn. She was leaning back against cool, curved metal. The metal arched above her, and came back down. It was like she was in some kind of tube. But not a tube. She knew this shape. It was a cone—badly dented, and deformed, but it was a cone. She was inside one of the scale funnels. Fighting her way up through the corn, she stood. She staggered out of the ankle-deep grain. She was in the parking lot, which was odd, because she had been up on the scale floor. The funnel had been on the scale floor, too. She was very confused.

There was a lot of fire, and she heard sirens approaching. All of Highway 262 seemed to be on fire. And the streets around Herky's and on into town. *Why are the streets on fire?* Her head was pounding, and she sat down in a pile of debris. *What a mess*, she thought.

The sirens were getting closer, and she heard people calling. Then she heard something else. It sounded like a man, screaming. She wasn't sure where it came from, but it seemed like it might be coming from the fire at Herky's.

A wave of nausea swept her, and she vomited. The screaming continued. She wanted to do something, but she couldn't even stand.

She wished she knew how to pray, because she wanted to pray for the man. Whoever he was, and whatever he had done in life, it couldn't be bad enough to deserve whatever was happening to him now.

Thirty feet away, on the south side of what had been the Head House office, Annie Dale pushed aside the debris that kept her pinned under her desk. Her head hurt, bad. In darkness she managed to crawl out, but there was no office. She could see nothing, but she could feel that the ceiling was resting on her desktop, at an angle. She crawled ahead as if she were in a tunnel, and soon she was in a tunnel, with a light at the end. Her knees and her palms were getting cut, but she knew she had to keep going. It was getting hard to breathe.

There were sirens. A fire? Was that why it was hard to breathe? She emerged from her tunnel into the August afternoon. Immediately before her was a horrendous tangle of rail cars. *Railroad accident*, she said to herself. *I thought that the El had exploded.* Looking across the wreckage, she could see her church, battered but standing. Her head was throbbing now. Swiping her hand across her forehead, her hand came away bloody.

"I'm hurt," she told herself aloud. Looking right, and then left, she repeated, louder. "I'm hurt." There was no one to answer her.

Probably all went home, she thought. *Not much to do around here, till we get everything picked up.* She looked again at the blood on her hand. She looked up at the church. She began moving toward it. When she got to the rail cars, her course was ill-defined, but she managed to pick her way through. Everything smelled like gas. There were puddles of it. She tried not to step in it. *Ruin your shoes*, she thought, not realizing she wore no shoes.

When she emerged from the wreckage, the church still awaited her. As she drew near, though, she saw that all the stained glass windows were gone.

"Oh, no," she said sadly.

Twenty: Unplanned Events

She entered the church, standing in the main door.

"Reverend Ackermann?" No response. She tried louder, but still nothing. She thought she heard his voice. Looking back to the El, she saw him—shouting, calling to people, moving debris. Her gaze returned to the sanctuary, and she moved forward into it. Stained glass was shattered all over the sanctuary floor. She began looking for the blue piece, the special piece, from the dove's halo.

She would never find it, but she would still be looking for it a half hour later when they found her, and drove her to the hospital in Mitchell.

Chapter 21: Aftermath

"Annie, this isn't right. It isn't right for you to do this," Reverend Ackermann said, standing beside her hospital bed.

"*You're* doing it," she said.

He was taken aback. "That's different, and you know it. I'm a man. It won't... matter as much. Long term. You need to think this through. Think about the effects. And say... I don't think you're supposed to know who's donating."

"I'm sure I'm not supposed to know. But people have a way of finding things out in Emery. Come on, Reverend. How long have you lived here, anyway?"

"Humph," he intoned, nodding to himself. "I suppose you're right, Annie. If I keep an eye out, I'll see Teapot Eddie making his rounds, even around here."

"Eddie..." Annie said with a burst of apprehension.

"...is just fine, Annie. He was at home when it happened."

Annie closed her eyes, and sighed. So many people she was thinking of now. She had already learned that Bob was OK, but there were so many others. So many lost to the explosions, so many lost to the flames

Out in the hall, Lewee lingered near the door, not trying to hear, yet staying close enough that hearing was a possibility. She knew the Reverend had been trying to talk Annie out of something. And she knew Annie's voice; whatever it was, Annie was still going to do it.

"Is she with someone?" a voice said behind her.

Twenty-One: Aftermath

Lewee turned to see a doctor, a doctor W. O'Shaunnessey, by his badge, a harried young man obviously in need of rest.

"Pastor, from her church," Lewee said.

"Ah," he said, nodding. "Good, good."

Suddenly the clergy visit took on a new light to Lewee: "Doc, is she okay? I mean, there isn't anything serious, right? They said it was just a bump on the head."

He eyed her. "Are you family? Because technically, I shouldn't discuss her condition, outside of family."

She shifted her weight. "No, I'm not family. But she doesn't have any family, doc. I mean, not.... She has a brother, but he's...." She struggled with diplomacy. "He isn't old enough to understand," she said, remarkably close to the truth.

"Well, no harm, I suppose. She's fine. I'd like to keep her for a while for observation, but we're actually going to have to bump her out of here. There are so many...."

"But you were glad her pastor was talking to her."

Dr. O'Shaunnessey did not reply.

"I think," Lewee said vaguely, "that he's trying to talk her out of something." She got no response, and that goaded her. "It's something you *want* him to talk her out of, isn't it?"

"I'm sorry, miss. We're really getting into things here that I cannot discuss."

The Reverend Ackermann, having noted the doctor's presence in the hall, had wrapped up his discussion; he emerged from the room.

"I'm sorry, doctor," he said, not seeing Lewee. "I can't change her mind."

"That's fine," Dr. O'Shaunnessey said quickly, with a slight tilt of the head to alert him to Lewee's presence. "They'll be needing you now, if you're ready." The doctor moved past them, into the room, and shut the door.

"She's doing okay?" Lewee asked the Reverend.

"Indeed she is. A remarkable lady."

Lewee wanted to ask him what was going on, what Annie was going to do, but she knew it would lead nowhere. Then inspiration hit. Had she heard Annie say that Reverend Ackermann was doing it too?

"Doctor said you were needed somewhere?" she asked casually.

The Reverend nodded. "There were a lot of injuries. A lot of burns. A lot of people in Emery need skin grafts."

"You're donating... skin?"

"The normal donor base is overloaded, and they don't have time to round up volunteers, however they do these things normally. They're asking anybody they can, because they need them now. Right now."

"Skin grafts? Where? Where do they take it from?"

"From the back, mostly. Nice, wide open area. Less noticeable."

"It leaves scars, doesn't it?"

The Reverend shrugged. "Some. Not bad, as I understand it. But you'll have to excuse me, I...." He had thought the young girl's concern for him was oddly much; she didn't even know him. He saw in her eyes what she had now deduced, though he did not know how; he had not realized she had heard him discussing it with Annie, had heard Annie say that the Reverend was donating, also.

"Young lady, I don't know how you found out what she's doing. But if you learned it through me, you have to understand—I am under an oath of confidentiality. If I somehow suggested to you what she is doing, then your telling anyone else will only make matters worse...."

"It's okay, Reverend. I won't tell anyone else. You go. They're waiting for you."

Twenty-One: Aftermath

Frustrated, the Reverend Ackermann considered his position. There was no way to undo what he had let her learn. Best, perhaps, to simply not make an issue of it. He moved off.

Lewee waited alone in the hall, waited for the doctor to exhaust his last efforts to dissuade Annie from the sacrifice she was going to make, waited for him to fail at all his efforts to talk her out of it, by warning her again of the scars that would ensue. Lewee actually heard little of the conversation. But now, knowing the background, the snippets she heard made sense.

Latching onto a passing nurse, Lewee pumped her for information as the nurse went about her business. Did they still need grafts? Who was allowed to give? And what would rule a person out?

"You understand," the nurse said, "that we're only taking grafts from men."

A polite lie, Lewee understood, to alleviate guilt among those whose vanity would not allow themselves to be scarred.

"I understand," Lewee said. "I'm asking for my brother. He wants to do it. But he's not sure he can. He's not sure he's allowed."

"Is he sick?" asked the nurse.

"No. No, he's got... he's got tattoos."

"That shouldn't be a problem. We can't take the tattooed area itself, of course. Are they on his arms?"

"Yeah," Lewee said softly.

"Then it's not a problem. We take most of the grafts from the back. As long as his back is clear. And as long as he hasn't had any work done in the last few weeks—traces of ink in the bloodstream, that kind of thing. He should be fine. Have him check in at admitting."

Lewee thanked her, and then wandered back in the direction of Annie's room.

Lewee wondered if she herself would have the courage to do what Annie was doing. Could she find, down within herself somewhere, the courage to offer such a thing, to scar herself in that way, and perhaps to save a life in so doing? She would never know. Her own foolishness had blocked her from that.

The door to Annie's room was open, but before she went in, Lewee leaned up against the wall, and waited, and wept.

Annie would never tell Lewee what she was about to do. And she would never ask Lewee to participate; Lewee knew that. No one would. No one would ask a nineteen and a half year old girl to scar herself for life in such a way. But she wished they would. She wished they all would—Annie, and the doctors, and even Mother. She wished they would assume she would be willing, and then badger her when she was not. And then, when their questions about her morality and her willingness to sacrifice had reached their peak, she would tearfully turn away from them. She would tear apart her blouse, ripping off her buttons, and then jerk the blouse down over her shoulders. In her fantasy, she could reveal to everyone her glory. She could reveal to them her shame.

* * *

Andrew passed in and out of heavily medicated slumber. One time, when he emerged, Ken was at his bedside. Andrew looked around for Arlene. She was not there. He wondered if Ken were really there; everything seemed very dreamlike.

"Andrew."

"Ken. Where's Arlene?"

"She's with the kids, Andrew."

"Andy?" There was a touch of drugged alarm in Andrew's voice.

"Andy's fine. He's just fine. He's going to be leaving the hospital soon. He can come stay with us for a while. All the kids can."

Andrew digested that for a while.

Twenty-One: Aftermath

No reason for the kids to stay with Ken and Arlene. They should come home. Ken was telling him that the kids couldn't come home. He was telling him, without saying the words.

"Joanie was at the El," Andrew said. "I saw her over at Herky's. Or was I dreaming?"

Ken shook his head. "No. You weren't dreaming. She was there."

"She was hurt, wasn't she? In the explosion. She was hurt."

"I'm sorry, Andrew. Joanie didn't make it."

Fading out. Fading in.

"Didn't make it," Andrew echoed. "She was...." His mind struggled to make the distance estimate. How far was Herky's from the El? "She was way over at Herky's. The explosion... shouldn't have...."

When it was clear that Andrew couldn't finish the sentence, Ken spoke: "There was a lot more than the explosion, Andrew. A lot more. Emery's gone. I mean, a lot of the houses are still there. But the businesses... the businesses are all gone."

"Emery. Gone? That's... crazy, Ken. Emery can't be gone."

Ken did not dispute him.

"Joanie. You're saying Joanie... is dead?"

"I'm sorry, Andrew."

Fading out.

* * *

"Is Bob okay?" Lewee asked.

Annie smiled as she sat up on her bedside, and fastened her robe around her. "Ole Bobby boy is just fine. He pestered Mrs. Finney into getting him an ice cream sandwich at Herky's. They were three blocks away when the explosion hit. Just one block away from the gasoline, when it went up."

"One block," Lewee said.

"Bob keeps insisting his hair got singed. Mrs. Finney says it didn't. She's taking him back to Redeeming Love today. Say, Lewee. Is your mother okay? Did she come through everything alright?"

"I don't know," Lewee said. "She hasn't come to visit. Hasn't even called. I had the neighbors go over and check. They said she isn't around."

Annie couldn't bring herself to speak what it was that she was thinking. Many people were unaccounted for. And because of the intensity of the fire, some never would be.

"She'll show up," Lewee shrugged. "When she's good and ready. And I'll tell you, Annie. If she doesn't, I won't be all that broke up about it. One more person, movin' on with their life."

"Oh, come on, Lewee. She wouldn't just up and *leave*."

Lewee tried to put on a wistful smile, and thought: *No reason she should be any different, Annie.*

Annie changed the subject. "So, Lewee. They get you all checked out?"

"Yeah, I'm just wasting space here. When are you going home, Annie?"

Annie stood. "Me? Oh, they've got some more things to check me out, on. I'll probably be here for a few days yet. Maybe more. We'll see. Actually, they said they would be up here soon to take me down for some more tests. I should get myself ready," Annie said. It was an artless lie, that Annie hoped would be accepted anyway.

"Okay," Lewee said, rising to give her a hug. A full, firm hug. "Okay, you go ahead, have your tests."

Twenty-One: Aftermath

For the next hour, Lewee Jorgesson—the only child of the perilous union of Franklin and Vivian Jorgesson—wandered the halls and lobbies. She wandered among the injured and the grieving and, most heartbreaking of all, the uncertain—those who suspected the worst, but who could get no confirmation of their tragedy. These touched her the most. They had nothing to console them, it seemed to her—nothing except for the fears that clung to them and tried to suffocate them.

How do they survive a time like this? she wondered.

The guilt she had felt over her tattoos, over her inability to help because of them, had struck her in an unsettling way. She was unaccustomed to feeling guilt; guilt was not part of her nature. That was why, it had seemed to her, Mother's tirades about her supposed improprieties with Billy had cut her so deeply: She was a good person, she was sure, and guilt was a stranger to her. Which made it so disturbing to have guilt thrust upon her by Mother in that way. Which made it that much more disturbing, when guilt seemed to rush in on its own, concerning her beautiful, beautiful tattoos. She did not like guilt when she had an answer to it—as she did with Mother. She liked it even less when she had no answer to it—as she did outside of Annie's room, before.

That guilt was subsiding. In its wake, however, it seemed she could feel the holes within herself—the very holes, it seemed, that Pastor Zack had described to her. But they seemed somehow unimportant now.

The pain of those holes, those gaps, was eased by a yet-unnamed sense of grace that walked beside her through the halls—a grace that temporarily filled those missing places within her. The missing places, the missing pieces which she had not yet come to understand. But for the moment she did not recognize them, until the time would come when she could understand them, and name them, and deal with them.

She paused in the hallway. A sheet-draped gurney rolled past her, and she was not disturbed by the ill-defined form it bore towards the elevators. She turned, and watched as the nurse's aide stepped around it, to press the elevator call button. Going down. She wondered over the fact that death, passing by so near, had not distressed her. But she understood it at once. There was one hole within herself that was being filled, just then, that was not temporary. It was the only one of the holes for which she knew the name.

She did so wish she could find Pastor Zack; he would be so pleased that this one would not, despite his suggestion, be the last hole filled—pleased that she had come to see it on her own, even before the other holes had been filled.

She laughed, quietly, but aloud, to herself.

"Well, glory hallelujah amen, after all," she said, smiling. For a moment, she thought of seeking out the hospital's chapel, but quickly dismissed the notion. *Leave the chapel for the mourners.* The hallway was her chapel; all of the hospital was her chapel. "So, Jesus. I guess we got us some business to tend to."

* * *

For the balance of his stay, Andrew Lanquist refused all visits from clergy. He wasn't bitter, exactly, at least not as Andrew understood bitterness. He even prayed, in much the same mode as the cool and distant sort of communications he now had with Barris.

He never knelt, or even sat, but conducted what spiritual matters he needed to while standing. And always alone. The prayers he prayed were the sort he imagined no other human being would understand. They were akin to terse business communications, from a junior partner who did not fully trust his senior, but who was committed by contract to his obligations.

If Joanie's life had been taken in payment for God's delivering of Andy (and to Andrew it was either this, or God was not involved in any of it) then Andrew was only partly angry at God. Much of the blame, he knew, lay with himself.

In his bargain, he had tried to specify all of the "loose ends", and close every loophole. But he had made the mistake of focusing on how

Twenty-One: Aftermath

God might cheat him on the "Andy end"—Andy living out his life sickly, or dying just a few years later anyway. Andrew had secured all of that. But in focusing there, he had neglected to nail down the payment terms: He had not made it clear that everything he offered was "payment in full". God saw an opportunity, and took it. It was Andrew's own shortsightedness that had allowed a spiteful God to take from him his wife—and to take from his children their mother.

But he had Andy. And so Andrew would keep his word. Every prayer issued, every Sunday morning spent, every dime donated, just brought him that much closer to the end of the contract that his remaining years now marked out. Enjoying Andy, watching him grow, was the closest thing to revenge he could hope for.

And in all of this anger, directed—so he felt—at himself for his foolishness, none of it was what Andrew would recognize, or label, as bitterness. But to an outside observer, the effects upon Andrew, in both the short and long terms, were indistinguishable from that very poison to the soul which had plagued all men, since Cain rose up against Abel.

In the bustle and confusion of the hospital, Zack Hennessey never managed to cross paths with Lewee, though he stopped several times at her room. He assumed, however, and rightly, that her ongoing absence from her room meant she was doing well.

Like many of the clergy from Mitchell, he counseled those whom he could. In some cases, they were people he knew. In many cases, they were strangers who just clearly needed someone, anyone, to talk to.

Most of his time was spent in the visitors' lounges, which were now overflow zones for the ER. The injured sat, or wandered by. Gurneys with dead were rolled past from time to time. There were always more gurneys, with more dead.

He did his best to cover his shock at the extent of the death. This was not, he knew, where he wanted to be. *Too much death*, he thought, as another gurney rolled by. *Too much death*. The phrase struck something in his subconscious, as part of his brain far away from his awareness worked through the anagram. And his conscious mind remembered the place, the place where he did want to be—the place he resolved to return to, when this horror had passed. He turned his attention back to the grieving man before him, and offered what words of consolation he could. But were they the right words, he wondered? Would they somehow, magically, help? Or might he be saying something that, owing to details of the man's life and history, would only make things worse? *What if I fail to read the signs?* The sounds of the hospital echoed more softly. *What if I don't pick up on the subtle clues the man before me gives?* He felt a chill.

A woman caught his eye, across the room. Seated, faced away—long brown hair with a hint of red.

"He was only twenty-five, father," the man was saying. Zack Hennessey forced his attention back, front and center.

"Too young," Zack agreed, nodding. *Too much death*, he thought to himself. And as he thought of the phrase, he remembered the meadow he yearned for. A place from his youth.

The woman across the visitors' lounge raised a half-finished cigarette.

"I keep thinking," the man before him said, "maybe if I just go home, he'll be there. It'll all be some kind of big mistake."

A big mistake, thought Pastor Zack. *Yeah. Maybe it all is. One big, big mistake.* The woman's auburn hair kept pulling his attention. He held the hand of the man before him, patting it gently, and as he did so his attention moved to the woman's hand, the hand that held the cigarette aloft. And his attention moved to her arm, where a thin line of red was slowly streaming down.

Zack Hennessey stood, in a dream, or in a trance. He knew the woman, and knew why she was bleeding. The hand of the man he had been comforting dropped away, and Zack Hennessey moved forward, across the hushed room, toward where she sat, past the silent injured, past the quietly grieving. She was the only one he needed to attend to; she was the only one he could help. This time he would understand her

Twenty-One: Aftermath

urgency; this time he would pick up on the clues. This was his second chance.

She should not be here, could not be here. But, he realized as he approached her, where else should she be? This was the place for the dead and the dying. Where else should she be?

He could see the deep gashes now, across her wrist. They were so deep, so deep... how could she even hold the cigarette? But she had to hold it. She always held a cigarette, all the times he had counseled her. She would not be complete without it. Why had it taken him so long to recognize her hair? It wasn't auburn, it was brown. It had always been brown. Until the time he had found her, and the blood from her wrists had stained that hair. He would never forget that color, he had told himself. But he *had* forgotten it, just a moment ago. He had forgotten.

He stood beside her. She looked steadfastly ahead. Then she turned her head, as if turning to face him, but not quite all the way.

"Saving the last dance?" she asked. "Saving it for me?"

He moved in front of her, knelt before her, eye to eye.

And it was not her. It was a boy, a fifteen year old boy, with short blond hair. And no cigarette. And no bleeding wrists. The boy looked at him, alarmed at the stranger's sudden proximity.

"Yeah?" the boy asked.

Nausea swelled within the pastor. *Too much death*, he kept thinking. *I don't know what I'm doing here. I don't know what kind of damage I might be doing.* The room shifted a little to one side. *What had she asked him? The last dance? What did that mean?* The room kept creeping to one side, and he shifted his balance to stay up. The nausea swelled again. The other girl, Margaret, or Lewee, or whatever her name was—he couldn't even remember why she had come to him.

He remembered her fumbling with the buttons on her sleeve. What if his words of encouragement led her to slash her wrists, as well?

Overwhelmed by the tragedy of the El, and aided by a past ghost animating present fears, Zack Hennessey passed out on the visitors' lounge floor. He was not alone. Several pastors, EMTs, even one of the doctors, had found that day just too much to cope with.

Like those others, he would—after a fashion—recover.

* * *

Lewee returned home, and kept things in order for Mother's return. In time, she kept things in order for her own sake. Eventually, without serious thought to whether Mother had simply left, or had been consumed in the inferno by the El, Lewee filed the paperwork to have Mother declared legally dead. Normally, without a body, such a declaration would require seven years' time. But the judge whom Mother had known, who had once stretched propriety for Mother's sake, now stretched it for Lewee's sake. The circumstances of Emery's disaster—the dead, and the forever missing—made that easier. The house was Lewee's, to live in, or to sell as seed money to move on. For the first time, Lewee was in charge of her own life.

Mother's disappearance was, in essence, the last gift Lewee would ever receive from Father. For in the preparations to approach his daughter and rekindle things lost, there were all manner of things that needed to be done. The most important of these was to ensure that no one would pursue, if Lewee was willing to come away with him. On the morning of August 8th, after Lewee had left for work, he had made sure that there was no one who would press the issue enough to track her down, no one who might suspect where she was. He had handled it well, and cleanly, in the fields outside of Emery proper, where turned earth was a sign that all was right with the world.

Shades of Thorne Creek

Chapter 22: Judgments

After all of the Federal, State and County investigators had taken their measurements and photographs and samples, the debris from the rail cars and from the El itself was removed. Teams of earthmovers and dump trucks, provided by Barris, hauled away scoop-load after scoop-load to a never-discussed dump site, until only Tunnels A and B and the foundations of the Head House remained. The tunnels themselves were mostly cleared of debris, but in time were partly filled with encroaching dirt from over the foundation walls, followed by snow. And thus the scar that was the Emery El lay throughout the winter, surrounded by hastily set posts holding up hurricane fencing.

In Washington, the political climate had calmed. The resignation of the President of the United States, which had kept the attention of the nation away from a small-town explosion and fire, was settling into the status of a fait accompli. The political outrage of a blanket pardon, in time, came to feel like just one more fading wave from that spasm. The bureaucracies did what they have unintentionally been crafted to do, by years upon years of natural selection: They continued unaffected.

While an official investigation trudged on, Emery's Town Council debated what to do with the grounds of the El. Barris had donated the property to Emery—an act of generosity that was wholly lost in the rancor it ultimately generated. Some wanted a park—benches, flowerbeds, maybe a playground—some sort of cheerful way to remember, while at the same time forgetting. Another faction wanted a plain grass field with a memorial marker, as a solemn tribute to those who died. Another faction, comprised mainly of the sullen Andrew Lanquist, and augmented by those few friends he had not yet managed

Twenty-Two: Judgments

to alienate and who felt a duty to support him, simply wanted all traces of the El gone. No park, no grass. Just an empty gravel-and-weed expanse as it had been before the El was built. As if the El had never *been* built. As though none of it had happened. The forgetting-wish of the playground faction, enforced by a sledgehammer blow.

The debate seemed to drag endlessly, from one meeting to another. Emery's mayor, in an effort to end the stalemate, sent a gentle and carefully worded letter to Ed Gulleif in Arizona. Would he like to contribute his thoughts, either by letter or in person? Should we use just the tiniest portion of the money Barris is lavishing at the moment to get an airline ticket, or two, for him to come here and address this?

There was never any response.

The mayor graciously let the questions posed to Ed Gulleif drop.

In the spring, as the formal investigations were drawing to a close, Andrew Lanquist tired of the endlessness of the debate. Renting a front loader in Mitchell one evening, he trailered it to Emery. Once night had set in, he resolved the matter to his satisfaction. By the loader's headlights, and by two street lamps nearby, he began.

He peeled up the fencing around the site, as if he were unzipping it, and piled the fencing to one side. Filling in dirt and debris at one end of Tunnel B, he improvised an earthen ramp down into the tunnels. There he scooped out the dirt and rubble and the remains of what wall remained between the tunnels, and drove it all up and out, growing the pile to the side of the El that had begun with the fencing. A crowd soon gathered, concerned but very quiet, to watch. The town Sheriff, Jack Crowley, quickly appeared. Just as quickly, he determined to limit his impact on the proceedings to crowd control, motioning people back as the front loader roared on through the night.

Andrew labored like a man calmly obsessed, never acknowledging the crowd, never seeming to see anything but the task before him.

Once the now-unified tunnel was reasonably clear of debris, Andrew approached the edges of it from up at ground level. He nestled

Shades of Thorne Creek

the huge shovel between the cement walls and the ground, and then he paused.

The loader idled, and the crowd waited. Andrew hadn't thought to get ear protection; even over the steady rumble of the idling engine, he could feel his ears ringing. He was sweaty, and greasy, and his knuckles were bleeding from where he had banged them while working the controls.

Thirsty. He was so thirsty. Someone was approaching, moving out of the crowd. Andrew revved the engine, stopping him. He adjusted the shovel where it rested between the foundation wall and the earth, and began again. He pried and pried until the first section of wall collapsed into the tunnel.

Someone in the watching crowd began an ill-advised attempt at starting a round of applause; the idea died quickly.

The crowd had grown to almost one hundred by then, all watching in silence. Many were sad, some were angry. More than just a few were afraid; Andrew was not who he had once been. Sullen and withdrawn, what were his plans for after his escapade? Would he turn the machine on the crowd? Those who wondered such thoughts still stayed to watch, but positioned themselves to the edges and the rear of the crowd, so they could more easily run for cover.

One of those who stood on the edges did so for other reasons. Unable to shed more tears. Waiting. Watching. A figure dressed in a long hooded raincoat for the storm that was promised in the hours before dawn. If Andrew were to turn the machine on the crowd, he would not run.

Andrew positioned the machine farther and farther along the wall, knocking section after section into the tunnel pit. With the last of the wall debris well below ground level, he picked a spot of ground opposite from the debris pile he had made earlier, and began scooping out the earth and dumping it into the pit. In time, the space that had been the El was smoothed, and packed by machine treads.

Twenty-Two: Judgments

As Andrew drove the loader back to its trailer, he stopped to make sure it was lined up properly. As it sat idling, the crowd began to approach—those within the crowd not held back by fear. They gathered around the loader. Andrew saw their faces, but could not read them—did not want to read them. They were happy, and angry, and proud, and compassionate. But to Andrew they were all just variations of the human masks he always saw now. Dozens and dozens of Pinocchios, all thinking that they were *real* little boys and girls. All counting time, until their strings would be cut.

He did not dismount to prep the trailer. He checked his fuel level. The blood from his knuckles had dried in streaks down his hands. He was still thirsty, but no longer cared. He looked to the fuel gauge again. E, and F. E and F. *Not that complicated*, he told himself. He read it again, trying to make his brain work, and he understood it; he had enough to make it.

Revving the engine up again, he backed away from the trailer, turned his machine, and moved out onto Highway 262. Northwest. To Mitchell. Through the small hours of the night, he lumbered along, to the rental facility, where he left the machine. He walked into town and found a motel, where he collapsed. In the morning, he would take a cab back to Emery.

In time the crowd around the El's grave dwindled. Sheriff Crowley let them disperse on their own, like mourners at a burial. In the end, only one remained, one who showed no signs of imminent departure. Crowley approached him slowly, reverently.

"I suppose..." Crowley began gently, and then by the light of the streetlamps he saw the face under the raincoat's hood. "Ed?" he whispered.

"Jack," Ed Gulleif said, with a voice more gravelly than Crowley remembered. Long pause. "I'd appreciate if you didn't mention it to anyone. 'Bout my being here."

Shades of Thorne Creek

After a moment's contemplation, Crowley shook his head. "Of course, Ed. Whatever you want. You got a place to go?"

"Mitchell. Got a motel room in Mitchell, me and Rose."

"You need a ride?"

Ed looked at him blankly.

"To Mitchell, Ed. You need a ride to Mitchell?"

Ed stared into him while the question settled, and processed.

"Naw," he said at last. Then, as a separate action, he shook his head. "Naw, I got me a rental." He tossed his head slightly to one side. Jack Crowley looked around, but didn't see the car.

Ed showed no signs of moving.

"It's late," Jack said gently. No response. "Storm's moving in, I think." A roll of thunder arose in the distance, as if in response.

Still no motion from Ed.

"Shouldn't you be getting back?" Jack asked.

Ed looked to him. "I just…. I wanna…." He looked away, looked to the ground. "I just need some time, Jack."

"Sure, Ed," Crowley said, nodding. "I need to cruise for a bit. I'll swing back, ten maybe fifteen minutes, make sure you're OK. OK?"

"Ten or fifteen. That should be fine."

As Crowley's car pulled away, the thunder was drawing closer. An occasional flash strobed over the freshly turned earth. Ed walked the plot of land, his foot kicking at the occasional clod of dirt that stood above the level. He looked to the west, to the storm clouds revealed by the half-moon in the east.

His lungs drew in air. He could smell the rain coming. Looking back over the fresh dirt, he nodded. *The rain*, he thought. He would return, after the rain. Trudging back to his car, he shed the raincoat and tossed it in the back seat.

Twenty-Two: Judgments

By the time he got to Mitchell, the rain had started. He left the raincoat in the car, and slipped into the motel room.

Rose sat at the tiny table, with the lamp and the phone. Ed sat across from her. He looked at the double bed, which was still undisturbed, and at the cheap landscape print that hung above it. Lightning flashed around the edges of the curtain.

"We should get to bed," he told her. "Pull out early in the morning."

"How early, Ed?"

"When the rain lets up. One more stop, in town. Then we roll out."

She stood up, taking his hand, and stood beside him. More lightning—and thunder, close behind now. And rain on the window panes, washing away dirt, and dust, and sins, and grain dust.

* * *

In the predawn light, Ed Gulleif stood again at the plot of earth. The rain had begun its work, flattening out the tread marks from the front loader. He walked around till he found a piece—a chunk of cement poking above the surface, that had been covered in dirt before. Dirt that the rain had removed. The hunk of concrete block protruded like an old bone. Ed knelt, and pushed it, and pulled it, and worked it loose. It was about as heavy as he could safely lift. He carried it to the pile Andrew Lanquist had made.

Ed tried to get his hand under the block, to boost it up as it went out, to get it up on the pile. It just landed at the base. Not as dramatic as he had hoped for. Fitting. A halfway gesture, without any real meaning.

But at least, he told himself, he had done *something* to clean up the mess.

Shades of Thorne Creek

He returned to the car, and Rose drove to the airport, so they could fly away to Arizona. So he could count the days, and wait for the time when he would find out how much of the blame he bore—from the only source of opinion that really mattered.

Ten days later, the minutes of the Emery Town Council included two notations.

It was moved that Tarkin, Inc., be contracted to haul away the final rubble pile from the site of the El. Funds to be drawn from the Barris reparations account. Seconded. Passed by acclamation.

It was moved that all discussions, past, present and future, regarding use of the property formerly occupied by the El, be permanently tabled. Motion seconded. Motion passed by acclamation.

* * *

The formal investigation concluded that the primary responsibility for the disaster at the Emery El lay with Barris. Their pockets were the deepest, and so it was inevitable, as well as largely fitting, that most of the blame fell on them for using the El in a way for which it had not been constructed, and for which it had never been properly retrofitted.

Harkin, the provider of the scrubber system, shared a fraction of the blame. And, by the happy but curious coincidence that tends to follow such matters, they had proportionately less available cash to contribute toward the settlements.

And so, mostly from Barris' pockets, came the monies to erase all of the horrors— to fully compensate those who had died by providing pensions to their survivors, and to fully compensate families for their lost fathers and mothers, brothers, sisters, children. And these acts of monetary contrition had an additional benefit: The entity within Barris known as The Board learned its lesson. It fired those who had the least internal political cover, demoted those who had more, and officially

Twenty-Two: Judgments

chastised all of the rest. Justice, such as is spun by earthly courts, was done.

And let it not be forgotten that, long before the courts determined what should be paid by whom and to whom, Barris stepped forward with a gesture of compassion over the entire situation. They provided, free of charge for those families willing to accept them, fully engraved but otherwise identical soft-pink granite grave markers. These were provided for all the dead from the blast at the El, both the direct victims and the indirect—for the ensuing fires had claimed more lives among the citizenry than the blast had claimed among the workers. The markers to this day stand in the Thorne Creek Cemetery at the edge of Emery, and would have served as a never-ending reminder and memorial to that event—if any monument or plaque had been posted explaining them. Perhaps once those who lived through the events have all passed, and the rawness of the emotions has faded, the town will be ready for such a memorial to be installed. But it will then need to be placed quickly, before emotions cool further, into forgetfulness.

Aside from Barris, there were others who shared in the guilt, who pressed on with their lives without the cleansing effects of public shaming, without whatever purifying effect the paying of a cash settlement can offer.

Ed Gulleif knew, every day for the rest of his life, that history would have unfolded differently had he pressed the Barris representatives, when they first tendered him their offer in 1972, about what their intentions had been.

Andrew Lanquist knew that if his management style had been more proactive than reactive, then lapses in his barely-adequate safety procedures would not have occurred, or at least would not have endured and compounded until the critical hour. And he knew that if he had not felt the need to prove the soundness of his trust in Hector years before in the post-party incident, then he would have hired someone to officially fill the post of Plant Foreman. Someone who would not have allowed things to go the way they did.

Shades of Thorne Creek

As for Hector himself, he was spared the agony of soul searching, by the equivocal blessing of fatal, blunt-force explosion trauma. He may for a moment have sensed what was happening, but no doubt had no time to connect it to any failings, genuine or not, on his own part.

Many others, in reading the official report of the catastrophe and hearing the news stories and gossip that arose, sensed with grief where their own hands had contributed in minor ways. Those with the courage to see their own blame no doubt took too large a share, unable to see how events needed to work together, how everything unfolded only when *all* of the tumblers aligned. Perhaps they took some comfort from understanding that. Perhaps not. Perhaps it is not strange that the town collectively and silently decided to erect no memorial, to post no plaque, in Thorne Creek. While the dead may not want to be forgotten, many of the living desperately need to be.

Shades of Thorne Creek

Chapter 23: Secrets

The specially designed drill bit dug through the metal box cover with Lewee, Annie, and Mr. Burkett of the Home Federal Savings Association watching as earnest witnesses. Box 79 had belonged to Mother since just before Lewee's third birthday.

They were in the basement of the facility, but it reminded Lewee of no basement she had ever been in. Climate controlled, Mr. Burkett would have been proud to explain, had they asked. Temperature controlled. Humidity controlled. Well-lit, of course. And the air was quite pure, except for the smell of scorching metal that now crept about in curling wisps.

Without knowing where Mother had spirited the key, there was no simple, clean way of accessing the large safe deposit box. But access was Lewee's right, now that all of Mother's assets were Lewee's, by law. Even though Mr. Burkett insisted she would not need to bring the document along again for the opening, Lewee had the court papers tucked in her purse. That was Annie's idea, and Lewee was glad Annie had suggested it. Every "t" crossed, every "i" dotted. Lewee had waited long enough for this. She couldn't bear another delay. It wasn't an anticipation of anything specific; Lewee had no idea what was in the box. That, in fact, was the source of the nagging curiosity. Why would Mother have had such a box? If not for the arrival by mail of the yearly bill, Lewee would never have guessed that there was one. The box was bigger than Lewee had expected; ten inches high, almost a foot wide. And as for its depth, she had no idea.

The drill squealed through the metal. Lewee had never dealt with a safe deposit box before. She thought it would be more... private. She had wanted Annie there, but once the door was opened Burkett and the workman would be able to see whatever was inside. She wasn't happy

Twenty-Three: Secrets

about that, but what could be done? The workman had to be there to get into it. And Burkett—well, that was procedure, it seemed.

The drill fixture finished digging its circle around the lock, and the lock mechanism popped loose and bounced around inside the fixture cylinder. Withdrawing it carefully, the workman slid a gloved finger into the hole, tripped the mechanism, and swung the door out.

"Thank you, Hank," said Mr. Burkett. Stepping up, he carefully slid out the metal bin that had been exposed. "If you'll wait just a minute, you can begin cleaning up while the ladies examine their box." Lewee was relieved to see that the box which emerged was enclosed on all sides. Burkett led them to the end of the wall of safe deposit box doors—some small, some large, but none larger than theirs—to a bank of private viewing rooms. All of the viewing room doors were open wide, and he stepped into the first. Setting the box onto the table, he withdrew, and once Lewee and Annie had slipped in, he shut the door behind them.

The table was tight up against the rear wall. Two chairs were on either side, with barely enough room to squeak into them, and a third chair was on the side facing the door. Lewee chose this one in which to sit.

"You sure you want me here for this?" Annie asked.

Lewee just patted the table beside her, unable to take her eyes off of the box. Annie slipped into the chair on Lewee's left, as Lewee lifted the hinged lid.

"Looks like paperwork," Lewee said, lifting out a three-inch thick expandable folder. It was not labeled. It was tied with a simple cord closure. She set it in front of herself. She pulled out the next folder, about an inch thick. This one was labeled: "Legal—Louise Margaret". No doubt the paperwork and the final court order that shooed Billy away. She set it in the empty space, to her right.

She pulled out the last folder, almost as thick as the first.

"Legal—Frank".

Shades of Thorne Creek

Lewee read and re-read the title, without breathing. Legal. Frank. Her father, Franklin Jorgesson. An unreasoning rage boiled within her. Her father had not left her. He had been forced away, by court order. More of the same kinds of lies, she knew. *She* had done it. *That woman* had driven them, both Father and Billy, away. Her hands tightened on the folder, twisting its edges. She wanted to curse her mother aloud. She knew the words, had heard them from others, though she had never used them herself. But now she could not speak them.

"Lewee?"

Lewee dropped the folder atop the unlabeled one in front of her.

And then the rage passed, for a time. It was replaced by a wave of relief, and joy. *He didn't leave me. Just like Billy didn't leave me. Not really. There's nothing wrong with me. It was her. It was all her.*

Annie's purse had a handkerchief tucked in an outer pocket. It was intended as decoration, but it was full-sized when unfolded, and she passed it now to Lewee, who wept into it briefly.

"Annie? I'd like you to know. If you don't mind. It's none of your problem, and I guess I shouldn't dump this on you. But I'd like you to know. About Mother. About what things were like. Is that OK?"

For about twenty minutes, Lewee filled Annie in on the parts of the story of Billy that Annie did not yet know—the court order, and the lies that surrounded it. Annie's picture of Mother grew, and darkened at the same time. The things about Lewee's mother that Annie had observed over the years, and had assumed were flukes—the occasional public harangue, the oddly over-protective reactions—these were not flukes, Annie now knew. They had been warnings Annie had missed, signals of a dysfunction that Lewee had been steeped in, and from which she had somehow emerged unscathed. *Except*, thought Annie, *perhaps not altogether unscathed.* She thought of meetings Lewee sometimes had with their pastor, Pastor Zack. *There are many kinds of demons. And many kinds of exorcisms.*

Twenty-Three: Secrets

Lewee passed the "Legal—Louise Margaret" folder to her, and Annie read for herself the documentation of one aspect of Mother's deceits and pathologies.

Lewee, bracing herself to discover a new set of lies, opened the folder marked "Legal—Frank".

Another twenty minutes passed, as they worked through their respective folders. Lewee worked page by page, while Annie skimmed.

"Oh, Lewee, I'm so sorry," Annie said, setting down the folder. "You must have felt like a prisoner."

"Kinda," Lewee said, slipping a document back into place in the folder. She sighed deeply. "Annie, I can't make any sense of this. It looks like they started divorce proceedings, but it doesn't look like anything was finalized. It jumps all around. There's court orders, investigators' reports, it all gets jumbled up. You wanna take a crack at it?"

"I can try. I'm just not sure I should be poking around in this stuff."

Lewee slid the folder to her, and took her hand. "I know. Part of me wants to just burn it all, so nobody ever sees it. But I feel better, now that you know. About Mother, and all. I don't want to broadcast it to the whole world. But I feel better now that *somebody* knows."

Annie took the folder—a master folder of smaller, manila folders. She decided to start at the back, and skim her way forward. Lewee had not yet even begun looking in the other, unlabeled folder, at the newspaper clippings and miscellaneous documents, when Annie drew in a sudden breath and held it.

Lewee looked to her. Annie's grip on the folder was trembling.

Annie had never been one to curse casually, and since attending Pastor Zack's church with Lewee these last several months, she had grown even more averse to it. Even so, the words left her lips like a gasp:

"Oh my *God*."

Lewee waited, fearful, for a moment.

"Annie?"

Annie slid the folder back in. She drew out another, scanned it for a second, and slid it back. The same with the next. The one after that, she scanned longer. She leaned into it, trying to read around the tears she was forming.

"Annie...?"

Annie looked to her for a moment, and then looked away. She blindly groped for and found the kerchief she had given Lewee.

Lewee spoke in a whisper: "Annie? You're scaring me."

Annie held the cloth to her face, let it draw out her tears. She breathed through the fabric, as if it could filter and purify the air in the tiny space, which now seemed so contaminated.

"Lewee. Don't read anything else. You can't read anything else until you know what's in *here*."

Lewee slid a bunch of clippings back into her folder.

"OK. What's... in there?"

Annie shoved the kerchief into her purse. She slowly turned to Lewee, telling herself she *would* maintain her own composure as she spoke.

Annie saw a different Lewee sitting beside her. Still the Lewee whose father had left so long ago. Still the Lewee whose heart had been broken by a boy who left so recently. Still the Lewee with the shrewish mother. But now a Lewee who was more. A Lewee who was all of these, *with a reason*.

Who am I, thought Annie, *to tell her this?*

"You still talk with Pastor Zack," Annie said.

Lewee nodded.

"I mean, in private. Kind of like a counselor?"

Twenty-Three: Secrets

Lewee nodded again.

"I think," Annie said, "maybe he should talk to you about this."

"Annie. You're my friend. My best friend. Annie, I want *you* to tell me."

Annie nodded, in an ongoing motion. Her hand found Lewee's. Finally, the nodding stopped.

"OK, Lewee. I'll tell you. But please. Let me do something first. Let me call Pastor Zack, and have him come here. I want him to be here. I need him to be here."

Lewee nodded, and Annie arose and left the room. Lewee heard some whispered discussion with Mr. Burkett about how long the room would be needed, but she could not make out all the words. She could tell Annie was asking for a phone.

She had noticed that Annie had gone to the end of the legal file. Lewee stood her own file of papers upright.

"Don't read anything else," Annie had said. An utter impossibility. Lewee could stay away, for now, from the papers that had upset Annie so. Whatever they were, they frightened Lewee. But she couldn't *not* look at *everything*. If the end of the legal papers were important, maybe the end of these papers were, too.

The defiant Lewee—the one who had strode confidently into the viewing room to expose Mother's lies—that Lewee was gone now. A smaller Lewee remained. A younger Lewee. Almost a child.

This younger, smaller Lewee still needed to examine the box's contents. But not to expose Mother. To expose herself, she now feared. What else could upset Annie so? The truth about anyone else, *that* truth Lewee knew that she could face, and Annie knew that she could face. But this—this had to be something about herself.

She had read much of the Bible, and committed a fair amount to memory. It was helpful to call up the right words, at the right times. But a passage bubbled up now, unbidden, from within her. "'I will fear no evil'" she quoted. And then: "Lord Jesus, give me strength."

Shades of Thorne Creek

Lewee moved her fingers to the back of her folder. Everything seemed to be ragged, yellowed newspapers. One sheet caught her attention, a sheet that was not newsprint. She pulled it out. It was a photocopy of a section of newspaper, an Elk Point newspaper. Elk Point—way down in the southeast corner of the state, if she remembered right. One article had been outlined in yellow highlighter.

Area Man Arraigned in Stepdaughter Abuse Case.

The words *Man Arraigned* and *Abuse* seemed to clutch at her throat. She thought of Annie, of how she had acted. Lewee shook her head. But this said *step*daughter. Surely that meant it wasn't *her*. Unless there was even more she didn't know? It couldn't really be that Father was only her stepfather?

Her eyes caught the date at the top of the paper. June 7, 1950. 1950? It was five years before she was *born*. She leaned back, relieved. It wasn't about *her*. Whatever it was that Annie had found, it wasn't *that*.

"Thank you God," she whispered. "Thank you Jesus, that it wasn't *that*."

Even so, she found that, for reasons she could not explain to herself, she could not read more of the article. The upper left corner was torn away, and she quickly saw that the article had once been stapled to a photocopied document, behind it in the folder. The same second-self within her told her not to read this paper either. Though she willed them away, her eyes kept returning to the page—a court document, an arraignment in Sioux Falls, June 6th, 1950. The arraignment announced in the newspaper. Her eyes skimmed here, and then there, until they caught the words *Franklin Jorgesson* filled in for *Accused*. It listed an address in Elk Point. When had Father ever lived in Elk Point? Further on, lost in paragraphs of text detailing the accusation: ...*sexually fondling his two year old stepdaughter*....

She looked back to the thick folder, *Legal—Frank*, that had disturbed Annie so. The documents Lewee had seen, before passing them to Annie, had been dated in the late 1950s. Dated from when she herself had been two, or three.

Twenty-Three: Secrets

Lewee let the earlier court document slip from her fingers. *This wasn't me*, she knew. *Not me. My predecessor.*

Lewee arose, her eyes now locked on the thick folder of Father's legal proceedings. The unlabeled folder was about Father's apparent first marriage, and about his step-daughter. But this folder, the *Legal-Frank*, this was about *herself*. She backed awkwardly through and around the chairs, coming up against the viewing room's door. She pressed back against it, unable to look away from the folder, unable to look for the doorknob.

Just over a minute later, Annie returned. She calmly, methodically talked Lewee away from the door so she could enter. Standing, holding each other tightly, they waited, and wept, and prayed.

* * *

Zack Hennessey knew at once that he was out of his depth. And this went beyond self-doubts over past failures. This went to basic questions of what kind of counseling he was even trained to do. This... this was a whole different league.

On the phone, Annie had told him only that she and Lewee had discovered something, and needed him urgently, and she had given him the address of the bank. With all three together in the tiny space, Annie explained what she had learned—about the court case severing Jorgesson's parental rights to his daughter, and why.

Lewee explained what she knew—that the other file, with its time-jumbled pieces, held Mother's research, including Father's history, and the time before marrying Lewee's mother. The time of Father's first marriage, down in Elk Point. The time, it seemed from the papers, that his behavior first emerged. And then Annie ventured just a bit further, as far as she thought Lewee could bear, into the later accusations and court proceedings that led up to Frank Jorgesson's flight.

It was clear to Zack Hennessey, in all of this, that his seminary training in counseling was insufficient to such matters. He directed

Shades of Thorne Creek

Lewee to John DeCrik, a psychologist Zack knew and trusted. In good conscience, he had to direct her to a psychologist rather than a psychiatrist—for Zack Hennessey disdained psychiatrists both in their general philosophy and in their reliance on medication. He had to give her over to someone like John; he had no choice, with issues this deep. But even so, he didn't feel right about it. He had come so far with her; he wanted to see her through to the end. His own fears—of mishandling the counseling, of things going terribly, terribly wrong—had been held in check. But her core problems, he now knew, were beyond him.

So one set of fears that he had not yet put down—that he would counsel her poorly, or misread danger signs—were given over to another more insidious set. That turning her over to another counselor could itself be a mistake, that if John failed her, that would be Zack's failure as well. This second set of fears would wear Zack Hennessey down worse than the first, for there was no way to dispel them.

Standing between Lewee and Annie—holding them, hugging them, praying with them, it struck him how very, very small the space was. He never thought of himself as claustrophobic. At least, never before.

Shades of Thorne Creek

Chapter 24: On Death, and Life

Miles gave way to miles gave way to miles, as Zack Hennessey's pickup truck made its meandering way west, creeping slowly along the map laid out on the seat beside him. He didn't need the map per se. He had set it there just as a matter of course, because it is what you do at the start of a long trip. But he had not referred to it once. There are some things you never forget, he knew. And the way home was one of those.

From time to time he repositioned and resettled himself in the seat. The scars where the skin grafts had been taken only rarely bothered him these days. Long drives, mostly. Those scars were the only visible trace left upon him of the disaster in Emery. But there were other marks upon him, as there were upon the survivors of the blast itself. The explosion at the Emery El had not impacted Mitchell greatly, but through his connection to Lewee Jorgesson, it had impacted *him*. It had not started anything that was not already in motion, but it had helped things along—accelerated things.

He turned north onto County Road 15, marveling at how unchanged some parts of the journey were. Was it just a trick of memory? Were some scenes along the route truly so precisely the same after all these years? Or were the new images just rudely crowding out the old, hushing them before they could protest their displacement?

He preferred to think it was the former, preferred to think that some things were forever fixed. Too much in life was shifting beneath his feet, especially in the aftermath of the El; this whole drive felt like a stumbling into an oasis of familiarity, of sameness.

Rolling his shoulders, he pressed back in the seat to massage his skin.

Twenty-Four: On Death, and Life

Pastors see death. It is part of the package. Pastors, and doctors. And families; there is always someone left behind. And after the Emery El, there were many left behind. Lewee was the only one of the Emery survivors he had known before the explosion. He had come to know several others afterward, though, as did a number of Mitchell and Sioux Falls clergy. The clergy in Emery had been overwhelmed with the counseling requirements. In truth, "the clergy in Emery" would have been overwhelmed by just about anything.

Zack Hennessey shook off the thought. *Judge not*, he reminded himself. The pastor of the Lutheran Church in Emery may not have been much for strength of conviction, but Pastor Hennessey knew that he himself now stood in no position to cast aspersions on the strength of anyone's faith. But at the time, he had cast aspersions, silently, inwardly—after several meetings with the Reverend Hunt Ackermann. Perhaps, at least in part, that was the reason for the dream, and for the doubts that crowded in around him these last few months. *As you judge, so shall you be judged.* He squeezed his eyes shut for a moment as if to force the thought out of his mind, and then returned his attention to the road.

So now you try to force from your mind, he thought, *the very words of the Living God?*

This was getting him nowhere, he knew—this vicious bouncing around, as though he were sparring with himself. It was like trying to slip stealthily through a well-lit hall of mirrors.

He wondered about Lewee Jorgesson, about how she was doing in the therapy he had encouraged her to start. He wished that confidentiality rules didn't preclude his asking John DeCrik for *something*, some sense that it was going well. Short of that, just a word from Lewee herself. She and Annie Dale still came to church together, regularly. But it did not surprise him that she was not discussing her therapy with him. Her scars, he was coming to understand—all of her scars—ran deep.

Lewee often seemed unhappy, and he wondered if she was making progress. And if she would be making more progress, had he not passed her off. On some level, he couldn't help but feel he had failed her. Rational or not, that feeling kept creeping into the mix. But whatever he fretted and worried over concerning her, he knew that Lewee Jorgesson was in the hands of God. She was not the lost soul that had sought him out that Wednesday night, over a year ago. She was a child of God, now. Whatever trials she was facing, her destiny was heaven. He knew that. But it is the sort of thing that is easier to be convinced of for others, than to be convinced of for oneself

The flat plains of South Dakota began to yield to the rolling foothills of the Badlands. He was miles and miles from the actual Badlands themselves, but the rolling terrain heartened him. He was nearing home.

And then, in the distance, a sight he dared not believe: Where 334 crossed County 15, it looked like the diner was still there. After all these years. He had assumed it had been torn down, or had collapsed from neglect, years ago.

The sign still read "Roadside Inn". After all these years, the diner still stood. And with the same name. Maybe the trip would pay off. Maybe he could convince himself that not everything fades and dies, that some things remain. Perhaps he was still who he had been when he had left here for Mitchell years ago.

Slipping into the parking lot, he positioned his pickup amongst the older, more worn trucks of the local farmers.

The diner's outer door was secured open. The inner screen door, though spring-driven to close, pushed easily aside. The bell mechanism attached at its top was broken, and failed to announce him. That suited him.

The red and white checked floor tiles—those were more faded than he recalled. Time, he reminded himself. Time. In a few spots the tiles had been replaced with the brighter colors he recalled. Mindlessly, he avoided stepping on the replacements. Unnoticed by the smattering of customers, he slid into a spot at the counter, pulled a menu from a battered stand, and perused the wonders of health-free dining.

Twenty-Four: On Death, and Life

"Jimmy?" came a voice. "Jimmy Hennessey?" The name, like the voice speaking it, had a distant and welcome familiarity. *Jimmy*. It had been so long since anyone had called him that. Hennessey raised his head, but did not turn to the speaker who approached him from far down along the customer side of the counter. He let his mind roll over the voice casually, taking his time in placing it. The white clad figure was almost to him, and Zack worked it out: Who else would be working at the Roadside?

"Rory," he said, smiling as he turned.

The T-shirt, the apron, the white hair-shielding cap, they all were the same. But that, of course, was illusion. They had been worn out and replaced many times over the years. The one true constant, and the one thing that looked aged, was Rory.

"Jimmy Boy," Rory said. "Oh, I can't believe it boy." Rory's hands were filled with food-laden plates, which he clearly wished were gone. "Hold on, Jimmy Jim," and he passed on by to a table, delivering his goods without ceremony. He returned to the counter.

"You still preachin', over in Mitchell?"

"Still preaching," the pastor said with a grandiose nod.

"May!" Rory yelled out. "I'm breakin'!" From the kitchen, the unseen May did not respond. Rory settled into the adjoining seat, and the stream-of-consciousness reminiscence began. Jimmy "Zack" Hennessey let the words pour over him like baptizing waters, and he smiled, and nodded. Rory's face was a bit cragged, and his wiry black hair had flecks of white, but beyond that the years had not been cruel. Apparent, but not cruel. There remained, as always, a faint trace of stale cigarette smoke on him. It was Zack... which is to say Jimmy... who had introduced Rory to the coffin-nail habit. Jimmy had quit before ever getting hooked. He had felt guilty, in those bygone years, when word got out about how bad they were for you. Now, seeing that his old neighbor still used them, James Hennessey felt even worse.

The words came to him, imagined, from the back of his mind. Rory's bubbled ramblings masked them, but the words still came:

Shades of Thorne Creek

"Introduced him to them, didn't you. Introduced him to his death." It was the voice from his dream.

"Jimmy? Jimbo! Hey, stay *with* me, boy!"

Hennessey snorted out the scent of stale cigarettes, and smiled as his attention returned to his friend.

"Sorry, Rorr. You just take me back. A lot of memories, boy."

"Hmm, boy. Don't I know it. You in town for long?"

"I dunno, Rory. Probably not. Just poppin' in, poppin' out."

The pastor ordered a turkey sandwich, and ate while Rory regaled him with their history. It cheered him, and he welcomed that, but he was in no mood to add cheer to the conversation. Eating gave him cover, and he used the white bread and white meat like a shield—to ward off any impulse to expand the nostalgia. Rory was doing fine, on his own. "Jimmy Boy" soaked up the good cheer, like a willow in a drought, despite himself.

After his meal, Zack Hennessey begged off of any more old-time-musings, offering some lie about needing to get into town. He turned his truck toward town, and was away. After cresting the first hill, he knew he would never go all the way to town; not on this trip, at least. He was here, at the place he suddenly knew was his destination. At the base of the hill there was a slightly-beaten footpath off to the right. It led to the meadow. The hang-out meadow. Huctooth Mead, as it was officially known. Mead, he had learned long after leaving town, was a poetic word for meadow, still used in places in England. How it came to be used here, he hadn't a clue. Huctooth, he assumed, was some family name from the early years, the settler years.

In fact, the name Huctooth Mead did date back to the days of the first settlements. But there had never been anyone named Huctooth. Huctooth Mead was an anagram, chosen by one of the few survivors of an extended family decimated by a smallpox outbreak. They had named it after burying their relatives here, a cemetery whose existence was now long forgotten. Perhaps, at some point in the distant past, a young Jimmy Hennessey had heard about the anagram, and then forgotten it.

Twenty-Four: On Death, and Life

Or perhaps his subconscious worked it out for the first time in the hospital, after the El's explosion, when he had been surrounded by too much death. In any case, his conscious mind knew nothing of it.

Pastor Zack "Jimmy" Hennessey left his truck at the roadside, and followed the path. He climbed the slight rise that was itself the low-lying juncture between two greater rises, and looked out over the meadow.

Meadow was a misnomer. It was the rolling prairie equivalent of a meadow. No plush rolls of grass, but plenty of yellow to yellow green (depending on the season) prairie grasses. It was spring now, and hints of greenish yellow were tucked in amongst the brownish yellow.

He began walking toward the craggy dead oak that stood on a rise near the center of the mead. He walked the grounds where kites had been flown, and model rockets had been launched, and numerous eternal pledges had been made and ultimately forgotten. And, he reminded himself, where some pledges had held.

He could not feel—had not felt, for too long a time—the presence of the living God. That presence, his sense of that presence, hung always just before him—out of sight, out of reach, like the memory of a name that you know, that you know that you know, but that will not come forth. Zack knew the feel of it, the form of it, that presence of God he had once felt. But the substance of it escaped him now.

He became aware of his own breathing, of the moist spring air in his windpipe sliding forth and back, as if through a snorkel. Soon, if the mead was quiet enough, he would hear his own blood rushing through his ears, as he did most nights of late.

He focused again on that uncallable memory: The presence of God. Surely here he would feel it. Here, in the midst of nature, in the face of creation. Here. Where he had felt it, as a boy. Here, where he had set his life on the course of the ministry.

He shuddered. Worse than an uncallable memory, for in time memories always come. What if this were more like some fading dream, whose details were now washing away, leaving behind only the sense of their emotion? Once such a dream had faded, it was gone. Forever.

It had to be the stubborn memory, he told himself. Not the fading dream. Not the fading dream. He stopped short. His thoughts were flooded now, not by some metaphorical dream, but by an actual one. He had dreamt it only once. But it was not the kind that faded, no matter how he wished it would.

He resumed walking, but seemed to be getting no closer to the tree. His mind beat its way, once again, through the dream.

He had been sitting up, alone, late, watching an old movie. Some sort of epic wannabe, whose title he could not recall. He had dozed during a ballroom sequence. A masquerade. With the music from the television feeding him, he had dreamt of himself at a masquerade ball—on the floor, moving deftly among the dancers. Not dancing himself, but feeling entirely in place. He seemed to be wearing a mask, but one that did little to obstruct his view.

Someone else moved along the floor without a partner, someone who stood out, but stood out only, apparently, to Zack. No one else seemed to notice the figure. But Zack's attention was riveted on it.

The figure's costume was as bright and ornate and cheerful as any of the others. But the mask was a death's head, a papier-mâché skull that fit very close, allowing the eyes, surrounded with black makeup, to seem to float within the skull's sockets. The figure had done something creative around the nose; the actual nose did not seem to protrude through the recessed nasal cavity of the mask.

Had he been awake, Zack would have been shocked at the inappropriate tastelessness of the display. But within the dream, he was fascinated, watching the figure glide among the waltzers. Often the figure would reach out and nudge the mask of a dancer—a man here, a woman there—setting it slightly askew. Then it would move on, not waiting for any reaction. Some did react, readjusting their masks. Others did not. But everyone danced on.

Twenty-Four: On Death, and Life

The figure was drawing close. With a sense of playfulness, Zack waited for it.

"You won't push aside my mask," he thought to himself. The figure drew closer, and someone called out—a woman's voice, urgent, he wasn't sure where. And, with his attention diverted, he suddenly felt his mask pushed to an angle, partly blocking his view. A moment before he had been playful, but now he was angry. Straightening his mask, he looked to the death's head. The figure was faced away, swaying as if dancing, and seeming about to move off. Then, maintaining its moves, it turned its head toward Zack, then its whole body, and smoothly moved up to him, taking Zack's hands as if engaging him in dance.

Zack did not move.

The figure leaned in toward him. Zack could see a tuft of hair poking around one corner of the mask—one tuft of auburn hair. The figure spoke:

"Dance with whom you will, behind your mask. The last dance is with me, when neither of us shall conceal."

Was it a man's voice? Or a woman's? The figure released him, and moved off. Had the figure been holding Zack as if leading, or as if being led? The figure was lost in the swirl of costumes.

And Zack had awoken. He had never been right, exactly, after that. Maybe, a fellow pastor advised him, it was all the death of the Emery El disaster, finally catching up with him. He had counseled too many people to be unaffected by it.

But what should it matter? Zack wondered. The only thing that had happened at Emery was death. And death held no fear for him. Or at least it shouldn't. Death was his chance, at long last, to stand face to face with his God, and his Savior. His chance to understand all the mysteries that had perplexed him. It was the final, ultimate beginning.

Zack reached out, and leaned against the oak. Boards had been nailed into it, forming a crude ladder. They had been added long after his time. When he was young, anyone wanting to get up into the branches had to master the climb. He had never been a tree climber, and that had made the effort that much more rewarding. Somewhere along the way, somebody had nailed in cheats. But that didn't bother him. Not at all. He was too old now to disdain help from any quarter. The nailed steps seemed to lead only to the first of the many branches. But it was only the first branch that interested him anyway. That branch shot out at right angles to the tree, forming a ledge—the perfect vantage point to survey the mead.

He put a foot on the first step. He thought again of the end of his life, of the passing from life, to death, and beyond.

But that was just it, he thought. That was the point. You're supposed to be alive. And then you die. And then you stand before God. But Zack had already died. Something, somehow, inside of him had died. He knew it. He could feel it. He was just marking time, now, waiting.

He hoisted himself up the first step, and then another. The nails were rusted, and the wood was worn, but the step held. He leaned his forehead against the old, dead bark.

"Oh God," he said, and then had no idea how to proceed. "Oh God. I don't want to be dead. I want to live again."

He turned his cheek to the bark, and looked out over Huctooth Mead. The view was better from up on the branch still above him; but even from here he could see that it was as he remembered it. In all the years, all the summer afternoons, he had only climbed it once, one late fall afternoon, just days before the school year started. On his way down he had fallen and broken his arm. And that, as they say, had put an end to that.

He climbed the steps, and settled in. One leg ran out along the branch, and one hung over. He sat there, opening his eyes to look around the mead, and closing them to retreat into himself.

In time, he noticed it. Beyond his extended foot, there was a small tuft of green. And beyond that, another. Small packets of spring leaves, beginning the long slow process of unfurling. Sprouting, from the very

Twenty-Four: On Death, and Life

dead branch on which he rested. He looked up to the main trunk extending above him. Several more green packets were there. The outermost branches were, in fact, dead. Nothing grew from them. But the tree itself... the tree lived.

He wondered. Had the tree really been dead all those years, and just now miraculously sprung to life? Or had it just always looked dead, from a distance? Had these same tufts of green sprouted every year, unnoticed by all—except for those who actually climbed up here?

And then, it really didn't matter. Either way worked for him.

Looking out across Huctooth Mead, it struck him how very, very large the world was. And how funny, that he had once thought himself claustrophobic.

Chapter 25: Longings

Lewee set the cardboard box of files on the kitchen table of her small basement apartment in Mitchell. She shifted it into the center of the table, and then she sat and studied the outside of the box.

For a time, she had wanted to buy a small safe to store the papers. She did not want the endless, albeit slight, expense of another safe deposit box ticking away at her resources. Her job covered the apartment and food and modest living expenses. The sale of Mother's house was covering her therapy. But there was no end in sight for the therapy—two years running, so far—and there was an end in sight to the resources from the sale of the house. It made no sense to pay money to the bank every month for a box.

Annie had talked her out of the safe. And wisely, Lewee had come to realize; any thief who might break in to her apartment would be tantalized by the safe, and would do what he could to remove it and open it elsewhere. And that would be the last she would see of it. It was safer as a box, tucked into a back corner of her closet.

Her apartment was no social hub, no regular scene of parties whose tipsy guests might boorishly paw through her things. She had guests from time to time. Even dates, intermittently. There was no one who stayed the night. One tight cluster of people knew of the box, and its contents, and they would never pry to learn more of its secrets. Those others who might from time to time be in her home were never occasioned to see it, let alone wonder about it.

The box was safe. Even, it seemed, from her. In the two years she had been seeing John DeCrik, she had not been in the box more than a dozen times—and all those in the first few weeks after the discovery of

Twenty-Five: Longings

the papers in the safe deposit box. In those dozen torturous forays into the archives, in those little more than a dozen days, she had found enough material to keep her sessions burdened for the nearly 800 days that had followed.

She had already known almost everything in the legal file with her name upon it. She would have disregarded most of what was in her father's file, would have considered it to be more lies from Mother, if not for the contents of the third. There, in disorganized clumps, was the information that had, in her mind, changed her father's file. Transformed it, from a tattered tissue of Mother's delusion into what Lewee now saw it as: The achingly damning record of her father's betrayal of her.

She had come to recognize her father as an abuser who derived his satisfaction, not from direct pleasure to himself, but by generating and witnessing sexual pleasure in his young victims. Perhaps a more traditionally-understood abuse would have been easier to understand, and deal with—where the betrayal is marked by pain, and even physical damage.

Her wounds from her father were more insidious, where the premature awakening of her sexual nature was shrouded, swaddled, in sexual pleasure.

Victims of a more traditional abuse often have issues of guilt, of feeling that they are somehow to blame for what has happened to them. Those feelings of guilt are compounded, however, when the formative sensation of the experience was not pain, but pleasure. This is a guilt which, rather than standing opposed to reason, seems buttressed by it.

It took a long time to understand what her father had, in this sense, done to her.

Her father. She smiled. It was her psychologist that had first pointed it out to her. Mother was still referred to as Mother. But the man who had been "Father"? He was now "my father". The name had been reduced to a title, a label, a clinical definition. She had tried, briefly, calling him Frank—dissociating him from the fatherhood role he had played, or should have played, in her life. But "Frank" was too casual, too familiar, for this monster that had shared her childhood home. Franklin? That had lasted an even shorter time, but for a different, more troubling reason—a reason it had taken weeks to explain to her counselor. Franklin was too cold, too distant, for a man that, despite everything, despite her hatred and her rage, she still....

It was hard enough to say it to herself. How had she managed to say it to her psychologist?

She still loved her father.

Even now, after all the sessions discussing it, she did not, could not, understand what that meant. Did she love him for what he should have been—was this a feeling of purity and goodness? Or was her love for him some twisted psycho-sexual product of the pleasure he had given her—a feeling that sickened her and, despite the kind and directing words of her counselor, made her hate herself?

When she thought of Billy, and his eager and clumsy but essentially good-natured attempts to paw her, when she warmed to the memory of his desire for her, was it the attention of an earnest young man that thrilled her? Or was he simply reawakening something within her, something she now hated so much that she would gladly cut it from herself with a knife?

And on those rare occasions when she succumbed to the desire to accept a date? Was it the promise of a relationship, perhaps even the hope of a marriage somewhere in the distance, that drove her? Or a base and primal urge, to recapture something unspeakable? This was perhaps the most insidious aspect of his damage to her. The longing for a father, for the warmth of his touch, being all swept together in sexual yearning.

Her therapy was aground upon these rocks. Her therapist was directing her away from obsessing over a need to divine her true feelings for her father: Even if her deepest feelings actually were that most horrid thing she imagined—that was his fault, and not hers. Her task was to focus on what she felt now, to make her relationships with men fulfill what she needed now, not worry about whether she carried damage from her father. She did carry it, and always would. Her task

Twenty-Five: Longings

was not to root out the evil inside her, so that a new and pure sexuality could grow unsullied. She needed for the evil of her past to be choked out by the healthy relationships of the here, and the now.

Appealing words. Rational philosophy. All dashed upon the rock of the mystery that was Franklin Jorgesson, the mystery that was her father. What had he been? What had she been? She needed to know this, in order to know what she was now.

She pulled the box toward herself. Would reading about him demystify him, break his hold over her? Or was she behaving like an alcoholic, craving one more drink to "settle the nerves"?

She drew out the folder, and started from the beginning, methodically. Mostly they were newspaper clippings; references to hearings and arraignments. There was assorted paperwork that didn't fit logically into either of the files on the two legal proceedings Mother had initiated. One paper was a photocopy of an arrest report on her father, a year after he had left. Drunk and disorderly, in Sioux Falls. She scanned it, doubting there would be much of interest, until one detail caught her eye. Identifying marks. Upper arm tattoo. Her eyes locked on that. She thought she was nodding. In fact, she had begun to rock slightly, forward, and back. Forward, and back. Upper arm tattoo. Upper arm tattoo.

Her stomach shifted. The broth she had had for supper did not sit well.

She let her eyes move further on the page.

USS Colorado, it said. *Sounds like a ship*, she thought. He had been in World War II—one of the few tidbits she had gleaned from Mother. The USS Colorado.

Skull and crossbones.

Her rocking slowed, and stopped.

There were other words on the page. But they did not seem to relate to the tattoo, so they were shapes without meaning, strings of symbols from some forgotten tongue.

Shades of Thorne Creek

Her father was tattooed with bones.

Her eyelids, as if under a puppet master's control, closed. She sat in darkness. It was an involuntary darkness, but not an unwelcome one. She could not have reopened her eyes had she wished to, but she did not wish to. *Skull*, she thought. *Crossbones.* She willed herself not to visualize them, willed herself to see them neither in memory nor imagination. She leaned back. But not in an uncomfortable kitchen chair. She leaned back in a comfortable nothingness, a dark and silent nothingness. There was a tickling along the edges of her face, a warm tickling... water. She was lying back, face up in water. And that was the silence; her ears were under the water. The eyes of her memory opened, and she saw the muted colors of the upstairs bath. And she saw the arms that cradled her, the arms that eased her down into the water. And she saw the funny picture, the funny, funny picture. The smiling face. She was too young even to associate it with pirates and sailing ships. A smiling face, atop crossed sticks. The funny picture smiled at her, and she smiled back.

And then other feelings swept her, feelings stronger than the laughter at the smiling picture—feelings stronger than the comforting warmth all around her. Good, good feelings....

Lewee's other eyes opened, the eyes that let in the light of her apartment kitchen—and yet other eyes opened as well, the deeper eyes, that let her see the truth that she had feared: She was what her darkest fears had foretold. She *was* the child enrapt in the sexual power she was exposed to. She had enjoyed what had been done to her.

Leaping up, she slammed herself forward into the kitchen counter and vomited into the sink. *This man with the skeleton tattoo did this to you*, an inner voice said, as she vomited again, *and now you have skeleton tattoos all over you.* Her stomach heaved again, but brought up nothing but traces of bile. *Isn't it obvious*, the voice said, *that you long for the tattooed man? That you long for what he did to you?*

Her hand groped wildly for the faucet. Finding it, she yanked it on, and focused on the sound of the running water. The cold running

Twenty-Five: Longings

water of the now. She ran the water over her face, then through her hair. She let it wash over her, and wash, and wash.

Leaving the faucet on, she toweled her head mostly dry. She stared at the wall over the sink, waiting for the voice to return. It did not. She went to the phone.

"Annie?" Lewee barely recognized her own voice as she spoke. Her words were soft from the weakness her body felt from the retching. But quiet as they were, her words were driven by urgency. "Is it late? I'm sorry, I don't know what time it is."

"It's... it's only eight. Lewee? Is that you?"

"Annie? Can you come? Can you come now?"

There was some muffled conversation on the other end, as Annie spoke with someone. And Lewee realized: She had interrupted Annie in a date. Probably that young doctor she had been seeing, Walter. When Annie's voice returned, Lewee tried to back out of her request.

But Annie did come, and stayed with her through the night. Most of the time they were awake, and most of that time Annie read to her from her Bible. Sometimes the passages were chosen with care, sometimes they were chosen at random. But they were all, uniformly, right.

On the day of the El's explosion, Lewee had given up her protestations against hymn-singing and praising God, the whole "glory hallelujah thing" as she had once called it. She had found, in God, a father she had never known, growing up. That had been fractured, or at least stunted, the day in the bank basement when she learned of the evil that a father could do. It was unfortunate but, her psychologist assured her, not unexpected. And not irreversible.

That night as she learned, as she finally understood, what her tattoos had meant, she could have veered into spiritual disaster. Her image of God as father could have been poisoned further, as she saw the sway that Franklin Jorgesson had held, throughout all the years, over her. But instead, she moved ahead—leapfrogging over the place Annie Dale had been years before, one night in Thorne Creek

Shades of Thorne Creek

Cemetery. Lewee was comforted by Annie, and by the words Annie read her. But most of all, she was comforted by a father she had always needed, always longed for, and who had always, *always* been with her, waiting. A father whom she was too distraught to push away from any longer.

The hardest lesson, the one that the following years of counseling would try to hammer home, was that the two yearnings—for a father who loved her, and for sexual fulfillment—were confused and conjoined not by Lewee, but by another. One over whom she had had no control, nor even influence. It had been Franklin Jorgesson's job to protect her; it had been Lewee's job to trust him. Only one party had failed.

But her tattoos—her wonderful, her beautiful tattoos—spoke to her a different story every time she saw them in her mirror, every time she caught a glimpse of them on her forearm.

They spoke to her the words of that inner voice, the voice that her counselor worked to convince her was a lie, the voice her budding faith urged her to ignore. But knowing that certain words are lies does not mean that those words go away. Sometimes it only makes them speak louder:

Isn't it obvious, that you long for the tattooed man?
Isn't it obvious, that you long for what he did to you?

* * *

Six years and counting after the disaster at the Emery "El", Lewee Jorgesson sat in the waiting room of A. A. Anderson, Tattoo Removal, in Minneapolis.

During the initial meeting, several things were discussed:

The nature of her tattoos: Major, but far from being beyond what they had dealt with in the past.

Twenty-Five: Longings

The time: She would be in Minneapolis longer than she had expected, but she would stay for the whole procedure, rather than making a series of trips. She wanted it done, and wanted it done as quickly as possible.

The costs: Substantial, but within the realm of what she had saved and could scrape together as time went by.

The pain: Which, she assured them, she was prepared to endure. And, they assured her, they were authorized to prescribe medication to ease her through it, if need be.

A. A. Anderson had seen many people, with many forms of tattoos, with many reasons for wanting them removed. Sometimes the reasons were explained. Sometimes they were not. One thing was clearly noted in the initial interview papers: Lewee Jorgesson, whatever her reasons, was dedicated to having her tattoos removed, and to having it done as quickly as possible.

It had taken her years to come to grips with her past—with what had been done to her, and with what she had later done to herself. Her psychologist had encouraged her to wait about having the removal done until everything was settled in her mind. She had waited as long as she could. Her time was now.

Shades of Thorne Creek

Chapter 26: Redeeming Love Convalescent

After my initial conversations with the groundskeeper Ray Tucker (the graves keeper, as I have come to think of him, though that appellation does not sit well with him) I only had the barest outlines of what had happened in Emery, back in 1974. It would take a long time to gather all the pieces. But one place I had to start was Redeeming Love Convalescent, in Mitchell. There, Ray Tucker believed, the former minister of Holy Redeemer Lutheran was a resident.

RLC was an unremarkable building. Although reasonably well maintained, its dowdy architecture revealed its true age, not unlike liver spots on a well-manicured hand.

Removing my bike helmet, I approached the desk attendant—an extremely Nigerian-accented male nurse—and realized abruptly just how little planning I had put into my inquiry.

"I'm looking for someone. A resident."

"Yes?" he said, with an upward leading tone that hinted at limitless patience. I hoped I read him right. *Harry G*, his name tag read.

"I'm not sure of the name. He used to be a pastor. A Lutheran pastor, in Emery." Harry looked at me with an expression somewhere between curiosity and concern. "Holy Redeemer Lutheran," I added proudly, as if this would somehow establish my credentials.

For a moment he paused, as if weighing his options. To tell me the name or not, I was hoping. How to make me go away quietly, I would soon learn.

"And why do you wish to see this gentleman?" he asked.

"I...." In a flash I ran through my options. *I just want to ask him a few questions.* As if I were a cop on official business. Which I clearly

Twenty-Six: Redeeming Love Convalescent

wasn't, and even if I looked the part, I doubted that that would grant me entrée. *I just wanted to talk with him.* Great. Provide no valid reason, but manage to come off like some stalker of Lutheran ministers. Spill it, I decided, just after I had paused long enough to damage my chances further. "I wanted to talk with him, about Emery. About what happened, back in 1974."

Right eyebrow lift, with pause. Not good.

"I'm sorry sir. I'm afraid...."

"I understand. Does he maybe have some relatives in town? Maybe I could talk with them, get the OK from them...."

He shook his head apologetically: "I don't think the Reverend has any relatives...." Harry realized his multifold mistake at once. He had admitted that the person I sought existed, and confirmed that he was a Reverend. And revealed that he had no relatives... surely, privileged information.

"Perhaps you could speak with the Administrator, Mrs. O'Shaunnessey." Harry picked up his phone.

I opened my mouth to speak, but was too slow in declining. The dreaded Mrs. O'Shaunnessey, no doubt 300 pounds of blue-haired menace, was already on the line.

"Yes, ma'am," Harry was explaining. "And he is looking for a Lutheran minister, from Emery. Back in 1974. Yes. Yes, I'm sure it is. No ma'am; I was sure you would want to talk to him. Thank you ma'am." He hung up the phone and looked up proudly. "She will be with you, presently."

Gee, Harry. Thanks.

But the dreaded Mrs. O'Shaunnessey was nothing like I had imagined. Middle aged, yes. But trim, and attractive, and as pleasant as her role of gatekeeper would allow.

She escorted me to her office, and sat behind her desk. I declined the chair she offered me, and as I explained the odd circumstances that had brought me to Redeeming Love Convalescent, I wandered about and read the plaques on her wall. I focused only on her commendations, all the time failing to note her full name, where it was repeatedly spelled

Shades of Thorne Creek

out. I admired the photos she had framed. On a table at the back of her office, I examined the curious wicker basket that had been lined with a tattered, stained cloth.

I told her of the graveskeeper at Thorne Creek Cemetery, and the fragmentary stories he had relayed to me. The basket held nothing of interest, just five small smooth stones—three were clustered in the center, and two were at the edge. As I spoke of Ray Tucker, I picked up one of those stones from the edge.

Tucker had told me many things, I explained, but there was much he did not know. The stone was unpolished, and had not been run through any grinding and polishing machine; it simply appeared water-worn.

I was a writer, I told her, and Tucker's stories intrigued me. Setting the stone down in the center of the basket, I finally took the seat before her desk.

As soon as I sat, however, she arose. I continued my explanation, as she moved out from around her desk. I told her of my interest in pursuing the stories, and I did not turn to follow her as she moved to the back of the office. She was, I was sure, standing at the basket I had disturbed. In retrospect, I am sure that as I explained my interest in the Reverend from Holy Redeemer, and my hope that he might flesh out some of these stories, she moved the stone I had displaced. From the center. Back to the edge.

As she returned to her desk, I could see she was listening patiently. But I could also sense the gears of her mind working up the list of reasons I would not be allowed to meet with the Reverend.

"I'm sure you understand," she concluded, after politely rattling through the list she had tallied.

"Of course. And there are no relatives I could speak with?"

She shook her head sympathetically. Then, almost as an afterthought, she asked:

"Was there something specific you wanted to ask him? About what happened?"

Twenty-Six: Redeeming Love Convalescent

"Nothing specific, really. A hundred things. I just want to find out everything I can about what happened. About the explosion."

She sighed, and in an instant she seemed to age. Five years? Six?

"Does it need to be the Reverend? Maybe I could help you."

"You were there?"

She smiled a humorless smile.

"Oh, I was there. Right in the middle of things. I was in the El. I worked there."

My eyes flashed to her name badge. *A. O'Shaunnessey*, it read. *Administrator*. Her hair was a mixture of blonde and grey. A straight, simple cut. I did some quick arithmetic, guessing how old she had been in 1974. I hesitated a moment, then realized I had nothing to lose.

"Annie?"

She was slightly taken aback, but then cocked her head unconsciously.

"Yes?"

"Annie Dale O'Shaunnessey," I said in wonder.

"Yes. I don't think I know you. Have we met?"

It was awkward; I once again felt I was being pegged as a stalker. I managed to convince her that "Annie Dale" was among the precious few names Ray Tucker had given me. I asked her:

"How did you end up here?"

"Well, there was no El anymore. Almost no Emery for a while; it took some time to rebuild. RLC needed an accountant, I needed a job. And it meant I could see my brother every day."

"Your brother, Bob. Ray Tucker said you had a brother living here. Oh, he must be thrilled having you work here."

She smiled a smile I hadn't yet seen, and her eyes were still on me, but not straight on.

"Bob died, last year," she said.

"Oh Annie," I said, not realizing the strange familiarity I had fallen into. "I'm so sorry."

She nodded. "But to answer your question, yes. He was very happy to have me working here. We got to spend a lot of time together. It was good."

"There's so much you could tell me. If you're up to it, if you don't mind. There was a young girl, with an unusual name."

That same look, the off-center gaze. I knew I wasn't going to like this.

"Lewee," she whispered.

I nodded, suddenly unsure how steady my words would be, if I were to elect to speak.

"Lewee sold her mother's house, after the El. Got an apartment here in Mitchell. She got a job somewhere… where was it, now? I don't seem to remember."

"But you stayed in touch?"

"Oh yes. We were a lot closer after the disaster than before it, actually. She even started me going to the church she was involved with. A little Assembly of God storefront."

"Just down the street from the tattoo parlor…."

"This Raymond Tucker seems to know a lot."

"A lot of years, talking to cemetery visitors, I guess."

"Hmm. Yes, Pastor Zack's church. I still attend there. Pastor Zack is gone, died in 1995. But I'm still there."

"And Lewee?"

"Some time… I think it was 1980, maybe… she went to Minneapolis, to see a skin specialist."

"About the tattoos?"

Annie's eyes narrowed. "Ray Tucker, huh? I'm going to need to pay a visit to Emery, have a talk with Mr. Tucker."

"But it was about the tattoos?"

"Yes. There was a man there who specialized in tattoo removal. Gang-related stuff, mostly. Lewee was a big job. She relocated to Minneapolis while she was having the work done. After a while, I lost

Twenty-Six: Redeeming Love Convalescent

touch—my letters went unanswered. Eventually they were returned; no such addressee. I think it was late '81 when I finally heard from her again. She wrote me from ShiningStone."

"They're a rehab outfit, aren't they?"

Annie nodded.

"So what was it? What had she gotten herself mixed up in?"

"I don't know. She never said. But I've found out that tattoo removal can be a pretty painful process. Especially if the subject insists on having it done quickly. They may have had her on pain pills. I've always figured that was what started it. Because she wasn't the type, really. Not a recreational user type. After about six months, the letters I sent to ShiningStone started coming back."

"Finished the program?"

"Dropped out. Disappeared. In a month she was back in. Her first letters from then were pretty incoherent. But they got better." She left the thought there, as if she had no plan to go on.

"And?" I said, as gently as I could.

"And. And, in two months I got word that she was dead. Some kind of overdose."

It would be months of discussions before I came to know Lewee Jorgesson anywhere near as well as Annie had, but even so, with the little knowledge I had, I felt the loss. And sitting in her office that day, Annie and I cried together.

To this day, no one can speak with any certainty about the circumstances surrounding Lewee Jorgesson's death. Did she take something to help take the edge off of her withdrawal, and then things spiraled out of control? Or did she leap whole heartedly back into the addiction spawned by her tattoo removal? Or, saddest of all, did the tragedy of her life circumstances catch up with her, consume her, and persuade her to overdose intentionally?

There are theological debates, hinging on the meaning of this scripture or that, about the nature of the Christian concept of salvation. Having once believed what must be believed, and having done what must be done, is a person's place in heaven forever secured? Or can

Shades of Thorne Creek

one, in the depths of depravities, lose the promise that had once been theirs? I have neither the training nor the wisdom to know which camp is right. But I thank God that it is not my job to decide the fate of the Lewees of the world. And I thank God for the passages warning me not to even think to assess any one person's fate.

At first, I thought of Lewee as having succumbed to the horrors of her past. But she lived to about 26 years of age; 24 years after her last contact with her father, almost eight years past the disaster at the El. I'm inclined to think of her as a survivor. As Bob Dale and Pastor Zack Hennessey served to remind me, all people die. Some people die way too soon. Some days, I feel that all people do.

With Annie's gracious help, I came to know and even understand Lewee Jorgesson. As the final keeper of all of Lewee's notebooks, there were some things Annie has never let me see. Other things that Annie elected to show me, I have decided not to reveal here.

With a great trepidation, I have chosen to reveal one further item, an untitled and apparently unfinished poem she wrote some years after the El, during a period of extensive therapy. It was a work she had shared with her friend Annie, a sequel, of sorts, to her poem *Hall of Mirrors*.

A Father holds his Daughter; infant child, wrapped for bath.
I see you both—the hallway long, the mirror imperfect—
But still I see you both.
A door is opened, and through it you have passed.
The child laughs, and smiles;
The splash of water warm, Father's strength of touch and voice,
And all she knows is joy.
And she then feels more than she was meant to feel.
She does not know betrayal
Nor understand the unseen door through which I see you pass.
And the cruelest thing of all?
The gentleness of your touch, and the pleasure you instill,
And the patterns and the pathways of corrupted love.
I understand the hallway now—

Twenty-Six: Redeeming Love Convalescent

Its odd turns, and reflecting lies.
Only its architect remains a mystery—
A mystery whose resolution I do not pursue.
Your marks, within, without, cry for their own undoing,
My own flesh proclaims the

Which, apparently, is as far as she ever got with it.

It is an awkward thing—weighing, on behalf of one who has passed, the dignity of privacy versus the value in letting their story be known. But I have revealed what I have, in the hopes that others might glimpse what I have seen—that what happened to Lewee Jorgesson can be viewed in other terms:

The Emery El was felled by a deadly pentangle of fuel, oxidizer, confinement, dispersal, and ignition. The grain dust, the air, the tunnels, a blast of air, and a spark all did their work. Similar forces were at work in Lewee's life. It appears that, toward the end, counseling helped reveal these things to her. Her father's abuse, her passage through puberty, her mother, young Billy's influence in, and then disappearance from, her life— these forces, too, did their work. The tattoos began to spread across her like a fire. But where the El succumbed in an instant, Lewee Jorgesson lasted for years. I think that, in the end, she understood what had driven her. I think that was why she was having the tattoos removed. The El was just a building; it never had a chance. Lewee Jorgesson had fought back.

And Lewee Jorgesson did escape the curse that her father had laid upon her. She did not escape it completely, or cleanly. It was no storybook, happily-ever-after escape. But she did escape; I believe she left this world with her soul. As Poe might have said: "With only this, and nothing more." But it was enough.

I would have wished better for her. But, it was enough. God willing, when I cross over, it will be to the place where Lewee is. After all she and I have been through in the writing of this, I do so look forward to meeting her at last.

Shades of Thorne Creek

For the rest of that September day, Annie told me of the events of that terrible afternoon in 1974, and of the days that led up to it, and of the things that followed. It took a long time for her to trust me fully. It wasn't until the following summer, in the heat of the prairie days, when I noticed her consistent choice of blouses with long sleeves. I commented on how it reminded me of Lewee, and Annie felt she knew me well enough to tell me why she wore what she did.

Short sleeves would work for her. But they just came too close to showing what she did not want shown, what she did not want known. Her arm held at an angle just so, someone might see the scars. For, like many of the survivors in Emery, she had gone ahead with the procedure—the procedure which Lewee was forced to decline. She had given up large patches of skin from her back. Along with those others, she had saved lives in that first dark day, before volunteers could be secured from farther afield.

And as for the preference for longer sleeves, it was not that she was ashamed of her scars. Neither was she proud of them. She simply preferred not to have to explain them.

On that first day of our meeting, she was not prepared to reveal all of these things. But there was much she did tell me. We moved from her office, to the staff lounge where she allowed me to pilfer some food, and eventually to an empty lounge near the main entrance. I learned much from her that day—many pieces of the puzzle that Ray Tucker knew nothing of. And when the sky outside was darkening, a figure in a walker approached me slowly from behind. I tried to ignore him, unsure what to expect.

"This him?" asked the gravelly voice.

Annie looked up at him, then back to me, and up to him. She was trying, it seemed to me, to make a quick decision. In thinking about it later, I realized it was a question of how to address him: In general, or by title. To conceal, or to reveal.

"Reverend, a little early for your evening walk, isn't it?" Annie's eyes came back down to me, and I realized what she had just done, and

Twenty-Six: Redeeming Love Convalescent

the implicit permission she had just given me. "Why don't you sit and join us."

It took her five minutes to maneuver him into a chair, and as she herself was about to again sit, an agonizing cry came from down the hall. She looked to Harry G's station. Harry was elsewhere.

"Excuse me," Annie said, heading down the hall, toward the terrorized cries that continued. "Go easy," she admonished me as she hurried off, and she was gone.

"He's one," grumped the Reverend Ackermann, a thin shell of a man, with sparse white hair, and a generally annoyed expression. He maneuvered his quad-cane beside his chair, and laid his forearms across his thighs. Seeing that his words held no meaning for me, he resigned himself to explaining. "From the Emery El. One of the explosion people. He was one of them."

"Who? Who is?"

The cry resounded down the hall.

"Him. Mr. Screamer. Diddling himself again."

"Excuse me?"

"He just diddled himself. Masturbated, boy. What do they call it, these days?"

I wondered just what the state of Reverend Ackermann's mind was.

"Happens every time. Can't keep his hands off himself for more than a day or two. Then when he does it, it happens to him all over again."

"What happens?"

"The El. The explosion. The fire."

"He relives it? Flashback? Why?"

"Ah, who knows. Nobody even knows who he is. Got caught in the fire, most his clothes burned up. His ID too, if he even had any, which I don't think he did. Damned mystery man."

"And he doesn't remember?"

"Who he is?" snorted Ackermann. "Ah, he knows. Just doesn't want to tell anybody. From out of town, I figure. Some kinda crook, I figure. Getting ready to rob some place when it all came down. Herky's Market, maybe. That's where we found him. And there was a car in the lot—a stolen car. So *you* put it together."

I wondered if it could be.

"Do you know anything about him? Anything at all?"

The retired Reverend moved his elbows up onto the arms of his chair, and brought his hands together. He studied me over steepled fingers. My interest had seemed to intrigue him, and he seemed to be trying to read me. It was a little creepy.

"Been here ever since he left the hospital, after it all happened. Wheelchair case. But I think he's here on a mental, too, on account of not being able to remember who he is. So he says."

"And there was nothing identifying him."

"Has a tattoo, but it isn't much. First part of it got burned, so nobody knows what it was supposed to say. 'El Dorado', is what I think. *Something* Spanish, anyway. But who knows. *H*e sure isn't saying. Crazy, that's mainly what I do know. Got trapped by the gasoline fires, and it got all turned around in his mind. Thinks he's reliving the fire, and he thinks he's in the fires of Hell, all at the same time."

"Really," I said.

"That's the problem with all this *biblical literalism* people in these parts are so fond of. They think Hell's a real place, with real fire, and they're gonna burn forever. Then some poor sap believes it so much, he gets all screwed up in the head."

"But you don't think it's true. Hell."

"Ah," he said, waving his hand. "There's enough Hell right here on earth. What's God need with any more of it?"

I wondered then, even as I do now. I don't have the training to dispute the reasoning of a seminary-trained ordained minister. But be that as it may, I'm not at all sure that Reverend Ackermann was right.

Twenty-Six: Redeeming Love Convalescent

What I do or do not believe about Hell isn't at issue here. But I would observe this. If Hell does exist, and it is eternal, it seems some people feel a need to prepare for it, like a pitcher warming up in the bullpen.

Maybe this unknown resident has built his own little bullpen, getting himself ready for what he knows, in his heart, is coming. And if he is who I think he is, and if the stories I pieced together are, in part, true—then he probably feels he has a lot of warming up to do.

I think Annie O'Shaunnessey, nee Dale, is doing the same thing, in such a very different way. I think that every day she is getting ready for what she knows in her heart is ahead for her.

Ray Tucker thinks there are ghosts, shades, still hanging about at Thorne Creek Cemetery. Personally, I don't think so. I think that what lives on from each of those who are buried there has long since moved on to what awaits it.

But as a writer, I can't help but feel that the stories do persist, restless shades seeking the chance to be known, dreading the thought of being slowly lost, forgotten.

And if the stories that inhabit Thorne Creek Cemetery have taught me nothing else, they have taught me to be ready. Because one day I will sink down through the grass, much like I imagined on that late afternoon, almost a year ago now. The ground will receive me, and a stone will appear like magic; a stone with a date of death. Not August 8th, 1974, but some date—a date that is unknown to me, and unknown to all those born of women and men. But a date that *is* known, I trust, by God.

Shades of Thorne Creek

Chapter 27: Thorne Creek

Before noon on the final day of that initial trip of exploration and discovery and preliminary interviews, I began biking from Mitchell toward Emery and home, planning to meet my son's van enroute. We were to coordinate via cell phone, with the aid of mileage markers and GPS. And I decided to make a last stop in Emery. At Thorne Creek Cemetery. That was, after all, how my adventure had begun.

Nearing the town, just after the green sign identifying the town, but before the cross streets and scattered residences, I now noticed a long gravel driveway that I had ignored before. At the highway was a mailbox, whose weather-worn lettering had passed right through my field of vision before, but which now could not pass by without seizing me.

A. Lanquist.

I stopped just past it, and then rolled myself back. The possibilities, I thought. Andrew? Andy Jr.? Or no connection at all? But how many *A. Lanquists* could there be in a town like Emery, South Dakota? With no thought of how I would explain myself, I rode up the driveway.

It was a long haul on gravel, but a house appeared, and outbuildings. And between these, parked prominently, was a huge machine I took to be a combine. At its side, a lone man toiled. He wore coveralls that at one time may have been grey or blue, but were now primarily grease and stain and tear. The strain about the waist suggested an incipient paunch, not present when the garment was purchased.

I slowed, but continued. What *was* I going to say? The man wore a broad straw hat. Beneath it, he had a full grey-tinged beard that

Twenty-Seven: Thorne Creek

seemed to have been choosing its own course of growth for some time. He saw me. I stopped pedaling, but continued to coast.

"Hello!" I called.

Turning from his machine, he waved. He wore no shirt under the coveralls. Hair sprouted from his chest and shoulders. His back, as well, I would learn. A common result of certain medications.

"I'm looking for Mr. Lanquist," I said, stopping a few feet before him.

He ambled toward me, with a gaze at once both wary and anticipatory.

"You found him. Do I know you?"

I stumbled through an explanation as best I could. Somewhere between my noticing the dates at Thorne Creek and Ray Tucker's mention of his dad's name, Andy called over to the house:

"Hey Luce! How 'bout some ice water?"

Presently Lucy Lanquist emerged, with pitchers of water and lemonade, and we sat in the shade of the combine, and talked. There were a lot of details Andy filled in for me, including everything about his surgery, the remarkable details of which I was only hearing for the first time.

"You're quite some individual, Andy Lanquist."

"Aaah," he said dismissively, swilling more water. He had to move his beard aside each time.

"Do you ever wonder?" I asked. "What it all meant? If you were… I don't know… meant for something important?"

Andy tipped his head.

"Well. Raised two kids. They turned out to be not half the delinquents that I was. That's something, I guess."

I smiled. "Maybe that's enough."

Shades of Thorne Creek

Lucy reached out and stroked his arm, in a way I thought might mean something. If it did, it was something I was not meant to know.

"Still a young man, though," Andy said. "Barely fifty years old. Who knows what's ahead of me?"

I asked about his father, and was surprised to learn that he was in residence at RLC. Annie Dale O'Shaunnessey did not yet, it seemed, trust me enough to offer any unsolicited information about those in her charge. Or at least, not about her former boss. I suggested I'd like to talk to Andrew Senior. Things grew very quiet.

"I'll have to ask you not to do that," Andy said, civil but firm. "The El, what happened that day, our mom dying. It hit Dad pretty hard." *Dad*, I noticed. Not *Pop*. "Things were always different after that. Different with him, I mean. He wasn't the same guy."

I understood. Or I thought I did. I was thinking of a man losing his wife. Which is life-changing enough, by itself. But Andy had meant more.

"You asked if maybe I was meant for something," Andy said. "I'd like to think so. I'd like to think there was a reason for it all. But then there would have to be a reason for my mom dying, too. I think that's what gave Dad the hardest time. It was easier to think her death just happened, that it didn't mean anything, instead of thinking that God meant for it to happen. But me, I just kind of messed that up for him. He could never look at me and think that God isn't involved, that God doesn't control things."

"And that made your mom's dying all the harder to accept."

"I guess so."

"What about you, Andy? What do you think it all means?"

He struggled up to his feet and stretched.

"I dunno what it all means. Except..." He looked across the fields. "Except, it means something. I guess that's enough for now, till I can figure out just what."

Twenty-Seven: Thorne Creek

I passed by the gates to Thorne Creek Cemetery that afternoon, without entering. I was a little too close to everything just then; the emotions were just too raw.

That situation worsened as I began to research, and learn more and more of the details which have filled this story. I visited Emery and Mitchell often during the writing. But never Thorne Creek.

* * *

Annie Dale O'Shaunnessey never would explain to me what meaning that basket of stones held for her; she never said anything of it, beyond explaining its origin in the Sunday school lesson of the young David preparing to battle a fearsome Philistine. I have my own ideas about what she thinks it means—of the message, or the sign, that she thinks God is giving her. But in the end, my speculations are of no more value than those of anyone else. Perhaps one day, when some giant has been felled, she may drop me a note to let me know—to tell me what that giant was, and which stone (that is to say, what person in her circle of acquaintances) was instrumental in the deed. But I will not press the issue unless and until she raises it.

In the months that have ensued since I first met Andy, I have had occasion to think over his words on his farm that day. It is normal, inevitable, to seek out the greater meaning in life's big events. Births and deaths. Catastrophic explosions, and inexplicable deliverances. Andrew Senior could never accept that there was meaning in Andy's survival, without also believing there was some plan in his wife's dying—and the idea of God's intent for Joanie Lanquist to die, and to die in the way that she did, has stood for the rest of Andrew's life as a barrier between Andrew and God.

I wish I had, for my benefit as well as for Andrew's, some simple platitude that would reconcile all of this. I do not. I do not think of Joanie Lanquist's death as a punishment upon her, nor do I think of the

Shades of Thorne Creek

El's explosion as a judgment upon Emery. In fact—and dismiss this as radical musing, if you will—I do not think the explosion even *changed* very much, in the overall arc of people's lives. I think of the explosion of the El as an accelerator. I think it took the courses those lives were on, and pushed them to those destinations more quickly. But perhaps this is simply the sort of philosophizing that comes easier when one is biking, carefree, through September prairie—or sitting behind a computer monitor, far removed from events by both distance and time.

A year has passed since my first visit to Thorne Creek Cemetery. The book, shy of this epilogue, is finished. I roll in to Thorne Creek again. But this time it is no rest stop of scheduling convenience. I am here via car, and with a very specific task in mind.

I do not meet with Ray Tucker, although he is here. I do not, I will not, talk with him on this visit. Because I do not want the answer that I know he can give me, whether it is positive or negative. This is a quest I have to follow alone.

I search all of Thorne Creek, grave by grave, no longer looking for a date of death in 1974. Rather, I seek one much later. I have no reason to expect that the grave will be located here, and every reason to hope it will not—because I know how I will react to it. But I cannot move on from this project, cannot put it to rest, without trying to find it.

Early on, I find some graves I had hoped I would not stumble upon—the Dale family plot. Mr., Mrs., Bob. I do so wish I had not found that; I really don't need to be reminded of them, just now. There is a combined stone for the parents, a separate stone for Bob, and a space to the side, presumably for Annie. I hope she will not use it, but rather will choose to have a spot somewhere else, with her husband. I think of her, coming here, to visit. I think of her, looking at Bob's grave, and remembering the prayer she had prayed one night, a lifetime ago. I hope she never comes here. She deserves better, than to put herself through that. She has a life; I hope she lives it fully, freed from the hauntings of the past, freed from sins for which only she holds herself accountable.

Twenty-Seven: Thorne Creek

And I rethink my regret over finding this set of graves. They remind me of something important: That we are, all of us, headed for Thorne Creek. There is no other way for our stories to end. We're either here, or we're headed here. The Hectors, and the Bobs, and the Zacks, we're already here. The Reverend Ackermanns and the Franklin Jorgessons, we're just counting down our last days. Even the Annie Dale O'Shaunnesseys; our plots have been purchased, and they await us. Whatever we are going to do in life, the time to do it is *now*.

Later in my search, I find something else—a grave I had not expected, or even contemplated existing.

Vivian Jorgesson, it reads. A date of birth is given, but there is no space allocated for a date of death. I will later learn that the grave is empty. The plot and the marker were commissioned years after her disappearance, by her daughter. Perhaps as a mark of respect. Perhaps as some sort of closure. Looking out across the fields and the occasional gentle rises that surround Emery, I wonder if indeed she is buried, somewhere nearby. In my darkest musings, I wonder if she is buried alone.

Still further in my search, I find another—even more unexpected.

Rachel Saunders, it is engraved, *Cherished Daughter*.

I thought Rachel, waitress at Herky's Market, bride to never be, had survived the explosions at the El. A quick check of the date of death— December 4, 1974— confirms she did survive. But I know that date. It was something Annie Dale O'Shaunnessey mentioned during our extensive interviews following our initial encounter. And then I remember that date, and what that date was meant to be. And then I realize that Rachel did not survive the disaster of the Emery El. Not really. The El took many lives. And it took them in many ways. With a tinge of shame, I remember now my first excursion into Thorne Creek, months before. I remember the idle stories I spun when I first wandered among these graves and read these stones, and I think about one story in particular—the first that I imagined here.

It was a story about different people in a different time, but, I now sense in rereading Rachel's date of death, it was a story that might well

Shades of Thorne Creek

be Rachel's story. Looking at her grave, I regret having so blithely, almost light-heartedly, fabricated those imaginings before.

The events that deliver people to Thorne Creek are sometimes heroic, sometimes tragic, but always deserving of more respect than I showed that earlier day. With my hand upon Rachel's stone, I apologize to her, with words too personal to relate here.

And then I continue my search. I take all of the day, but I find it. It is plain and simple and cheap, and whatever bureaucrat filed the requisition processed it under her birth name:

Louise Margaret Jorgesson
2 / 23 / 1955 ~ 11 / 17 / 1981

But that is not all. Sometime after the initial inscription, perhaps sometime, even, after the placement of the stone, something was added. I do not know by whom, and this is another question I will not attempt to pursue; whoever commissioned the change deserves their anonymity. I imagine it to be some other survivor, perhaps one of the workers from the gallery floor of the Head House. Just a few simple words. *Fly, Lewee-bird*....

Shades of Thorne Creek

Appendix: The Sixth Air Vent

Near the end of Chapter 6, a procedural loophole is mentioned—a loophole which resulted in a critical one-way air vent never being installed at the Emery El.

When Barris had purchased the El, they had invested well in upgrading equipment, particularly safety equipment. The purchase of the Harkin Air Scrubber had been a part of those moves. Not trusting the workmen at the El, Barris had hired Harkin to perform the install. And Harkin, being in the height of the install season, had quietly hired an outside contractor to install the scrubber. Dooley Services were no strangers to this work. They had installed a Harkin Air Scrubber once before, and many of the "kinks" that can happen on a job had been worked out on that job.

The matter of surplus parts was one example. On that first job, Dooley had damaged more parts than expected, and the surplus parts Harkin had initially sent along had not been enough. There had been delays while additional parts were shipped, and no one had been happy about that.

For the El, Harkin sent more spare parts than seemed necessary, and mandated careful tracking to make sure the unused parts were returned in the end, and to make sure that Dooley paid for the ones damaged by their carelessness. And so, this time, there were no delays. As for the damaged items? It made no fiscal sense to ship them back to Harkin in the hope that this part or that part of some assembly might be salvageable. The shipping costs back to Harkin for the ninety-five percent that were ultimately unsalvageable anyway outweighed the cost savings on the other five percent. And so, assemblies marked as damaged were to be disposed of at the install site, with the rest of the installation debris. Simple, clean, efficient.

Appendix

There were six duct lines leading to the scrubber from the El's tunnels, drawing off dust-laden air. Two ducts serviced the current silos, and four more ducts were in place and set to handle the towers that Ed Gulleif had always hoped to one day install—the towers that Barris was sure they would install, soon enough.

And each of these six ducts was designed with a one-way air vent, to ensure dust-filled air always moved *from* the tunnels beneath the silos *toward* the scrubber, and never the other way around.

Yet somewhere in the course of things, only five vents were installed. The sixth lay piled with one of the two spares that Harkin had supplied. The second spare's carton had suffered a horrendous gaping puncture during handling, along with some attendant damage to the vent itself—though damage not nearly so severe as the carton's condition seemed to suggest. Still, it had been piled with the damaged parts by the worker who had noted it; Dooley management and Harkin could argue over whether it was salvageable or not, he had figured.

All was well up to this point. In the final accounting, three unused vents would have been tallied (two good and one damaged). Three remaining vents, when only two spares had been supplied, would have raised a red flag; the error would have been caught, and the final vent would have gotten installed.

An El employee, however, knowing the damage to the vent was minimal, and hating to see the waste of an almost pristine vent assembly, chose to spirit the vent away. He did not realize that such "innocent pilfering" would certainly be noticed and would bring about grave recriminations.

But of course, due to the assumptions of the accounting process, it was not noted, and thus there were no recriminations: Six vents were to be installed—Dooley had received eight vents, and had returned two. The numbers balanced; everything, it seemed, had been accounted for. And a needed one-way safety feature was thus never put in place.

Also from Alan Havorka

Within a Sheltering Darkness

On a planet known as Mirrus, a people living in endless night send out a sailing ship on a dangerous journey, whose mission is understood in full only by the Mirrans' ruling authorities, and by one man on board. That man reveals to the crew this much: Their voyage will take them to the waters of the DevilsEye. There, twenty-one years before, the lives of a crew were killed in a horror which still haunts sailors and land dwellers alike. But what none of them knows is that the DevilsEye will only be the beginning.

On a planet known as Earth, an astronaut sets aside his private demons to participate in an experiment— an experiment that should serve as a stepping stone to the expanded exploration of space. Instead, it propels him 50,000 light years from home. There he is set into the midst of a people intent on casting him in a role he must adamantly refuse.

In time, a mind-wrenching truth will emerge: The man is more than he imagines, more than the Mirrans dare to imagine. Within him lies the key to resolving what stands between the Mirrans and their creator, the one known them simply "The God Who Is Silent".

Also from Alan Havorka

Critical response to *Within a Sheltering Darkness*:

Havorka thinks past the basics and delves into the minds of the anxious but determined explorers....

...the author has planned this book out, and his words feel well-weighed and carefully crafted. World-building is kept to the necessities, and the pacing is even and fairly quick. These are all things that I really like to see in these books—they give me the sense that the author had his readers in mind as he wrote....

Lovers of the Age of Exploration should get a kick out of this, as should fans of Christian parable. Even as a member of neither of these groups, I quite enjoyed this imaginative and thinky novel, and wouldn't mind seeing more of Mirrus and its people in later books.

Erin Stropes, Self-Publishing Review

http://www.selfpublishingreview.com/blog/2009/08/within-a-sheltering-darkness-by-alan-havorka/

Havorka's world-building is carefully crafted and believable, his characters on the Mirran world as well as Alex are quirky and have substance.

Gerry Dailey (Ancient Reader) on Amazon.com

Also from Alan Havorka

Excerpt from the pending *Shadows, Forward*

The moon cast cold light across the Earth, and threw its own shadows across the night. Millions upon millions of square miles of the Americas were dimly lit, all by the same moon, the same light. Yet everywhere that light touched, it illuminated uniquely; no two surfaces caught it in exactly the same way.

In one North American suburb, the moonlight passed undiminished through a domed plastic skylight, through the calm and cool air of a home's high-ceiling entryway. The light played across ceramic floor tiles, across the wood and fabric of a chair, across the cool, gray metal of a gun, and across the pale skin of the hand that held it.

In the moonlight, the gun's cleaning oils made it seem more alive than the flesh cradling it. But from time to time, the flesh moved. Rachel would turn the pistol, examining its machined recesses and mechanisms, then re-aim it at the entry door before her. Only her arm, her hand and the gun were in the moonlight. She had placed the chair purposefully at the center of the room, facing the door. Facing the door—there were no other considerations. She had meant neither to hide herself, nor to expose herself. This was all about the gun, and the door. And what would soon enter.

The door was solid-core oak; she hoped it would stop the bullet. But would Lee even close the door behind him? What if the bullet passed through his flesh, through the opened doorway, across the street and into a neighbor's house? What if, against all odds, the bullet penetrated the neighbor's wall, and struck some innocent within?

While she had steeled herself to commit cold murder, she was repulsed at the thought of committing involuntary manslaughter. Irony, she thought.

She sighed, her eyes closing; the bruise on her cheek smarted. That repulsion over murder, at least, meant she was still human. Not like the thing for which she waited.

She swallowed, and clenched her teeth.

Blind determination. That was how she had gotten to this point... how she had managed to convince herself to kill. To murder.

Also from Alan Havorka

Thou shalt not murder.

She had told herself that he wasn't human, not anymore. That particular prohibition no longer applied. While no court would agree with her, she knew it was true.

The courts would not know, the courts *could* not know. They would find her guilty. If she survived this night, and if Lee did not, then she would be convicted of slaying him. But it was not the verdict of jurors that concerned her. It was not the condemnation of society, nor the shock of their neighbors. It was not even the utter disbelief of their congregants. In the only court that mattered, God would judge her. His was the only judgment that she dreaded. God's judgment of her if she killed this man. Or God's judgment on her if she did not try.

Picking a corner of the door's inlay as her practice target, she went through the steps.

Grip.

Sighting, ball in the V. There was not enough light to see the ball, or the V. She pretended they aligned.

Breathing.

Exhale and hold.

And she imagined the slow steady squeeze.

Just like Ben had taught her. Center of mass. Always aim for the center of mass.

She breathed, and lowered the gun. She was ready.

Could this really be happening? Could she be about to gun Lee down? An hour ago, it had all been so different. There had been hope—hope that Lee was not a monster. Not a murderer. She turned toward the Victorian table along the wall. It was barely visible in the darkness, but the moonlight's diffuse reflections allowed her to see its vague shape. She could not see the leather-bound notebook laid upon it. She could not see its faux-silver overlay trim. She could not see the black ribbon sticking out, marking the page.

She could not see it, but she remembered all of it from before she had turned off the lights. She remembered finding that notebook. She remembered what was with that ribbon that now served as a horrid bookmark.

Also from Alan Havorka

Tightening her grip on the gun, she knew: Her dithering these last weeks was done. She had to act.

The sound of a car on the street caught her ear, and her breathing became rhythmic, even as her heart sped up unevenly. *Autonomic reactions*, she thought bitterly. Her hand retightened along the gun handle's contours.

Another false alarm? Just another neighbor returning from some nighttime errand?

She heard the vehicle slow. Headlights flashed across the entry sidelites; the car was in their driveway. A wave of nausea swept her. Her life as she had known it was about to end. One way or another. She gingerly touched her swelling cheek.

He had been forced to park in the driveway: In preparation for his return, she had pulled her car out of the garage, and centered it in the driveway so he could not pull around.

Her thoughts returned to the front door and whether it would be closed when the time came for her to shoot, to the scant but real risk to some neighbor.

A thought flashed through her like an electric shock: Lee could use his garage door opener. He could walk into the house through the garage. *No*, she thought, *no need to panic*. If he did come in through the garage, he would need to come up the stairs. And those stairs fed into the entry. He would appear via the hallway, just off to the right. She could still do it if he stood there, as surely as if he came in the front. *It's Ok. It's still Ok.*

The car door opened, and then closed. Rachel forced her breathing to remain steady, but her heart pounded harder, faster. And she decided. She would put a 'fleece before God': a forced sign to, hopefully, reveal God's will. If the monster closed the entry door, she would shoot him dead. If he left the door open, she would wait for him to approach, and take the gun from her, and do to her what he had done to those before her. She would either be executioner, or slaughterhouse stock. She would leave it in God's hands; the door would be her sign.

She had always disdained the 'fleece before God' concept. It was an easy substitute to the weightier and more spiritual approach of actually seeking God through prayer. *Prayer*, she chided herself. *What*

Also from Alan Havorka

a novel concept. There had been far too little time spent in prayer. But there was no time left now. No time to clear her mind, to try to sense God's leading.

She realized she was hearing no other sounds through the transom's gap. No approaching footsteps, no opening of the car's rear hatch. No garage door opening. He was neither approaching, nor unloading whatever purchase he had deemed essential to the night's unspeakable proceedings.

What has he doing?

Then it occurred to her. She saw it, as clearly as if she were looking out the living room window: He was looking at her car, parked ahead of his in the driveway. He was feeling the hood, and judging how long ago she had arrived. The temperature would tell her tale. It was cooling; she must have arrived shortly after he had left. And so, she had been here long enough, long enough to know. To know everything.

She swallowed. But *did* she know everything? Or were there more things, maybe buried in the garden? More than just some nuisance aquarium fish? Did she really know all of it, she wondered? But she knew enough.

No. She shook her head. Both their cars were electric; there was no 'hot hood' to gauge. No matter. Whatever the reason for his delay, in her mind's eye she saw him now, standing, looking at the house. He was looking at the windows, all the windows. All those darkened windows. He had left several lights on; she had turned them all off.

So, he knew from her car that she was home. And from the darkened house lights, he knew that… he knew that she *knew*. And so, he would be wary. She tightened even more on the gun's grip. Would her hand cramp, once she really needed it to work?

Footsteps, approaching on the sidewalk. She shifted in the chair.

He was at the door. The doorknob moved, and met no resistance from the lock. He had locked the door when he left. She had unlocked it in preparation. He was pausing, processing that. She cocked the hammer. A chill ran though her.

Let him hear the hammer cocking, she prayed. *Let him hear it, and let him run away. Get in his car and flee into the night.*

The knob turned the rest of the way.

Also from Alan Havorka

Prepare to die, she thought. She meant the words both for Lee, and for herself. She held the gun level, and surprisingly steadily. The door opened inward, incautiously.

Lee stepped in.

He closed the door behind him.

Her breathing stopped. She had been certain he would leave the door open, certain of the sign from God that she could surrender and die. Now she realized she might live. There was no thrill, no joy at the thought of it. Just revulsion at killing the monster whom she once loved. Whom she still loved, somehow. Her trigger finger did not act, did not shift or flinch. She waited. She could only make out his outline in the dim, rebounding moonlight. She saw more of his silhouette than of him.

His voice, the voice she knew so well, the voice she had heard so many times, countless times, spoke softly to her. Not as though calling out into the house. But rather, as though speaking to someone near at hand:

"Rae?"

"I'm here, Lee." She sensed his head turning. Then he seemed to stop, and she was sure he now fixed on her arm, and her hand, and the gun, which must have seemed to float ghost-like in the moonlight from the skylight. She sat almost entirely in moon-shadow. Her disembodied arm and hand and the gun had likely presented a nonsensical shape to him initially. But perhaps his eyes had adjusted better now. Or perhaps he just thought it through, and realized the inescapable logic of what was waiting for him.

"You can't mean to use that," he said with a quiet calm.

"I *mean*... to kill you," she said. She wished now that she had not already cocked the hammer; she wanted to use the 'click' to warn him to stand his ground. Why? So she wouldn't have to shoot him? Was she losing her resolve?

"It's me. It's Lee"

"Dear friend. Beloved husband. Trusted *pastor*. And more. Yes, I know it's you, Lee."

Outside all was gray— gray gradients of the near-full moon. But all was not lifelessness; through the throes of Autumn the crickets

Also from Alan Havorka

chirped and the tree frogs resounded. A thousand creatures offered sounds as their proof of life.

But in one moment all that fell still: A lightning-like burst of light flashed out into the night through the sidelites' glass, and a thunder-like clap was instant upon its heels. A splinter of wood sprang from the outside of the door, trailed by atomized blood. The wood bounced along the sidewalk. By the time the splinter settled from its gyrations, the bullet had crossed the street, penetrated the neighbor's vinyl siding, and passed cleanly through spun glass insulation between two wooden studs. The battered lead slug lodged harmlessly in the interior sheetrock, leaving the wall with only a minor outward dimple to hint at its presence.

Those few in the neighborhood who heard the crack dismissed it as something harmless. No calls were made. No alerts were sounded. And nothing drew attention to the darkened house across the street.

About the Author

Alan Havorka began his college career at the University of Minnesota as a Math major with a Physics minor, making the Dean's List early on. During his time at the U of M, he won 3rd place in a Science Fiction writing contest; his short story was published in the Minnesota Technolog—the periodical of the University's Institute of Technology.

After the University, Havorka eventually settled into the family business for a number of years. During this time the company computerized, and Havorka developed a database to mimic an elaborate paper tracking system. Ultimately, he left the family business and became an Application Developer, which he likes to describe as being "a computer programmer with an attitude".

Shades of Thorne Creek is his second novel, having gone to print in 2023 with the science-fiction fantasy *Within a Sheltering Darkness* (with only a few chapters of science, and nary a dragon, troll or elf to be found). He is currently working on his third novel, *Shadows, Forward*, and has plans for a sequel to *Within a Sheltering Darkness*, tentatively titled *Beneath the Burning Eye*.

Havorka lives in Minnesota. He rarely works now as an Application Developer, but he still maintains "an attitude". He has been blessed beyond measure in many ways, not the least of which (and not the greatest of which) is to be able to write far more freely than he had once imagined.

www.ingramcontent.com/pod-product-compliance
Lightning Source LLC
Chambersburg PA
CBHW031408290426
44110CB00011B/309